# HOW TO READ AFRICAN AMERICAN LITERATURE

# How to Read African American Literature

*Post–Civil Rights Fiction and the Task*
*of Interpretation*

Aida Levy-Hussen

NEW YORK UNIVERSITY PRESS
New York

NEW YORK UNIVERSITY PRESS
New York
www.nyupress.org

References to Internet websites (URLs) were accurate at the time of writing.
Neither the author nor New York University Press is responsible for URLs that
may have expired or changed since the manuscript was prepared.

ISBN: 978-1-4798-9094-1 (hardback)
ISBN: 978-1-4798-8471-1 (paperback)

For Library of Congress Cataloging-in-Publication data, please contact the
Library of Congress.

New York University Press books are printed on acid-free paper,
and their binding materials are chosen for strength and durability.
We strive to use environmentally responsible suppliers and materials
to the greatest extent possible in publishing our books.

Manufactured in the United States of America

10 9 8 7 6 5 4 3 2 1

Also available as an ebook

*for Alyssa*

# CONTENTS

# ACKNOWLEDGMENTS

I am grateful for the opportunity to thank friends, family, colleagues, and mentors who supported me through the writing of this book. It is a book I couldn't have written without years of training under the immeasurably generous Michael Awkward. I thank him for his mentorship, for our many conversations that helped to shape my thinking, and for being my toughest reader and strongest advocate. I am also indebted to Martine Watson Brownley who advised me throughout graduate school, engaged seriously with my thoughts before seriousness was merited, and made heroic efforts to rein in my neuroses.

Several extraordinary people read drafts of the manuscript in its entirety—some more than once. For this, I thank Madhu Dubey, Michelle Kuo, Alyssa Levy-Hussen, Cherene Sherrard-Johnson, and Jeff Steele. Madhu offered especially thorough and incisive feedback and helped me work through a conceptual problem that had me stuck. Michelle has read nearly every word I've written for over a decade. Her editorial eye is both generous and shrewd, but her friendship is all generosity. I thank her for challenging me, encouraging me, and seeing me through the bests and worsts of young (to middle) adulthood with unfailing loyalty and unconditional high esteem.

Soyica Colbert and Robert Patterson are dear friends, prized interlocutors, and exceptional peer mentors. I thank them for reading portions of the book in progress and for many valuable conversations about its contents. Robert has supported me at every juncture of personal and professional development: He is an inexhaustible source of insight, affirmation, intellectual generosity, and comic relief. Thanks, too, to the rest of our Emory University graduate school crew—Brittney Cooper, Susana Morris, and Yolande Tomlinson—for making the early years of professional development rich and pleasurable and for their continuing friendship.

I am grateful to my wonderful colleagues at the University of Wisconsin–Madison, who welcomed me, read drafts, and gave generously of their time and insight: most of all, Leslie Bow, Russ Castronovo, Christy Clark-Pujara, Ramzi Fawaz, Susan Friedman, Terry Kelley, Caroline Levine, Keisha Lindsay, Linn Posey-Maddox, Ellen Samuels, Cherene Sherrard-Johnson, Jeff Steele, Nirvana Tanoukhi, Tim Yu and David Zimmerman. Leslie and Russ are exceptionally giving mentors, readers, and advocates. Ramzi is a dear friend who always comes through at crucial times, reading drafts, talking through ideas, and offering pep talks and warm camaraderie. Susan is a brilliant reader and a generous and savvy advisor. Among many kindnesses, Caroline commented on works in progress, talked me through challenging stages of manuscript submission, and introduced me to the heartening genre of the shadow c.v. Cherene consults with me on all problems big and small, offering smart, rigorous feedback on drafts, always sound advice, and reassurance at times when I need it most. Nirvana has been a savior at moments of conceptual and critical impasse, giving generously of her time and her inimitable brain. More important, she is a sister-friend who has helped make Madison my home. I thank her for sharing genuinely and wholeheartedly in my moments of happiness and for making my times of unhappiness feel bearable.

At New York University Press, I would like to thank Eric Zinner and Alicia Nadkarni for their investment in this project. In addition, I am profoundly grateful to Darieck Scott and an anonymous reviewer whose thorough and insightful feedback helped me to see the book's focus and stakes in a new light.

I could not have completed this book without generous support from the University of Wisconsin–Madison, where funding from the Anna Julia Cooper Postdoctoral Fellowship and the Institute for Research in the Humanities allowed me invaluable stretches of uninterrupted writing time. My time at the IRH was enriched by generative workshops and conversation under Susan Friedman's incomparable leadership. The University of Wisconsin–Madison Graduate School of Arts and Sciences also provided generous funding for writing and research.

Much of this book was written during time away from teaching secured by the Woodrow Wilson National Fellowship Foundation. I would like to express my gratitude to Caryl McFarlane and Ina Noble, and most of all to my faculty mentor, Madhu Dubey.

Long before I began this book, the Mellon Mays Undergraduate Fellowship Program at Harvard University played a decisive role in determining my professional trajectory. I am indebted to this invaluable program and to my fabulous mentors there, Jason Glenn and Christy Medrano McKellips.

Shelly Fogelman was another early mentor since I had the unexpected good fortune of working for him during a year away from college. I am grateful for his premature confidence in me and for his wisdom, whimsy, and unflaggingly generous spirit. He is a true mensch who has always accepted me fully and without qualification: an extraordinary gift.

My parents, Ahmed and Fumie Hussen, were my first and best examples of intellectual curiosity and perseverance. They have lovingly cheered on my academic ambitions for as long as I can remember. My sister, Sophia Hussen, embodies all the best qualities of big sisters. I thank her for a lifetime of best friendship, for mitigating my weirdness, and for her bighearted love.

My dog Melvin has been a dedicated companion for the last twelve years, spending many early mornings and late nights with me in front of the computer. Although he would vastly prefer more food to being acknowledged, I would be remiss if I didn't mention him as a source of unconditional love that has sustained me since he came into my life.

Most of all, I thank my wife, Alyssa Levy-Hussen. It was my great good fortune to meet her over a decade ago, at a graduate school recruitment event. Since then, my debts to her have accrued beyond imagination. She is my confidant and co-conspirator, my counselor, my muse, my cheerleader and ferocious defender, my ally in all things personal and political, and my ideal companion. That I have found her and that she loves me are the most outrageously lucky facts of my life. This book, like everything I do, is for her.

# Introduction

You know, they straightened out the Mississippi River in
places, to make room for houses and livable acreage. Occasionally the river floods these places. "Floods" is the word
they use, but in fact it is not flooding; it is remembering. . . .
All water has a perfect memory and is forever trying to get
back to where it was. Writers are like that: remembering
where we were, what valley we ran through, what the banks
were like, the light that was there and the route back to our
original place. It is emotional memory . . . . And a rush of
imagination is our "flooding."
—Toni Morrison, "The Site of Memory," 1987

The psychoanalyst is a historian who shows us that our histories are also the way we conceal the past from ourselves;
the way we both acknowledge it and disavow it at the same
time.
—Adam Phillips, *Becoming Freud*, 2014

In her 1987 essay "The Site of Memory," Toni Morrison describes the
work of the African American novelist through a metaphor that links
black cultural memory to the seasonal floods of the Mississippi River. In
this metaphor, the author's romanticized floods defy spatial restrictions
installed by levees, dams, and dikes. Moreover, they disrupt the common
temporal assumption of forward-moving time, for instead of progressing
along a projected course, the waters burst through modern infrastruc-
tures of containment, reverting to their "original places" by way of an
organic "remembering." Countering the cliché that time marches on,
Morrison proposes that time turns backward in an eternal and inevitable pattern. Similarly, she asserts that black writers are summoned by
a powerful "flood" of collective, cultural memory that overwhelms the

boundaries of the individual and interrupts the unidirectional flow of time, returning the author's imagination to the unredeemed origins of the African presence in the New World.[1]

Morrison's identification of a powerful, recursive force acting on the modern black writer's consciousness accounts for a historical turn within her own oeuvre: Published in the same year, "The Site of Memory" and her Pulitzer Prize–winning novel, *Beloved*, inaugurate the author's protracted literary exploration of the history of American slavery. At the same time, and as her generalized language suggests, Morrison is describing what was by then an ongoing re-orientation of African American literature toward the psychic, moral, and documentary problems posed by the African American slave past. This literary phenomenon, retroactively consolidated under the name "contemporary narratives of slavery,"[2] begins in the twilight years of the modern Civil Rights Movement and continues robustly into the present, having gained considerable momentum since the late 1980s from Morrison's brilliance and celebrity.[3] Collectively, contemporary narratives of slavery dramatize African Americans' enduring attachments to an unresolved history of racial trauma that appears at once as a site of unresolved suffering and an object of reparative desire. Concurrently—and controversially—this thriving genre has worked to enshrine the slave past's "primacy in black critical thought." As Stephen Best opines, the unabated proliferation of contemporary narratives of slavery and their attendant criticism have exerted such influence that, "currently, it passes for an unassailable truth that the slave past provides a ready prism for apprehending the black political present."[4]

What accounts for the extraordinary potency of the contemporary discourse on slavery in black literary studies? I argue that this power derives in part from the widely shared assumption that the contemporary narrative of slavery embeds an enticing promise to the reader. This promise says that the act of reading will compel a difficult, emotional, and productive psychic labor; it will deliver you to a new and self-revelatory state of consciousness with both personal and political implications. On this view, Morrison's "route back to our original place" describes more than the undertaking of the black writer inundated by historical memory. The "route" charted by contemporary narratives of slavery also extends itself as a *hermeneutic of therapeutic reading*. The principal tenets of this hermeneutic include the elevation of textual immersion over critical distance taking and the pursuit of transformative pain. Its rewards include self-knowledge, authenticity, and psychic healing.[5]

Consider the well-worn literary figure of the modern black subject who renounces slavery's governing power over fictions of the self.[6] Her life in the present is marked by anxious self-policing and the elusiveness of psychic fulfillment, the contours of which only come into view when she begins to apprehend within herself "feelings and a host of subliminal memories" that attend the lost histories of her ancestors.[7] Through the smallest of imaginative leaps, the contemporary reader may put herself in the place of such a protagonist, as a present-day subject in need of a historically directed consciousness-raising experience.[8]

For example, Lizzie DuBose, the protagonist of Phyllis Alesia Perry's novel, *Stigmata* (1998), is born into the Southern black bourgeoisie in 1960. Her father is a respected doctor, famous for his ostentatious red convertible; her mother is a well-spoken sorority hostess to whom she playfully refers as "Mrs. Dr. Sarah Lancaster DuBose." As a teenager, Lizzie inherits an ancestral trunk from her deceased great-aunt. The trunk is full of disintegrating artifacts that connect Lizzie to a hitherto unfamiliar matrilineage, stretching back to the Middle Passage. Opening the trunk, Lizzie comes upon a crumbling "sheaf of papers" that bears the testimony of Lizzie's great-great-grandmother, Ayo, as dictated to her daughter, Joy: "I am Ayo. Joy. I choose to remember. This is for those whose bones lie in the heart of mother ocean for those who tomorrows I never knew who groaned and died in the damp dark beside me. You rite this daughter for me and for them."[9]

Joy's conspicuous misspelling of the word "write" calls attention to its homonyms, "right" and "rite," foreshadowing Lizzie's efforts to repair a legacy of historical trauma through repeated acts of suffering and bearing witness. In the twenty years that follow her inheritance of the trunk, Lizzie is seized by a series of dream-like possessions, through which she is made to re-inhabit the tortured lives of her great-aunt, great-grandmother, and great-great-grandmother. These traumatic experiences operate as rituals of shared physical and psychic pain, ultimately initiating Lizzie into a trans-historical coterie of "forever people" who live "at the bottom of heaven . . . in [a] circle [of time]." Indeed, although Lizzie loses years of her life to her demanding and injurious past—including fourteen years in a psychiatric institution—she ultimately concludes that working through generations of historical trauma is essential to her freedom in the present. The joint enterprises of remembering and processing, she concludes, "cured me of fear. Made me live with every part of myself every day. Cured me of the certainty that I was lost."[10]

Lizzie is the chosen heroine who experiences the redemptive power of memory, but the novel also proposes that her conversion is transmissible and replicable. In one scene, her cousin, Ruth, rescues Lizzie from a trance. As Lizzie comes to, Ruth grabs her wrist, and a "searing pain" travels from Lizzie's body into her cousin's. "[Ruth's] eyes widen and she looks otherworldly, her body rigid with pain, her hair hanging limply against her chin."[11] The reader occupies a position parallel to Ruth, a voyeur who witnesses Lizzie's pain and is invited to absorb it. Lizzie is our guide, and pain our vehicle: Following Lizzie's lead, we are meant to eschew the repressive forces of the contemporary moment, to reclaim history by enduring its punishments, and to "right" the unredeemed past and the amnesiac present. Indeed, Perry herself endorses such a reading of her novel when, in a 2009 interview with Corinne Duboin, she criticizes contemporary culture's reluctance to "deal with the emotional" effects of the slave past. Pushing back against this perceived norm, Perry positions her novel as a vehicle for "[going] deeper [than facts] in our own psyche" and confronting the fact that "we inherit other people's pain."[12]

Marked by the twin gestures of historical reclamation and psychic conversion, the hermeneutic of therapeutic reading strains against normative academic conventions of critical reading, which, to paraphrase Michael Warner, valorize distantiation, scrutiny, and judgment.[13] Nevertheless, this approach to textual encounter has attained enormous critical purchase, persisting, through decades of African Americanist scholarship, as a popular perspective on how we should read the fictions of racial remembrance that dominate today's black literature. The appeal of therapeutic reading is anything but mysterious: Its promise of reparative return speaks to the desire to make sense of an unredeemed past and its painful legacy and to locate agency and a capacity for social change in the act of reading.

But if, for some critics, the new discourse on slavery "[engenders] a liberatory effect on the reader" by "[compelling] survivors (and we are all survivors) to face the truth,"[14] then for others, this discourse makes dubious claims on historical memory and manufactures false hope about the possibilities for historical repair. On this view, therapeutic reading threatens to channel the reader or critic's desires into toxic and unactionable patterns. It teaches a fixed and misguided concept of racial identity, it cultivates an insatiable desire for recrimination, and in its preoccupation with history, it forestalls or even forecloses imaginative engagements with the present.

The latter position presents itself as the opposite or "outside" of therapeutic reading, yet ironically, it is also predicated on the idea that we are meant to experience fictions of trans-generational, racial remembrance vicariously or, at least, as an instructive model for redressing the ailments of contemporary consciousness. Thus the most vehement complaint that the contemporary narrative of slavery inspires is not about craftsmanship, style, or even subject matter. Instead, it is the notion that this literature compels us to think about history and identity in the wrong way: "It redescribes something we have never known as something we have forgotten and thus makes the historical past a part of our own experience."[15] From this point of view, fictions of historical return are dangerous and to be avoided. In Chapter 1, I name this critical orientation *prohibitive reading*. Prohibitive reading is not the opposite but the inverse of therapeutic reading. A false alternative, it ironically absorbs the premises of therapeutic reading—that contemporary narratives of slavery will transport and transform their readers—as its own. What it offers is not a different way of reading *Stigmata* (for example) but the conclusion, based on its replication of therapeutic reading, that we should not read such novels at all.

Throughout this book, I first try to think against the assumption that therapeutic and prohibitive reading are the only ways to approach contemporary narratives of slavery. I do not preclude the possibility that literature may enable transformative psychic effects. However, I contend that a critical over-investment in the promise or danger of therapeutic reading has crowded out inquiry into how therapeutic reading operates as a *literary figure*: inviting decoding, engendering a diverse range of direct and indirect psycho-affective responses, and accommodating a variety of competing interpretations. My point is this: The plots neither compel nor prohibit identification with the traumatic past. They desire identification while recognizing the terms may be strained, disappointing, elusive, inhibiting, inassimilable with modern life, or otherwise non-cathartic.

Approaching therapeutic/prohibitive reading from another direction, a second aim of this study is to interrogate the premise that re-experiencing historical pain is transformative and necessary. I expose the psychic logic and moral economy that undergird the notion of redemptive suffering, and I look into how narrative forms are made to hold contradictory desires for healing or psychic liberation, on the one hand, and for the revitalization of historical injury, on the other. If we are to produce a robust accounting of black literary studies' historical turn, then we must clarify the role of pain in fantasies of historical repair and think through the irreconcilable wishes that live within the desire to re-inhabit the slave past.

As a critique and intervention into how we read African American literature now, this study focuses primarily on the genre that has dominated the field since the decline of the modern Civil Rights Movement and the hermeneutic most common to its surrounding criticism—the contemporary narrative of slavery and therapeutic/prohibitive reading, respectively. Yet, even as I underscore the importance of assessing the logic and resonance of black literary discourse's historical turn, I am also concerned with how therapeutic reading's claim to moral urgency may inadvertently produce rote habits of canon construction and interpretation, blinding us to contemporaneous works of African American fiction that expressly disavow an orientation toward the past. Thus I undertake a third critical effort to uncover a shadow archive of post–Civil Rights black literary production that imagines narrative frames other than the slave past for thinking about racialized experience, feeling, identification, and desire.

In short, what follows is a book about how post–Civil Rights African American writers and their critics have come to understand the work of black literature and the enterprise of reading, particularly in relation to questions of history and historiography. This query is staged through analyses of a subset of black literature—including but not limited to the contemporary narrative of slavery—that expressly dwells on the methods, investments, and political implications of encountering the past through today's African American literature. The texts that I study em-plot proxy readers, quests for origins, overt or ironic eschewals of his-tory, historian-protagonists, and other strategic literary devices. Among the authors I study are Toni Morrison, David Bradley, Randall Kenan, Octavia Butler, Gayl Jones, Andrea Lee, James Alan McPherson, Alice Randall, and Charles Johnson. Read together, they produce a meta-literary and meta-historical discourse that guides my critical engage-ment with the hermeneutic of therapeutic/prohibitive reading.

Alongside a survey of this self-reflexive sub-genre, I develop a body of theories—derived from, but not entirely reducible to, psychoanalytic theory—that offers insight into how social injury and collective grief in-habit and drive the stories we tell about race and racism, trauma and sur-vival, past and present, and, to borrow a phrase from Saidiya Hartman, "the afterlife of slavery."[16] This book is organized by three particular psychoanalytic idioms—trauma, masochism, and depression—through which the grief and desire of African Americanist writing and reading attain clarity. But, more fundamentally, the heart of the theoretical ap-paratus that I put forth consists simply of the belief that narrative and critical desire are not always transparent, literal, or self-announcing and may manifest in unexpected, intricate, and inconsistent ways. With an eye toward such possibilities for textual misdirection and opacity, I re-examine certain reading practices that have solidified into habit and he-gemony to open the question of how, and with what effects, we might read African American literature differently.

## Psychoanalysis and African American Literature

Despite a number of formidable contributions to a psychoanalytic dis-course on African American literature and culture (notably by Badia Ahad, Anne Anlin Cheng, Arlene Keizer, Hortense Spillers, and Clau-dia Tate), it is an understatement to say that psychoanalytic methods remain unpopular in black literary studies. Tate succinctly notes that psychoanalysis "has carried a lot of irritating baggage that has made it virtually an anathema in the black intellectual community."[17] Indeed, African Americanist objections to psychoanalytic theory are various and often well founded. There is a long history of manipulating psycho-pathological discourses to shore up racist policies, practices, and beliefs;

psychoanalytic theory's claims to universal applicability are belied by the cultural specificity of its origins; and unveiling and interpreting the formal construction of interior life can appear to be an esoteric task, removed from urgent political imperatives for racial justice.

Except for my investment in re-valuing the immaterial, I erect no defense of psychoanalytic theory on these grounds. Indeed, a stronger caveat is in order because, although my thinking is often guided by psychoanalysis, my use of this theoretical paradigm is critical, non-exclusive, and often disloyal. Taking liberty with Adam Phillips's audacious decree that "psychoanalysts [should be] people who are only practising psychoanalysis until something better turns up," the chapters in this book unfold promiscuously, following categories of psychic processing that are first named and given shape in psychoanalysis but that subsequently accumulate proliferating, extra-clinical meanings.[18] For example, Chapter 2 is concerned with the logic and mechanics of masochism, but I am not solely—or even primarily—interested in what Freud says about masochism. I am equally interested in the appropriations and afterlives of this trope in everyday language, in feminist and queer theory, in cultural studies, and in political philosophy. Put another way, although a majority of the chapters in this book start with psychoanalytic theory, my aim is not to reify this mode of interpretation as the bearer of an ultimate truth but to use it as a springboard for thinking expansively about how we craft, receive, transmit, and revise stories about the experience and meaning of contemporary racialized subjectivity.

In this capacity—as an intricate and comprehensive grammar for talking about how narrative construction and interpretation reveal dramas of history, power, and desire—psychoanalysis provides an unparalleled resource. By shifting the interpretive endeavor from the *what* to the *how* of narrative meaning,[19] it allows us to decipher the ways in which psychic forms constitute rhetorical forms and, inversely, how rhetorical forms may be examined to reveal covert systems of attachment and desire.[20] Thus, ironically, in light of its original therapeutic uses, psychoanalytic theory is a tool that allows us to circumvent the literal or performative claims of therapeutic reading. Through psychoanalysis, we may approach the narrative construct of transformative, historical return as a coded story, to be read "more like [a dream] than [like] pieces of reliable documentary evidence."[21]

Moreover, as a capacious and versatile mode of theorizing the interior, psychoanalysis holds promise for African American studies in
particular, insofar as "race" itself is an entity whose legibility demands
an accounting for the phantasmatic. In the eyes of some, race may stubbornly presume to be the visible and self-evident mark of biological
difference, yet even the most vehement essentialists will find no easy
answer to Spillers's rhetorical question, "What is it that 'sees'—in other
words, do we look with the eyes, or with the psyche?"[22] In its most compelling descriptions, and especially after DuBois, "race" is a structure of
consciousness, a legacy of loss and injury (which is to say, of history),
and a cathected sign that mediates fictions of identification and desire. I
am interested in these abstract valences of "blackness" that accompany
and complicate materialist renditions of African American history: Psychoanalysis, however flawed, is indispensable to my interpretive task.

Reading a multi-authored collection of literature in aggregate,
through the lens of psychoanalytic theory requires one to make at least
a tacit appeal to some notion of collective consciousness. What psychic formation, then, is revealed in the exegeses that follow? Certainly,
the point of this book is not to unveil some distinct and cohesive entity called the Black Psyche. That African Americans differ from one
another, bearing individuated and idiosyncratic personalities, is the
most elementary disproof of racism. Moreover, and as countless critics, journalists, and pundits agree, the idea of a unified and coherent
racial identity has become increasingly untenable in a post–Civil Rights
America shaped by the end of de jure segregation, post-Fordist de-
industrialization and an ever-expanding wealth gap, and the growth of
the prison industrial complex alongside the unprecedented rise of an
institutionally assimilated black elite.[23]

Yet, given the history that establishes and subsequently constrains the
black presence in the New World, it is equally self-evident that African
Americans as a group are collectively subjected to a reductive system of
social interpellation—one with diverse and often catastrophic disadvan-
tages. As Dionne Brand elaborates, "The image which emerges from the
Door of No Return is public property belonging to a public exclusive of
the Black bodies which signify it. . . . One is constantly refuting it, or ig-
noring it, or troubling it, or parodying it, or tragically reaffirming it."[24] The
psychology of blackness, we might deduce, is not a singularity of mind

but an axis of identity formation that is experienced, on the one hand, as heritable and social and, on the other hand (borrowing Spillers's words), as "private" and "mine."[25] It corresponds to an array of primal scenes, prohibitions, and cathected objects, to which the individual psyche may respond in an infinite variety of predictable or unpredictable ways.

## Re-framing African American Literature's Historical Turn

A basic premise of psychoanalytic literary theory is the idea that the text and the psyche operate in analogous ways. Both produce meaning through narrative fictions that simultaneously articulate and repress one's history, affiliations, and governing desires; both rely on signifying processes that at once enmesh and individuate the subject from external structures of culture and history; both hover between the domains of fantasy and the "real." Extending the reach of this comparison, Susan Stanford Friedman proposes that we can read deliberately constellated books by a single author (such as James Joyce's fiction that features Stephen Dedalus) as akin to non-autonomous "serial dreams," which may unfold over a prolonged period of weeks or even months. Reading an oeuvre like a dream sequence, she elaborates, "requires an analysis of the gaps in each that can be filled in by the others—the traces of displacement, condensation, and secondary revision that can be deciphered by juxtaposing and superimposing the texts in the whole series."[26] Put another way, for Friedman, the interconnectedness of serial dreams provides the model and rationale for an intertextual approach to psychoanalytic literary criticism. Freud's notion of a psychic "common ground," which allows for the interpretive aggregation of discontinuous dreams, corresponds to the literary idea of a "composite text," in which an assemblage of resonant, consonant, and dissonant fantasies offers insight into a "whole series" of textual production.[27]

Although Friedman's translation of psychoanalysis to an intertextual mode of literary criticism pertains specifically to bodies of writing that are unified under the hand of a single writer, I extend her method to the study of closely knit literary sub-genres that, together, operate as an inconstant and discontinuous "composite text" about post–Civil Rights African American feeling, identification, and desire. Like serial dreams, the archive of meta-literary and meta-historical black writing I examine announces its interconnection through the repetition and revision of particular figures, images, and themes. Among these are the returning ancestor, the haunted modern subject, and the re-vivified slave owner or patroller; the scar, the heirloom, and the family secret; and intergenerational memory, vicarious or substitutive pain, myths of an original black innocence, and fantasies of narrative's reparative power.[28]

This common symbolic vocabulary appears even in a book like Andrea Lee's *Sarah Phillips*, to which I turn in Chapter 3. *Sarah Phillips* explicitly eschews the ideological orientation and backward gaze of the contemporary narrative of slavery. In the first chapter of Lee's novella, the eponymous protagonist "[awakes] with a start from a horrid dream in which [she] was conducting a monotonous struggle with an old woman with a dreadful spidery strength in her arms." Although Lee's plot cuts an aggressively different path from the contemporary narrative of slavery, focusing its narration on the present and near past, this departure is shadowed by the unanswered call of a familiar figure: a "dark and leathery" elder, whose surprising strength hints at the fearsome possibility of trans-historical abduction.[29] In this respect, *Sarah Phillips* is not simply a rejection but rather a "displacement" and "revision" of a primal scene familiar to the contemporary narrative of slavery. Its dissonant invocation of the fantasy of historical return betrays the text's psychic continuity with the very cultural imaginary that Sarah struggles against and renounces.[30]

In the chapters that follow, I read African American literature's historical turn as an articulation of collective racial grief that is temporally and psycho-affectively dense. The (lost) object of grief consists simultaneously in the unresolved trauma of the slave past and the political, civic, and psychic dismantling of the modern Civil Rights Movement. The principle that binds these moments of loss is something like the Freudian notion of deferred action (*Nachträglichkeit*), which posits that the temporality of psychic life is irreducible to forward-moving, linear causality. As Wendy Brown explains it, "Since grief inevitably recalls prior and contiguous losses, . . . whatever we are mourning most immediately might be the scene for discovering all that has gone unmourned."[31] Similarly, I submit that the crisis in black progressivism, following the premature decline of the Civil Rights and Black Power Movements, is experienced as a historically resonant psychic injury that reactivates the unresolved, original wound of slavery. Articulating the discovery of the present moment's unmourned past, contemporary black literature's energetic engagement with history reveals a temporally split, yet thickly interwoven, model of post–Civil Rights African American grief.

Consider, as a suggestive illustration of this triangulated psychic economy, James McBride's 2008 contemporary narrative of slavery, *Song Yet Sung*. The novel's primary action is set in 1850 and follows Liz Spocott, a fugitive slave traveling along Maryland's eastern shore. Anointed "The Dreamer" by a mysterious "Woman With No Name," Liz becomes a messenger of black political hope. Her prophetic visions of the future lend energy and teleological promise to the unfolding abolitionist struggle. In one such vision, Liz bears witness to Martin Luther King, Jr., the archetypal Dreamer of African American cultural history. Her vision begins as a distant, incomprehensible image of a "colored preacher" standing before a crowd of "white and colored, [holding] hands," "stretching as far as the eye could see." But it is brought nearer when the Civil Rights leader "[reaches] into the past and [shouts] a song from our own time!" Finding continuity between the suffering of her antebellum present and the salvific image of the March on Washington, Liz describes King's invocation of the antebellum "song" as the guarantee of a redemptive futurity: "I heard this preacher say [the last words of the song]," Liz foretells. "And when he did, them words changed the whole world somehow . . . 'Free at last. Thank God Almighty, I'm free at last.'"[32]

In this way, McBride draws a familiar connection between a historical pretext of African American enslavement and the redemptive telos of the twentieth-century Civil Rights Movement.[33] Yet this straightforward progress narrative is disrupted by another vision that persistently intrudes on Liz's consciousness, casting a shadow of doubt over the ostensible triumph of the "colored preacher." This second vision features "a colored boy . . . adorned with shiny jewelry—around his neck, his fingers, even in his mouth. A thousand drums seemed to play behind him, and as he spoke with the rat-tat-tat speed of a telegraph machine, he preached murder, and larceny, cursing women savagely and promising to kill, maim, and destroy. He shook his jewelry towards the sky and shouted, Who am I? Who am I? He seemed not to know."[34]

If a shared song produces a direct and obvious link from the abolitionist struggle to Civil Rights activism, then the rap song initially bewilders Liz with its violent unfamiliarity. (We will bracket, for expediency, the didactic respectability politics of Liz's prophetic visions.) Still, like King's speech, the rap song ultimately exerts a transportive power on The Dreamer, suggesting itself as another movement of the "song" of black political history. Staring into the eyes of the raging performer, Liz temporarily gains a privileged view of his subject position. "When she peered into [his eyes] she found herself inside him, looking at him through the generations and generations of who he was, and where he'd come from, seeing face after face until she finally came to a face she recognized."[35] Here, Liz's future-oriented gaze turns backward, so that the post–Civil Rights future becomes a lens through which she reencounters her own, antebellum context. What she recognizes in the sum of her visions is not only a face but also an unlikely genealogy. Both King and the anonymous rapper, we learn, are descendants of Liz's accidental ally, the Woolman: a slave turned maroon who bears the unsolidified potential for good or evil.

Adjoining the antebellum period, the modern Civil Rights Movement, and a post–Civil Rights era marked by cultural alienation and political disillusionment, the song reveals the teleological freedom quest folding back upon itself, as the moment in which radical political possibility has been lost rebounds upon a moment to which it has failed to arrive. Where King's speech inspirits Liz's orientation toward a future freedom, the rap song returns her to the slave past, in search of rehabilitative love and a moment of uncharted possibility. Seen in retrospect from a distant future, the Woolman's character gains new significance as he becomes an avatar for black political uncertainty and the search for meaning in the age of hip hop. Indeed, although the plot of *Song Yet Sung* is ostensibly pushed forward by Liz's mystical orientation toward the future, it is her revised vision of the past, routed through the contemporary rapper, that most tellingly elucidates McBride's project of novelized retrospection.

This selective summary of McBride's plot gets at the heart of my project insofar as it inscribes the attainment and loss of freedom as preconditions to the searching, recursive desire that loss compels. Similarly, I argue that African American literature's historical turn is governed by a desire born of post–Civil Rights political disappointment. But my analysis departs from McBride's portrait of Liz's clear-eyed, trans-historical vision, for in lieu of a prophet, I read through the caveat that we represent and witness the past always and only through the inventive prism of contemporary desire. On this view, the "history" the contemporary narrative of slavery sets out to name and grieve is not something buried intact that we may exhume and hold up for inspection. It is more akin to the psychoanalytic idea of memory, in which the past is an "echo" whose "meaning is made . . . in the revision consequent upon deferral."[36] Redescribing the painful past, fiction remakes its meaning in and for the present at a time of historically resonant, felt crisis.

I am certainly not the first to imagine that grief powers post–Civil Rights black writing or even that the object of its grief is temporally dense. Yet the story I tell about the psycho-affective contours of contemporary African American literature and criticism departs from a majority of the existing scholarship in its sustained interest in grief's propensity to be opaque to itself. Throughout this book, I assume that fictional accounts of the past function, not as a psychic portal into the past, but as an encrypted map of contemporary fantasies that circulate through the idiom of historical grief. Put another way, my premise is the belief that literature will carry not only its self-announcing content but also "disguised representations of forbidden" or disavowed "desire."[37] What fictions do we invent to describe the pained past that swells within contemporary experiences of grief? What do these fictions reveal, and what do they conceal? These questions lie at the heart of my inquiry.

In the first two chapters, I read black historical fiction on its own terms, with particular attention to how it imagines or projects its ideal reader and how it curates the reader's encounter with the past. Chapter 1 employs trauma theory to unveil the psychic structure of grief and desire at work in several canonical novels of historical return—Toni Morrison's *Beloved* and *Jazz*, David Bradley's *Chaneysville Incident*, and Randall Kenan's *Visitation of Spirits*. Against the grain of much of the extant criticism, I show how these novels unmistakably foreclose the promise of therapeutic reading, in spite of the desire for reparative return that persists within them. Whereas Chapter 1 challenges the viability of therapeutic/prohibitive reading as a prescriptive approach to black historical fiction, Chapter 2 suspends incredulity toward the promise of therapeutic reading to examine what the desire for this kind of transformative experience is made of. Through readings of Octavia Butler's

*Kindred* and Gayl Jones's *Corregidora*, I expose the difficult truth that literary fantasies of reparative return—though often interpreted as fantasies of gaining freedom—necessarily entail the pursuit of pain or self-injury. I turn to various theories of masochism to discern how African American literature navigates these uncomfortably joined desires.

Chapter 3 begins with the claim that many contemporary narratives of slavery minimize or disavow the modes and forms of grief that accompany the narrative frame of the present. By contrast, I identify several contemporary texts—Andrea Lee's *Sarah Phillips*, James Alan McPherson's "Elbow Room," and Alice Randall's *Rebel Yell*—that de-center slavery as a thematic concern and instead foreground such proximate sources of collective grief as the loss of black theo-political leaders, the end of the sixties and the spirit of white liberal backlash, and the rise of black conservatism. Articulating a range of psychic responses to the loss of what we might call, in aggregate, "Civil Rights idealism," I argue that this anti-historical archive contains those stories that black historical fiction cannot claim, the stories whose disavowal marks the boundary of the contemporary African Americanist literary/critical hegemony. If Chapters 1 and 2 examine how black historical fiction enshrines the ancestral past as the primary object of contemporary grief and trauma as the appropriate psychic modality for encountering that grief, then Chapter 3 reveals that prescription's remainder: a deliberately presentist literature routed through depressive states, such as defeatism, apathy, boredom, irritation, and fatigue.

Moreover, I propose that this body of anti-historical fiction allows us to re-imagine the contemporary narrative of slavery in a new light, as itself symptomatic of a melancholic turn, following the foreshortened trajectory of Civil Rights idealism. While I am not alone in characterizing contemporary narratives of slavery as melancholic, I diverge from formulations offered by scholars such as Kenneth W. Warren and Stephen Best, who locate melancholia in the pathos of a de-throned black elite or, more generically, in historical fiction's maladaptive attachment to the slave past. By contrast, my claim is that the melancholia of contemporary narratives of slavery reveals itself in how these novels downplay the importance of the post–Civil Rights present as an object of loss and desire. (Even in *Song Yet Sung*, the era of the misguided rapper only momentarily, and ephemerally, achieves representation.) To say this is not to diminish painful feelings in the present that we attribute to the slave past, nor is it to argue that slavery has been sufficiently grieved or that trauma offers an inappropriate lens for the study of contemporary black literature. Rather, I propose that historical plots of slavery may *simultaneously* represent a legitimate and transparent object of grief and work to forestall or encrypt other forms of unspeakable love and loss.

Taken together, the first three chapters contest the hermeneutic of therapeutic/prohibitive reading and propose alternative reading strategies, modeled on the psychoanalytic idioms of trauma, masochism, and depression (though these framing concepts, too, at times emerge as the objects of my critique). Rather than building toward a comprehensive or final word, I frame my analyses as an exploration of the messy richness of contemporary African American literature's engagement with history. I offer the fourth and final chapter as a provisional capstone: In it, I read together Charles Johnson's *Oxherding Tale* and Toni Morrison's *Paradise* to re-cast black literary studies' historical turn as a self-consciously ambivalent meditation on the past and the present, on the psychic labor that founds and confounds identity, on the medium of literature, and on the hydra-headed force of desire.

Let me stress that what follows is neither a guidebook nor a checklist but a series of provocations through which I aim to loosen the grip of an increasingly obdurate critical impasse in black literary studies. What would it look like to read contemporary black writing neither as the redemptive guardian of an "ethical relationship to the past"[38] nor as the nefarious guarantor of a prescriptive vision of black identity, forever tethered to the irredeemable wounds of the slave past? Is there an analytic lens through which we might richly apprehend the inextinguishable desire for historical return while also admitting into consideration the passing of time, the shifting political and epistemological grounds of "race," and the corollary emergence of what Randall Kenan describes as "new and hateful monsters [exacting] a different price"?[39] How might we cultivate a capacious, agnostic eye with which to survey and scrutinize those contradictions of time, scale, and desire that live at the heart of our critical enterprise today: then and now, crisis and mundane feeling, redemptive longing and its cynical disavowal? This book attempts to read African American literature toward such an end.

# 1

## Against Prohibitive Reading (On Trauma)

### "Wasness"

Among the many responses summoned by Kenneth W. Warren's contro-versial polemic, *What Was African American Literature?* is Aldon Lynn Nielsen's critical review essay, "Wasness," which appears within a printed symposium in the June 13, 2011, issue of the *Los Angeles Review of Books*. As the title of his essay suggests, Nielsen is wary of Warren's proposed periodization schema, and in his response, he seeks to trouble the points of initiation and closure Warren delineates. Whereas Warren defines African American literature as a "postemancipation phenomenon that gained coherence as an undertaking in the social world defined by the system of Jim Crow segregation,"[1] Nielsen retorts, "*Why would anyone be satisfied with such a procrustean definition of the field of African American literature?*" (Nielsen's italics).[2] For Nielsen, the claim of "was-ness" is arbitrary and ideologically motivated: Despite its capacity to inspire impassioned response, its ultimate aim is to narrow or foreclose the future of African Americanist literary inquiry. "Wasness," Nielsen argues, works to re-tool a conservative literary establishment that once exerted its regulatory power through pejorative questions about "isness" (i.e., *is* there an African American literature?).

Nielsen captures some of my skepticism toward Warren's periodizing hypothesis but stops short of examining what most interests me about the rhetorical uses of "wasness." In what follows, I argue that "wasness" serves as Warren's antidote to the object of his most virulent critique: a literary and critical rejection of linear, objectivist history in the years since the decline of the modern Civil Rights Movement. Taking particu-lar umbrage at the post–Civil Rights vogue in historical fiction, Warren identifies and derides what he sees as the pervasive, misguided desire of African American writers and critics to dissolve the fact of historical distance. Such desire, he argues, gains traction from its promise to posi-tion "present-day" actors "in the role of potential hero, or even freedom fighter, on behalf of a past that almost magically becomes our contemporary in terms of what it needs or demands from us."[3] Warren's claims against such aspirations to literary heroism are those of the pragmatist. Countering fantasies of trans-historical identification and agency with an appeal to epistemological metrics of discrete periodization (such as chronology, progress, and fact), he rests his case on the decisive claim of "wasness."

*What Was African American Literature?* exemplifies a growing body of criticism that casts black studies' powerful orientation toward the past as the new and misguided dominant of creative and intellectual culture. This criticism contends that proliferating representations of the past as a timeless, living, moralizing force offer a wrong account of history because they hinge on knowledge claims that deny temporal differentiation, "divesting history of movement and change."[4] No figure is more frequently invoked as the face of this perceived threat than Toni Morrison's voracious, beloved ghost who speaks the famous words, "all of it is now    it is always now."[5] And, the argument goes, the collapse of *what was* into our understanding of *what is* isn't just wrong; it's dangerous. Through this act of chronological defiance, history ceases to be about the facts of what happened and instead comes into view through the "radical expropriation" of subjectivity and meaning.[6] The experiential authority of the past's "true" victims is usurped by a contemporary discourse that presumes to speak in their place, on behalf of modern resentments and desires.

The principle of temporal collapse that so offends critics such as Warren, Stephen Best, Douglas Jones, Walter Benn Michaels, and Robert Reid-Pharr is the very principle that defines the reading strategy I call "therapeutic reading"—a hermeneutic premised on the reader's capacity for psychic transformation, by way of powerful textual encounters with the traumatic past. Michaels, for example, recasts the promise of therapeutic reading as its danger when he writes, "Setting out to remember 'the disremembered,' [*Beloved*] redescribes something we have never known as something we have forgotten and thus makes the historical past a part of our own experience."[7] In his view, books like *Beloved* are historical fiction in that they are novels about the past, but they are an insidious *something more* because they work to indoctrinate contemporary readers through the ventriloquized call of a pained and unappeased racial past.

The idea of "wasness" asserts itself as an epistemological check on contemporary authors and critics like Morrison, who in the name of impossible reparative desires, would compromise the singularity and boundedness of the irrecoverable past. Yet, as Nielsen anticipates, the critical mobilization of "wasness" works less to illuminate than to invalidate and end literary and critical interest in fantasies of historical return. As we will see, the point, for Michaels, is not to read *Beloved* in another way but to establish *Beloved*'s complicity in a toxic cultural formation. To describe this emergent mode of reading that compels the zealous rejection of an unfinished, accessible, or demanding past, I coin the term "prohibitive reading." Authored as a global rejection of therapeutic reading, prohibitive reading regards "narratives of historical continuity and temporal compression"[8] as strategies of inauspicious political conversion. On this basis, it aims to decenter—and often, to discredit—black literary studies' enduring preoccupation with the topics of racial memory and the history of slavery.

My critique of prohibitive reading is extensive but not unsympathetic; it is also distinct from an endorsement of therapeutic reading. In fact, I contend that both of these reading strategies are built on foundational misperceptions about how trauma manifests and circulates in literary discourse, and I turn to trauma theory to offer a third alternative. Trauma theory is informative not only because of the self-evident truth that slavery was traumatic but, more specifically, because it enjoins the psychic structure of trauma to an epistemological critique of conventional modes of historical representation. By describing historical catastrophe's disorienting effects on how we give and receive accounts of the past, trauma theory offers unique insight into the motives that compel the structure and style of black historical fiction and its criticism.

## Traumatic Time in Contemporary Black Novels

The fundamental effect of trauma, as it is theorized in contemporary, cross-disciplinary humanistic thought, is the profound disruption of the "narrative unity of life."[9] This conceptualization begins with the assumption that human life is made intelligible, and thus meaningful, through cohesive, temporally organized stories that we tell about ourselves and, through this process, master. One's sense of self, and of her place in history and the world, is determined in some measure by her grasp of history—the degree to which she achieves a sense of narrative continuity in, and narrative authority over, her life. Traumatic events interrupt the stories we tell about history and identity by introducing to our imagined life trajectory cognitively inassimilable circumstances of grand-scale horror or loss. Confronted by the unimaginable within the domain of the real, the traumatized subject becomes unable to wield history in the service of self-story. She can no longer coherently narrate her life because the crisis event renders her life incoherent to her. Thus, as opposed to the normative pattern in which people appropriate and arrange historical facts to tell their stories, the trauma victim becomes, to borrow a word from Cathy Caruth, "possessed" by history, haunted and claimed by a past that not only breaks from existing narratives of self but, moreover, appears to foreclose the very terms of conventional narrativity, such as chronology, self-consistency, and causality.[10]

I define *traumatic time* as a structure of narrative temporality prevalent in late twentieth-century and early twenty-first-century African American literature that defies chronological mapping and instead takes shape through repeated, affectively charged references to an original traumatic event. Traumatic time is non-linear, dis-unified, and re-generated by the impossible desire for a redemptive return to the past. Contemporary black writers emplot these psychic and temporal characteristics through "formal disturbance[s]" or "narrative rupture[s],"[11] as well as various figures, including but not limited to haunting, possession, time travel, fantasy, dreams, and flights of the imagination.

Nearly thirty years after its publication, Morrison's *Beloved* (1987) remains the best-known example of an African American novel structured by traumatic time, its influence manifest in the degree to which the figure of the sacrificed child of slavery returning in ghostly form has become a familiar trope within a broadly conceived American cultural imaginary.[12] In her foreword to the novel's 2004 reissue, Morrison describes her intention to reproduce for the reader trauma's core experience of unresolved shock: "I wanted the reader to be kidnapped," she writes, "thrown ruthlessly into an alien environment as the first step into a shared experience with the book's population."[13] *Beloved*, in other words, is not only a novel *about* the trauma of slavery; it is a text whose very structure reproduces trauma's disruptive gesture. A brief review of the novel's plot illustrates this point.

Although the historical premise from which the book derives is Margaret Garner's act of infanticide in the panic of being pursued under the Fugitive Slave Law, the reader does not encounter this tragedy in real time. Rather, as is characteristic of most accounts of post-traumatic memory, the reader realizes the catastrophe belatedly, partially, and in fragments. We first encounter the protagonist, Sethe (whose past is modeled on Garner's), in 1873, seventeen years after she fled a Kentucky plantation, slit her daughter's throat, and bartered sex for a tombstone engraved with the word "Beloved." Her experience of the present, metaphorized as the home she shares with her surviving daughter, Denver, is haunted first by an invisible, restless spirit and later by that spirit made flesh. In her human form, the ghost announces her claim to Sethe's past when she gives her name as "Beloved."

Insatiable, compulsive, and bound to a catastrophic past that defies comprehension, Beloved is the embodiment of Sethe's traumatic memory. Beloved's characterological core, and the core of Sethe's trauma, consists in the failure of mother love against the assaults of slavery. Unable to assimilate this failure to a plausible narrative of logic or meaning, Beloved obsessively mines Sethe's memory for a maternal response to a wish that has already been foreclosed—a wish for the saving grace of "enough" love. "She left me behind. By myself," Beloved's complaint goes. "She is the one I need" (89). Or again, "She don't love me like I love her. I don't love nobody but her" (137).

Much as trauma is said to operate through the "*possession* of the one who experiences it,"[14] Beloved threatens to consume Sethe, to overwhelm Sethe's day-to-day life with her impossible, too-late demand to be remembered, loved, saved *in time*. Through the incessant force of Beloved's grievance, Sethe herself becomes obsessed with the task of satiating the ghost. Her psychic life comes to mirror Beloved's singularity of focus, excluding the social and the possibility of a livable present as an act of fidelity to a past that refuses to be forsaken. "There is no world outside my door," Sethe claims as Beloved's hold on her approaches the absolute. "I only need to know one thing. How bad is the scar?" (217).

"The scar" is at once the daughter's fatal wound and the aporetic core of maternal memory that the wound produces. Sethe cannot escape the gravitational pull of the horrific past, but neither can her memory articulate or fully confront the original traumatic event. Instead, she "circle[s] the subject," "round and round, never changing direction" (189). The core of the "circle" that Sethe—and the text—asymptotically approach is, in Ann Snitow's words, "the vacuum, the absence" of "a gap in history, a blank in consciousness."[15] Although Snitow does not explore this line of thought further, her reference to the commanding power of an absence resonates with Shoshana Felman's influential description of post-traumatic consciousness as "a missed encounter with reality, an encounter whose elusiveness cannot be owned and yet whose impact can no longer be erased, in taking hold of the [witness's] life which will henceforth unwittingly, compulsively strive toward an impossible completion of the missed experience."[16] Emplotting just such a patterned dance between fear and longing, re-experiencing and forgetting, *Beloved* reveals traumatic consciousness as its psychic and narrative infrastructure.

It is by now commonplace to say that *Beloved* is a book about traumatic memory—yet, in an apparent paradox, many critics also cite *Beloved* to claim that the term "trauma" is categorically inadequate to the cultural and historical specificity of African American affective life. This criticism adheres to a different logic than the case for "wasness," which holds that traumatic time is inherently and problematically opposed to the "truth" of periodization. Rather, it points to the medical establishment's traditions of misperception, exclusion, and abuse to question the applicability of psychopathological terminology for discussions of African American expressive culture. Barbara Christian, for example, proposes that Morrison's "unique accomplishment" in *Beloved* consists in her recognition of an Afrocentric cosmology as *the* most appropriate prism through which to explore the phenomenon of intergenerational psychic damage in black communities.[17] And indeed, Morrison's own writing, in and beyond the oeuvre of her fiction, tends to disavow psychoanalytic language in favor of vernacular descriptions of black historical consciousness and mental distress. For example, her neologism "rememory," coined in dialogue between Sethe and Denver, describes something very much like the psychoanalytic concept of trauma but also registers the importance of indigenous claims to naming and explaining psychic experience.

Such resistance to medicalizing discourses, including psychoanalysis, must be taken seriously, as an interpretive orientation grounded in protracted historical precedent. Indeed, "race" itself—a Western cultural trope that produces the otherness it purports to name—has frequently marshaled its authority through false assertions of medical "truths."[18] An example famous for its unabashed absurdity is the nineteenth-century diagnostic category of "drapetomania," a psychiatric condition unique to enslaved African Americans, symptomatized by a pathological compulsion to run away! Finding ample evidence of such instances in which racial "sciences" of "psychic damage" are leveraged against the rights and freedoms of African Americans, the historian Daryl Michael Scott voices a popular view when he concludes, "Experts who study social groups . . . should place the inner lives of people off limits."[19]

Indeed, even the modern discourse of trauma theory, though it carries no egregious history of anti-black use, has habitually neglected or tokenized African American experiences, thus inadvertently alienating a significant contingent of contemporary black writers and critics. As Michael Awkward observes, despite the growing scope and influence of trauma studies over the last twenty years, "The psychic upheavals resulting from slavery and Jim Crow [remain] parenthetical asides and afterthoughts" in the field's most significant texts.[20] For example, Caruth's highly acclaimed and hugely influential two-volume special issue of *American Imago*, later consolidated as the edited collection *Trauma: Explorations in Memory* (1995), includes seven essays on post-Holocaust Jewish memory; one essay on women, rape culture, and sexual assault; one essay on the AIDS crisis; an essay about Hiroshima; and an essay about a community's response to a catastrophic, underground gasoline leak. Its anthologized essays make no mention, even in passing or as a relevant intersectional coordinate, of African American psychic life.

The diagnostic category of post-traumatic stress disorder famously took shape through lobbies for veterans' rights and sexual assault survivors, but trauma as a field of humanistic inquiry has most energetically emphasized the historically and culturally specific experiences of Holocaust survivors and their descendants. My point, of course, is not to diminish the horror or the widespread cultural effects of the Holocaust, nor is it to downplay the extraordinary intellectual and moral value of the prolific literature on trauma that has come out of Jewish studies. On the contrary, my ultimate position amounts to advocacy *for* exploring how the extant oeuvre of trauma theory produces widely applicable models for re-encountering black historical fiction in new and revelatory ways. Yet, as I turn to trauma theory, I wish to proceed with a cautious eye toward the ways in which trauma theory *as a discourse* has frequently, if tacitly, positioned black histories outside the purview of such foundational human categories as "historical crisis" and "modern consciousness." Such a tradition requires not only expansion but also critique, a point that Morrison may be said to underscore if we interpret her dedication of *Beloved* to "Sixty Million/and more" as an aggressive counter to trauma theory's systemic—though not all-pervasive—silence on the topics of black genocide, enslavement, and subsequent suffering.[21]

Morrison is not alone in her assertion of a black claim to trauma discourse: Trauma's recognizable idioms of loss, rupture, repetition and aporia saturate the genre of the contemporary narrative of slavery, and in recent years, black literary scholarship has increasingly looked to trauma theory as one tool for deciphering the psychic landscape of African American subjectivity, past and present. Scholars including Awkward (*Philadelphia Freedoms*), Keith Byerman (*Remembering the Past*), Ashraf H. A. Rushdy (*Remembering Generations*), Lisa Woolfork (*Embodying American Slavery in Contemporary Culture*) and Arlene Keizer (*Black Subjects*) have performed extensive trauma-based readings of the psychologically mediated relationship between contemporary black life and the history of slavery, and in related studies, Saidiya Hartman (*Lose Your Mother*), Samira Kawash (*Dislocating the Color Line*), David Marriott (*Haunted Life*), Fred Moten (*In the Break*), and Christina Sharpe (*Monstrous Intimacies*) have more subtly invoked the psychic structures of traumatic consciousness to explore what Marriott calls "the occult presence of racial slavery, nowhere but nevertheless everywhere."[22] My readings of traumatic time and my corollary intervention into the governing assumptions of therapeutic/prohibitive reading join this growing body of criticism, offering an application of trauma theory that works neither to discipline nor to cure but to contextualize and decode narrative patterns that emerge from world-shattering psychic experiences.

## Postmemory

"It would not be going too far," Best asserts, to say, "that [Morrison's] Nobel Prize in Literature in 1993 positioned *Beloved* to shape the way a generation of scholars conceived of its ethical relationship to the past."[23] If *Beloved* is prohibitive reading's exemplary antagonist, then the critique it inspires hinges on two basic assertions. The first is that it is impossible to transmit memory, especially across inter-generational expanses. The second is that the narrative premise of inter-generationally transmitted memory operates as an insidious vehicle for the eternal reproduction of an unappeased, black political identity. According to Michaels, "If *Beloved's* characters," enmeshed as they are in the real-time suffering of slavery and its aftermath, "want to forget something that happened to them, its readers—'black people,' 'white people,' Morrison herself—are supposed to remember something that didn't happen to them." Slavery, he says, is "the thing they are supposed to remember," and the *idea* that its ancient, unappeased horror never dies is the force that consolidates contemporary black political identity as such.[24]

But *Beloved* is a curious focus for prohibitive reading's definitive object lesson. Its narrative action confines itself to the antebellum and postbellum periods, and although its youngest character, Denver, never experiences enslavement firsthand, she is born before Emancipation and under the threat of the Fugitive Slave Law. Thus the inter-generational and inter-personal transmissions of memory that Morrison stages are contained within a temporal stage of contemporaneity. True, in extra-literary venues, Morrison has spoken of her authorly desire to induce in readers a sense of slavery's arbitrary brutality, but it is hardly uncommon for fiction writers to willfully manipulate the affect and identifications of their readers. Strictly speaking, *Beloved* presents no *technology* for collapsing the present into the past, as do time travel novels or plots of mystical trans-historical identification, which explicitly encourage the colonizing gaze of the late twentieth or twenty-first century. Why, then, *Beloved*? It seems that what proponents of prohibitive reading find objectionable, presentist, and uniquely illustrated in *Beloved* is the structure of memory through which Sethe describes her and Denver's relationships to her past.

In a much-analyzed scene, Morrison coins the term "rememory" to describe the spatio-temporal qualities of traumatic memories that appear to become permanent and fixed. "Memory," Sethe explains, consists of a selective chain of recalled events: "Some things you forget. Other things you never do" (43). By contrast, "rememory" is beyond the scope of cognition. Solid, inassimilable, unchanging and unchangeable, it is "a picture floating around out there outside my head. I mean, even if I don't think it, even if I die, the picture of what I did, or knew, or saw is still out there. Right in the place where it happened" (43). Moreover, rememory is voraciously redundant and feared to be transmissible. Thus, Sethe tells Denver, "If you go there and stand in the place where it was, it will happen again; it will be there for you, waiting for you" (44).

This promise of eternal repetition is the curse that prohibitive reading wishes to dispel. As Michaels frames it, the possibility that "Denver might bump into Sethe's rememory"[25] is tantamount to the threat that, because "nothing ever dies,"[26] contemporary blacks must live in fear of their enslaved ancestors' recurring pasts, which persist in damning and invariable exactitude. But in fact, Morrison differentiates between Sethe's sense that the past is fixed and re-inhabitable by others and her daughter's persistent feelings of exclusion from that past and its memory. Despite Sethe's vivid fears, Denver *cannot* "bump into Sethe's rememory." Indeed, even when Sethe's past materializes as Beloved, the ghost—while visible to Denver and even an object of her desire—is only interested in Sethe. "The two of them," Morrison writes of Sethe and Beloved, "cut Denver out of [their] games" (282). "She [Denver] came to realize that her presence in that house had no influence on what either woman did. She kept them alive and they ignored her" (296).

In *Beloved*, the intergenerational transmission of trauma is *not* the literal return to a durable site of original suffering. It is something more nebulous, like a shadow of the parental past that colors the early development of the child's fears, desires, and identifications. In a passage that could double as a description of Morrison's surviving daughter figure, Marianne Hirsch coins the term "postmemory" to describe the experience of trauma's second generation: "To grow up with such overwhelming inherited memories, to be dominated by narratives that preceded one's birth or one's consciousness, is to risk having one's own stories and experiences displaced, even evacuated, by those of a previous generation. It is to be shaped, however indirectly, by traumatic events that still defy narrative reconstruction and exceed comprehension. These events happen in the past, but their effects continue into the present."[27]

Born in the fugitive space of Sethe's northward escape from slavery and literally nursed on the blood of her sacrificed sister (Beloved), Denver is profoundly marked by a past she cannot remember. Morrison characterizes her as "[stepping] into [a] told story" (36) of dehumanization, fear, and murder, and she is haunted by "monstrous and unmanageable dreams" that ultimately induce her own symptomatic deafness (121). Nevertheless, Denver is not a creature of the past. She despises the past, rejecting all stories that do not or cannot make a bridge to her future. "The present alone interested Denver," Morrison writes (141). Or again, "Denver hated the stories her mother told that did not concern herself" (74). The past is the force that excludes her, not only because she did not experience it but also because, presently, she does not feel it. "Closed off from the hurt of the hurt world," Denver's affect and identifications are produced by a "[hungry] imagination" and a "loneliness" that "wore her out" (35).

Dominick La Capra has noted in passing a point that I wish to stress here: namely, that Michaels's hyper-vigilance in the face of Morrison's "haunting revenants" blinds him to the novel's "exploration of postmemory."[28] Generalizing outward, I am arguing that prohibitive reading apprehends the story of the re-appearing past to the exclusion of the story of familial continuance, when in fact the legacy of trauma always consists in *both* the astonishing force of the desire to return to and rectify the past *and* the infuriating impossibility of that desire. Thus Denver longs to feed and tend to Beloved, but she also rages against the stories that precede her existence or capacity to know. Denver's complex relationship to her maternal past does not amount to appropriation or incorporation of Sethe's trauma, even as Denver surely must forge a relationship to an inter-generational past in order to imagine a viable self that can step outside the haunted house. Like Hirsch's postmemorial subject, Denver's identification with Sethe's past is ambivalent and partial, characterized by a sense of displacement that conjures both resentment and desire.

Prohibitive reading casts the idea that trauma can be transmitted as a kind of false consciousness, based on an implicit disavowal of the distorting effects of mediation. Thus its proponents differentiate, again and again, between trauma's "true" victims and those who come upon traumatic experience secondhand. But in fact, Hirsch's definition of postmemory—and Morrison's emplotment of it—*foreground* the work of mediation. Postmemory, Hirsch writes, is "defined through an identification with the victim or witness of trauma, *modulated by the unbridgeable distance that separates the participant from the one born after.*"[29] It is as much a product of the succeeding generations' absence of memory as it is a product of the powerful narratives of un-making that pre-exist and interpellate the postmemorial subject. If, as the hermeneutic of prohibitive reading suggests, Sethe and Denver model the inter-generational transmission of trauma that is meant to extend further, to implicate the contemporary reader, then that model of transmission may hardly be characterized as fixed, transparent, or predictable. For what Morrison describes is not the immutable endurance of post-traumatic identity but the ever-mutating force of history as it produces new subjects, constrained by and straining against the ascribed terms of their legibility.

We can approach prohibitive reading more generously if we turn our focus from the "technology" of memory and its transmission to the potential political consequences of certain forms of memorial discourse. At the heart of prohibitive reading, there are warnings we would be wise to heed: that the meanings of "race" are historically contingent and in need of an adaptable rhetoric,[30] and that the moral rigor that sustains the dictate to "never forget" may also host a narcissistic presentism that un-self-consciously blots out the specificity of the very past it seeks to memorialize.[31] Moreover, these critics share a sense of skepticism about the political and psychical efficacy of imagining the self through the prism of past pain. The political philosopher Wendy Brown may well speak their mantra when she argues that to "will backwards" is to "[rail] against time itself"—and through this impotent gesture, to "install" the pain of one's "unredeemed history in the very foundation of [the demand for recognition]." Predicating a contemporary "I am" on an injurious "it was," the desirous return to an irredeemable past "can hold out no future . . . that triumphs over this pain."[32]

It is difficult *not* to be stirred by this line of thought, which enlists not only a substantive political case for recognizing historical contingency and change but also a seductive, unapologetic will-to-power.[33] But

I remain wary of the extraordinary vigilance with which proponents of prohibitive reading tend to condemn traumatic time's recognition of historical desire. The real history, they seem to say—the history that we can calenderically measure and record—is being threatened, overwritten, or dismissed in favor of an imposing *fantasy* of history that defies temporality, rationality, and objective study.[34] As Warren puts it, within contemporary African Americanist discourse, "Discrete periodizations" have been rendered "beside the point" and, more, have undeservedly acquired "a taint of injustice." The upshot of his complaint is that affective attachments to the past may persist, but they are beyond the rightful domain of academics or politics. They cloud and distort knowledge, obscuring the self-evident truth that, in order "to understand both past and present, we have to put the past behind us."[35]

But perhaps the truth of history is not so simple. If "wounded attachments"[36] to an injurious past undergird the writing of traumatic time, what kinds of attachments ground the ostensibly opposite desires for a clearly demarcated, discrete, or non-residual past? Is it in fact more true to read history as a conquerable object of knowledge than as an animating force that consists in both the events of the past and the desires—affective, narrative, political—that those events produce? My sense is that *Beloved* becomes an (imprecise) avatar for identity politics and its "poisonous" resuscitation of the past in large part because of a zealous, countervailing desire to intellectually secure the past as a fixed and detached object of study. *Beloved*, in particular, and the idea of postmemory, more generally, provoke foundational anxieties of conventional knowledge projects that work in part through colonizing and taxonomizing time. I do not mean to diminish the value of periodization as a way of knowing and encountering the past; of course, the idea of a future-oriented, progressive chronology gets at an enduring and compelling sense of historical truth. But I am interested, too, in *how*—and with what kinds of anxieties, desires, admissions, and foreclosures—periodization organizes and asserts the truth claims of prohibitive reading.

## The Historian's History

Whereas *Beloved* depicts the transmission of traumatic memory within the temporal range of legal slavery and its immediate aftermath, *The Chaneysville Incident* imagines the reach of slavery's postmemorial effects extending into the present. The novel was published in 1981, and its narrative present is 1979. David Bradley's title references a fictional sequence of resonant, catastrophic events, for the titular incident is not one incident but an intergenerational series of traumatic historical events that the protagonist, John Washington, discovers as his inheritance.

Recalling Sethe's idea of the spatio-temporal fixity of "rememory," Chaneysville, Pennsylvania, is a site of repeated racial trauma that exceeds normative ideas of linear chronology. Here, John's father, Moses Washington, commits suicide in a cryptic re-enactment of his grandfather's (John's great-grandfather's) death. Moses's ritualized suicide memorializes the tragic heroism of his own forebear, a former slave turned liberator shot in the act of guiding smuggled slaves to freedom, but it does so by forsaking futurity for the moral righteousness of memory. What Moses leaves for his son is not a pathway to the future but a mysterious collection of clues leading back to the ghostly and aporetic origins of the Washington patrilineage. Willing his massive archive of family history to John, Moses dictates the following instructions: "The only restriction is that you [John] are not permitted to sell, bequeath, or otherwise divest yourself of their ownership until you have examined all volumes, including personal memoirs."[37]

In spite of his portentous family history full of unassimilated feelings, John is a professional historian of Revolutionary America who adheres to a conservative, documentary model of historiography: Nearly all of *Chaneysville*'s readers have remarked upon his obsessive habit of collecting and organizing facts, in his attempt to capture a "truth" that inheres in the most basic articulation of what happened. Psychic experience and affective context are, for John, at best an unwelcome diversion. "There's no imagination in [historiography]," he tells his girlfriend, Judith. "You can't create facts" (268). This is how he describes his method:

> I went to work with my fountain pen and my india ink and my cards, going through the documents and leeching out single events, tearing them

away from the other events that surrounded them, recording them in bare, simple, declarative form on the white lined cards, in a hand as precise and unemotional as I could make it. I dated each one carefully as precisely as I could, with a string of digits—year, month, date—in the upper-left-hand corner. Then each one was an incident. A single event placed precisely in history, but apparently free of any cause. . . . The only truth—and that only a degree of truth—lies in the simple statement of the incident. (223)

Unlike Sethe's mystical declaration of the permanence of the past, John's attachment to facticity and order is easily reconcilable with critics who reject traumatic time on the grounds that it is phantasmatic, narcissistic, or un-provable. In similar, if exaggerated fashion, John posits that the sole route to historical truth consists in the sequential stringing together of unvarnished facts. This "true" history proceeds like an ordered stack of index cards: discrete, declarative, and decisive.

Yet ironically, although John attempts to exclude "emotion" from his research through a kind of numerical "precision," his neurotic method comes to bear a striking resemblance to a widely observed symptom of post-traumatic consciousness. Consider the striking similarity between his index card method—which takes as its hallmark a stubborn literality effected through de-contextualization and rigorous detail—and Caruth's depiction of "traumatic dreams and flashbacks." Caruth writes, "Modern analysts . . . have remarked on the surprising literality and nonsymbolic nature of traumatic dreams and flashbacks, which resist cure to the extent that they remain, precisely, literal. It is this literality and its insistent return which constitutes trauma and points toward its enigmatic core: the delay or incompletion in knowing, or even in seeing, an overwhelming occurrence that then remains, in its insistent return, absolutely true to the event."[38]

Like Caruth's stipulated trauma survivor, John insistently favors a vision of truth as the mimetic representation of the past. Moreover, both insist upon the moral value of such truth. For the Caruthian trauma victim, "truth" disallows the production of meaning because traumatic experience does not surrender, in the process of happening, to comprehension. Thus meaning can only be an amendment, a threat to the integrity of traumatic recollection. So, too, for John, the scene of archival discovery is "perfect" and vulnerable: "Anything I did, one false step, would destroy that perfection, would probably obscure whatever message might be in the scene" (140). In both cases, "the simple statement of the incident" is the only gesture that can legitimately approach and approximate the truth of the past.

Unexpectedly, then, John's very desire to periodize, to produce shape and certainty by putting the past behind him, mirrors the ostensibly opposite compulsion to re-*experience* the past—to go to the past, like Sethe, and "stand in the place where it was [where] it will happen again."³⁹ Like the traumatic flashback and Morrisonian rememory—those figurations prohibitive reading cannot abide—objectivist documentary historiography, with its essential feature of periodization, entails an impossible desire for exactitude, a compulsive and ever-unconsummated longing for mastery over the past.⁴⁰ Might we read the extremity of John's desire for objectivity as itself a symptom of trauma's overwhelming force?

John himself wonders, intermittently and reluctantly, about what his methodological approach may obscure or leave out. For although fact is his ultimate authority, he does not assume that its authority is comprehensive. Its truth, he concedes, is *"only a degree of truth"* (223, my italics.) What John misses, to his own chagrin, is a capacity for imagination. In one moment of self-doubt, he goes so far as to deride the very model of documentary historiography to which he is so inflexibly committed. Charging that documentary historiography misguidedly proceeds from the premise that meaning is to be found in documents, rather than the living context from which such documents arise, he scoffs, "Historians [lose] sleep over documents that they deem precious, but which, in the evaluation of people who have reason to know, are most useful as tinder, or mattress stuffing, or papier-mâché" (43). In flashes like this one, John's desire to know colludes with his desire to empathize, to imaginatively inhabit the psyche of historical actors, that he might interpret their actions with certainty.

The tension between John's seemingly inassimilable approaches to historiography builds when he learns of the immanent death of a surrogate father figure called Old Jack. Forced to face the mortality of his paternal line, John's curiosity about his historical inheritance is rekindled. He abruptly turns away from his professional, generalist work on early American history and resumes, with impassioned fervor, a previously discarded project of family historiography. Immersed in this work, John can no longer claim the disaffected stance of the objectivist historian-observer. He is forced to re-imagine historiographical work as a "dialogic exchange" between past and present, in which "knowledge involves not only the processing of information but also affect, empathy, and questions of value."[41] Initially, John is ill equipped for such a task, but the necessary process of methodological supplementation is helped along by the dying Old Jack, who reminds John of the epistemological foundations of African American oral traditions, and by Judith, John's psychiatrist-girlfriend, who insists upon the possibility of human knowledge that exceeds facticity.

Ultimately, *Chaneysville* is neither an endorsement nor a refutation of conventional historiography; it is an ambivalent engagement with it. It says: There are tangible and consequential limits to one's ability to know the past, there are facts and missing facts and "you can't create facts" (268). There is also a huge and inevitable transferential risk for the African American subject—perhaps for any subject—looking back in time. "One of the greatest fallacies that surrounds the study of the past," John tells us, is "the notion that there is such a thing as a detached researcher, that it is possible to discover and analyze and interpret without getting caught up and swept away" (140).

How can, and how should, accounts of the past address this Heisenbergian quality that haunts both history and memory? In his reading of *Chaneysville*, Warren argues that John's negotiation of conventional historiographical methods, ethical considerations, and his own transferential desire remains imperfect throughout the novel. On this point, I agree. But I disagree with the ways in which Warren's reading tends to strip the novel of its essential equivocations, its uncertainties, its unwillingness to "really, truly, utterly, absolutely, completely, finally, *know*" (264, Bradley's italics). For Warren, *Chaneysville* epitomizes the beguiling trick of traumatic time when it rejects the rational authority of conventional historiography in favor of a fantasy of the past as re-inhabitable, living, and seeking appeasement. He writes, "John Washington cannot finish the story so long as he persists in his thinking like a historian. The lesson of the narrative is that truth, in the final instance, demands belief, a belief that enables one to experience death as a passing and to hear songs born on the wind."[42]

But we may alternatively view the novel's ending as intentionally cryptic and inconclusive; Bradley himself has described the book as "a detective novel," whose mysterious ending compels the reader to "make of it what [he or she] will."[43] Indeed, the novel's final sentence lends itself to precisely such interpretive flexibility. Upon striking a match to sacrifice either the historical archive he has inherited or his own body, John pauses to wonder if Judith—and perhaps, by proxy, the reader-as-witness—"would understand when she saw the smoke go rising from the far side of the Hill" (432). What is it that John would want Judith to understand? That the finitude of bodily life is a Western myth from which African Americans may extricate themselves at will? That the rigidity and sheer mass of archival facts become barriers to the psychoanalytic process of working through historically accumulated racial wounds—but also, that the barrier can be burned? That historical "messages" consist in both context and intent on the one hand (the emotional experience of collecting materials, the purposeful lighting of the pyre) and reception and interpretation on the other? (*What* will Judith understand?)

*Chaneysville* makes plausible each of these interpretations but subordinates them all to Bradley's broader assertion that the *idea* of history may itself function as a kind of fetish object for the historian. In the novel, John proposes a model of the past as an incomprehensibly vast living organism, a sauntering dinosaur that we can encounter only in pieces. Against this imposing image, conventional historiography anxiously produces the fantasy of a visibly coherent whole that would hide from consciousness history's unconquerable immensity: its hordes of unusable facts, and its transferential production of excessive and impotent affect. By acknowledging historiography's fetishistic desires, Bradley does not suggest that the "facts" of history and their basic chronological arrangement are not true. He suggests, instead, that historical knowledge projects take shape as an encounter between a human subject—the historian, always burdened by the limitations of his knowledge and the particularities of his psychic need—and history—the unknowable animal that no amount of knowledge can fully subdue. No historiographical practice, *Chaneysville* implies, fully escapes the taint of non-neutrality, with which traumatic time has been so pejoratively painted.

We may accept this basic premise but still feel moved to ask, What is the role of the literary in traumatic time's historiographical critique? What kind of epistemological work do writers like Morrison and Bradley perform when they set out to "kidnap" us from the present or fill our ears with ghostly voices of the past? How do these novels re-envision the *reader's*, as opposed to the historian's, relationship to history? Here, after all, is the ideological crux of prohibitive reading. For its proponents position "literariness" as the propagandistic tool that curates, politicizes, and prescribes a narrow and specific affective relationship to the past—a relationship that turns on idioms of loss, injury, attachment, and irresolution. Best argues, for example, that "literariness is key" in establishing the moral-political agenda of what he calls "Morrisonian poetics." He contends that historical loss, as it is expressed in contemporary black studies, "is a feeling that literature produces" and sustains "because literary texts, as intentional objects, possess silences and ellipses that are structural, whereas silence in nonliterary discourse is not always the sign of an intention."[44] In a similar vein, Warren approaches a register of political alarmism when he describes the novelistic use of traumatic time as follows: "These fictions are defined by their commitment to making the past present to us *by any representational means necessary* . . . . [Their] vision of history . . . is one of recollection, which also becomes one of resurrection, as the dead are pictured standing outside their graves."[45]

Warren's polemicism is self-evident, but even if we understand these passages as a hyperbolic staging of his argument, such a reading does not dissolve its most basic implications. He suggests, in the first place, that any ideological desire embedded in traumatic time nullifies the truth claims of stories told in this mode. Furthermore, and reflecting the constitutive position of prohibitive reading, he posits that literature's representational "means" must be vigorously policed when literature encounters the past. Such a position makes sense if we understand traumatic time as a site of profoundly *political* controversy over the ethics or dangers of representing an oppressed group through the pained retelling of unresolved historical trauma. But to approach black literary study's historical turn in this way is also to overlook literature's generic capacity for self-consciousness—its implicit awareness of the non-fixity, perhaps even the capriciousness, of its truth. How else might we understand the literary truth claim, particularly in relation to a haunting racial past?

## Writing the Beginning

*Beloved*'s sequel, *Jazz*, is a book about a book—the material artifact— that envies humans, especially for our capacity for tactile and reciprocal love. Its narrator conceals its non-human identity until the final page, when it claims its desire in a sensuous address to the reader: "Look where your hands are. Now."[46] In this very explicit way, *Jazz* is about literature's constitutive lacks and longings. It is about how literature imagines, wields, and frets over the productive power of language, and it is about how literature envisions its intersubjective relationship with the reader as an embodied other.

*Jazz* is also a book about historical memory. Set in jazz-age Harlem, it is, in a traditional sense, historical fiction. More important for my purposes, it is a novel that attempts to look backward from its own narrative present, to contextualize and "know" the postmemorial foundations for its characters' formative traumas. An unconventional voyeur, the novel/ narrator describes itself, not as omniscient, but as "curious, inventive, and well-informed" (137). In remarkable contrast to Bradley's historian, who only belatedly comes to appreciate an epistemology of imaginative empathy, Morrison's narrator begins with imagination, though it later worries that it has over-valued this creative way of knowing.

Famously inspired by James van der Zee's post-mortem portraiture, *Jazz* begins with a love crime. Joe Trace, a middle-aged beauty product peddler, silently murders his betraying, adolescent ex-mistress, Dorcas. This sensational act, in turn, is quickly revealed as a story of displaced passions. "From the very beginning," Joe's wife, Violet explains, "I was a substitute and so was he" (97). For the narrator, who, throughout most of the novel, appears as an unidentified onlooker, the idea that love and desire operate through a substitutive logic motivates a turn to genea- logical investigation. It becomes preoccupied with the task of seeking out the respective roots, or original referents, of Violet and Joe's erotic desires. Significantly, the past that the novel/narrator seeks out is not a history of evidentiary truths. Instead, it looks for "evidence" in the psy- chic traces of the past as they manifest in the present—especially in the protagonists' fears of abandonment, ephemerality, and undesirability. Like a psychoanalyst, the narrator observes the redundant repetition of Joe and Violet Trace's failed desires in the present to vivify "coded stories about what [they] wanted in the past, and about what was missing in that past."[47]

An extensive and largely incredible origin myth ensues, in which the narrator's simultaneous efforts to understand and to fantasize a plausible history of the sensational love triangle yields an ancestral figure called Wild. Naked and pregnant, homeless and "berry-black" (144), Wild is the literary resuscitation of *Beloved*'s exorcised ghost. Like Beloved, she appears to live outside the domains of language and society, even as her mysterious, haunting power is central and constitutive. She is believed to be Joe Trace's abandoning mother, as well as the unexpected seductress of Violet's first true love, a mirage of a tragic mulatto named Golden Gray.

Perhaps it would be more precise to say that Wild is Morrison's re-imagining of Beloved from a position of meta-literary self-consciousness. If *Beloved* was a meditation on the psychic and identitarian devastations of black enslavement, then *Jazz* grapples with the question of how African American literature—particularly, the novel—belatedly approaches the unknowable history of slavery through its scattered traces. We must track and find Wild, the novel posits, not because she is a character in the story per se, but because present-day black identification and desire, as the presumptive objects of black literary representation, remain caught up in patterns of compensatory, substitutive attachments that stem from an original, unreconciled violence. Violet obliquely approaches this epiphany when she names the displacement at work in her marital love ("from the beginning I was a substitute and so was he"). But true to Felman's conceptualization of trauma as a missed encounter, the substitutive chain that the narrator follows leads back to a stunning non-presence, a missed encounter with a phantasmatic and unknowable character who leaves in her wake nothing more than an abandoned cave, used crockery, and a discarded dress.

In her famous essay "The Site of Memory," Morrison writes in harrowing first person about her authorial desire to unveil a historical black subjectivity obscured from contemporary recognition by the rhetorical norms of the day. The genre of the slave narrative, she reminds us, was over-determined in style and content. "In shaping [black] experience to make it palatable to those who were in a position to alleviate it, [the authors of antebellum slave narratives] were silent about many things, and they 'forgot' many other things." For example:

> Whenever there was an unusually violent incident, or a scatological one, or something "excessive," one finds the writer taking refuge in the literary conventions of the day. "I was left in a state of distraction not to be described" (Equiano). "But let us now leave the rough usage of the field . . . and turn our attention to the less repulsive slave life as it existed in the house of my childhood" (Douglass). "I am not about to harrow the feelings of my readers by a terrific representation of the untold horrors of that fearful system of oppression. . . . It is not my purpose to descend deeply into the dark and noisome caverns of the hell of slavery (Henry Box Brown)."[48]

Following the postmemorial traces of these autobiographers' silences, Morrison argues that the "job" of the contemporary black author is to find a way to "rip down that veil drawn over 'proceedings too terrible to relate.'"[49] Surely, this is a kind of historical desire: Morrison's wish to "rip down that veil" articulates a longing for accuracy, detail, and richly textured information. In this sense, her characteristic deployment of traumatic time (in both her essays and her fiction) would hardly seem anti-historiographical. Rather, and as in *The Chaneysville Incident*, traumatic time subsumes historiographical desire, recasting the latter as a symptom of its constitutive missed encounter. Historiography, in other words, is produced as a compensatory effect of the overwhelming feeling of belatedness that so pervasively marks traumatic consciousness.

But Morrison is also—indeed, most of all—interested in how the literary imagination reworks historical desire. *Jazz* in particular, with its unusual subject-making focus on the novel as such and its tenuous claims to the past as it was, deliberately puzzles through literature's affective relationship to the past. Literary historical desire, for Morrison, is related but not reducible to the historical will to knowledge that I have explored above. The seductress may be similar: In Wild, we find a figure reminiscent of the slave narrators' silences, whose absence is at the core of her enchanting power. With her stunning darkness and obstinate illegibility, Wild also harbors the cross-disciplinarily enticing idea of blackness *before* its Western encounter, untainted by the traumas of violence, acculturation, and objectification. But Wild most persistently references a uniquely novelistic fantasy of black origins. For we access her not through testimony, legal documents, or even family lore but through a series of literary clichés that the novel/narrator invokes to "track" Wild, that coveted and impossible subject, the foreclosed figure of African "purity" in the New World. Attempting to find Wild through the path of the "wound"—which is to say, through a survey of Western literature's offenses against blackness—the narrator leads us through various stock formulations of what Morrison elsewhere calls "the Africanist presence" in American literature.[50] There is a tragic mulatto, a primitivist heroine, a passing bourgeois, and a miscegenation scandal.

The narrator willfully envisions Wild but ultimately fails to produce her. *Jazz*'s fantasy matriculates, not to historical retrieval, but to an allegory for Africa's lexical encounter with the New World. This allegory begins with a symbolically saturated character called Golden Gray: a white-skinned, mulatto child of a Virginia aristocrat who has only recently, to his vengeful horror, discovered his black parentage. It is he who "discovers" Wild, startles her into a concussive fall, and abducts her in his ostentatious carriage. Wild, the love object that the narrator wants but cannot access, is to Golden Gray "not a real woman but a vision" (144). Her blackness blots out the possibility for her subjectivity, as she becomes, instead, a figure of his imagination. When she loses consciousness, he hopes that she will not regain it, that she will not threaten to become "something more than his own dark purpose" (146).

Reading *Jazz* alongside Morrison's nonfiction writing, Golden Gray comes into view as a symbol of the American literary establishment: an ostensibly, or at least, overwhelmingly, "white" enterprise that Morrison has described as ghosted by blackness, haunted by its constitutive yet disavowed hybridity.[51] In a gesture of paranoiac disassociation, Golden Gray (American literature) casts Wild (blackness) as "everything he was not": barbaric, grotesque, animal. Yet his assertion of difference is conspicuously compelled by his anxiety of self-identity, his need to "contain" and "identify" his internal wilderness. Golden Gray wonders, Might the "awful-looking thing lying wet in the weeds" be reconstituted through imaginative will as "proper protection against and anodyne to what he believed his father to be, and therefore (if it could just be contained and identified)—himself?" (149). This moment, when Golden Gray stumbles upon and captures Wild, is the moment of African American literature's missed encounter, that irrecoverable point of origin at which blackness is inscribed and subjugated within Western languages, idioms, and symbolic orders. It is a moment that the narrator (quite like Joe Trace) is frustrated by, grasps for, but always misses.

The encounter between Golden Gray and Wild—that primal encounter that the narrator misses and cannot resurrect—becomes the scene that the narrator cannot stop rewriting. It starts and stops. It holds a mirror to itself. It berates Golden Gray and then tries to appease him: "He is lying, the hypocrite" (154). "Aw, but he is young, young and he is hurting, so I forgive him his self-deception and his grand-fake gestures" (155). It "[sets], then [misses], the mark" (219). It worries that it "may be doomed to another misunderstanding." It takes imaginative risks nonetheless. It determines that "not hating him [Golden Gray] is not enough; liking, loving him is not useful. I have to alter things" (161).

Here, in the novel/narrator's concession of its own fallibility, and in its articulation of a world-altering *fantasy*, we find an important clue about the nature of the literary truth claim. Literature's truth, *Jazz* seems to say, lies in its explication of "[missing] the mark," in its nuanced engagement with affect and the unconscious, and in its desirous and imaginative reclamation of the irretrievable "trace." It is interested in the role of fantasy, and it can deploy fantastical modes to put pressure on the question of how to activate, or make productive, the desire for the inaccessible past. Might such desire matriculate to something other than delusional traumatic cathexis? Might it, alternatively or additionally, chart new and joyous possibilities for inhabiting identity and experiencing desire?

After all, the novel/narrator neither claims to achieve an accurate rendition of the past nor does it assert (as Michaels, Warren, or Best might fear) the fixity of black identity as an effect of the traumatic past's immutable force. To the contrary, the narrator's great discovery about historical trauma and postmemorial desire is that history does not— *cannot*—replay like an "abused record with no choice but to repeat itself at the crack" (220). *Jazz*'s past is a tragically lost object removed by an unbridgeable divide, but it is also a space of creative potential, an absence that fantasy reactivates in the service of a changeable present ("I have to alter things"; 161).

*Jazz's* ending is utopian. The novel/narrator imagines Wild's seduction of Golden Gray, as the dark woman stirs in the passing anti-hero "some brief benevolent love . . . and there is no reason [for him] to stay but he does" (161). What should we make of this seeing and staying, this quietly radical recognition? Wild is not only the narrator's impossible love object; she is also a mirror in whom the novel/narrator glimpses the image of its own non-humanity, its disavowed existence. The possibility, made speakable by fantasy, of someone looking at Wild with "her looking eyes looking back," thus emboldens the narrator's own pursuit of recognition, of the conferral of subjectivity by the knowing gaze of the other (221). "Look, look," the novel summons the reader on its final page. "Look where your hands are. Now" (229). *Jazz* thus culminates with anticipation: Its ending is the beginning that recognition initiates.

Let me attempt to voice a rebuttal from the perspective of prohibitive reading, one that begins with the claim that a different understanding of "recognition"—recognition as lucidity, or the capacity for unobstructed sight—is precisely what is foreclosed by the narrator's fantastical manipulation of the past. On this view, Wild overtakes and obscures the drama of the narrative present (murder, infidelity, desecration, racism, sexism, the economies of modernity). Moreover, the narrator's fantasy of Wild is itself an obfuscation of the truth of the past. Wild did not seduce Golden Gray, and more fundamentally, neither of these characters appeals to known standards of historical truth. Traumatic time, we must conclude, is doubly wrong. It is intellectually wrong in that it refuses the most self-evident principles of history: truth's necessary correspondence to documentary evidence and the linear progression of time. It is ethically wrong because it seeks to replace the unfolding story of the present with a moralizing and recriminatory narrative loop, grounded in an untenable fantasy of the past. "The real action of both politics and culture," Reid-Pharr insists, "always takes place at the surface and in the present."[52] From this perspective, Wild, John Washington's lost fathers, and *Beloved* are but sirens beckoning us away from the progressive course of socio-economic justice. They prey on our enchantment with the past, they bear false promises of redemption, and they leave us to starve on a desire that cannot be consummated.

This is not an argument I set up only to tear down. The ineffectuality of a present politics based on the past, the speciousness of claims to inter-generational "memory" as such, the self-obliterating poison of obsessive recrimination—these are clear and present dangers, evidenced in part by the degree to which they have concerned a wide-ranging and cross-disciplinary field of distinguished critics, theorists, and cultural workers. As the broader arc of my argument corroborates, I take seriously prohibitive reading's misgivings about trauma discourse and contemporary African American literature, even as I remain unconvinced of some of its corollary prescriptions.

Most of all, I am wary of the tendency of the proponents of prohibitive reading to frame their own desires not as *desire* but as positivism, anti-sentimentality, or common sense. Such rhetoric masks the probability that the will to eradicate affect from the domains of intellectual and political life is summoned by its own sirens, its own impossible desires: the desire for intellectual mastery over an affectively charged, often unpredictable or even incomprehensible social world; the desire for release from uncomfortable feelings of guilt or impotence; the desire for a present whose possibilities are radically unhinged from the constraints of the past. Such desires are not to be dismissed. Indeed, they are both timeless and timely. They appeal to a universal register in their longing to be unburdened of the past, even as they claim historical specificity in their demand for political presentism—for justice now, in and on the terms of the twenty-first century. But they are also made disingenuous by claims to objectivity and by their exaggerated projections of pathology, self-indulgence, or false consciousness onto competing articulations of historical desire.

What if prohibitive reading is not the conceptual antonym but the anxious mirror image of therapeutic reading? Like its purported opposite, prohibitive reading works from the premise that we may accept or reject in toto the embrace of the "historical past" as "a part of our own experience";[53] my argument has been that this premise sidesteps the messier and more interesting propositions of traumatic time and postmemory. In the latter formulations, the past permeates the present by producing the formative conditions for contemporary experiences of agency and constraint, lack and longing, identity and anonymity. Simultaneously continuous and discontinuous, obscured and revealed by our projective investments in it, traumatic histories persist, for the contemporary reader, not as the ghost daughter Beloved but as the unharnessable dream of her, whom Morrison calls Wild.

## Other Temporalities of Trauma and Repair

What traumatic time longs for is a reparative telos of inter-generational cohesion; its desire, to borrow a phrase from Reid-Pharr, is "tradition-bound desire."[54] Powered by the catastrophic loss of memory, culture, home, and family, traumatic time articulates an impossible yet ineradicable desire to return to a pre-contaminated site of racial origins and a foreclosed promise of progressive continuity. Caryl Phillips offers a succinct illustration of this concept in his neo-slave narrative, *Crossing the River*—a novel punctuated by a refrain that diasporic descendants direct to a guilty, paternal Africa: "Father, why hast thou forsaken me?"

Yet such an ideal is not the only or inevitable response to trauma. There are other ways of telling the story of trauma and its aftermath that replace the fantasy of a reconstituted generational time—the fantasy of a different "before"—with the fantasy of a different aspirational horizon. Exposing generational time's powerful attachments to hetero-patriarchal models of social organization, queer and feminist scholarship, in particular, has generated sites for new theories of post-traumatic reparative, liberatory, or utopian temporalities.

José Esteban Muñoz, for example, idealizes "a modality of ecstatic time in which the stranglehold [of straight time] is interrupted or stepped out of. Ecstatic time is signaled at the moment one feels ecstasy, announced, perhaps, in a scream or a grunt of pleasure, and more importantly during moments of contemplation when one looks back at a scene from one's past, present, or future."[55] Similarly, Elizabeth Freeman proffers an ideal of "queer time" as an un-co-opted alternative to "chrononormativity," the processes through which "naked flesh is bound into socially meaningful embodiment through temporal regulation," as in the time of courtship and reproduction, "work time," and "family time."[56] For both of these theorists and others, queer time is a utopian imagining of the otherwise that emerges in part from the traumas and hostilities of the now. Thus it is most often experienced as a fleeting, private, or phantasmatic glimpse of possibility, bounded by the trauma of its own negation. "The present," Muñoz writes, "is impoverished and toxic for queers and other people who do not feel the privilege of normative belonging." Yet it is precisely this toxicity of exclusion that forms the precondition for his utopian vision. "Queerness is always directed at that thing that is not yet here, objects and moments that burn with anticipation and promise."[57]

In Ann Cvetkovich's queer feminist critique, the problem with extant theories of trauma is not only their limited conception of reparative desire but also their limited conception of the shape and texture of traumatic suffering. She notes, for example, that trauma theory's archetypal references to the Holocaust as the original, extraordinary, aporetic event are inadequate to explain sexual trauma, which is often experienced as an occurrence *within* the range of normal, day-to-day experience. In this case, the notion of the "event" can prove less compelling than an understanding of trauma as concentrated in historically specific sexual encounters but also diffused into everyday experiences of gender and sexual identification and the negotiation of relationships and attachments. Without discrediting the prevailing idea that trauma may ensue from a singular or concentrated, originary rupture, Cvetkovich seeks to awaken trauma studies to "the way trauma digs itself in at the level of the everyday." She argues that if trauma theory is to make sense of what it means to *feel* trauma in late modernity, then it must address not only the structure and fallout of catastrophe as such but also "the persistence of the everyday in the encounter with trauma."[58]

Cvetkovich's move to privilege the ordinariness and minutiae of daily life in her theorization of trauma is broadly applicable but has unique value for describing traumatic experiences that are underscored by social marginalization and its attendant effects, from micro-aggressions to institutional discrimination to social and historical erasure. Because African American collective trauma is inscribed in both the incalculably vast historical "event" of slavery and the "ordinary" effects of systemic oppression, the concept of everyday trauma provides a useful theoretical supplement—and challenge—to the present chapter's central idea of traumatic time.[59] Specifically, it encourages the critic to connect the meaning of memory, "rememory," or the wish to remember the past, with a sense of what it means to live in the mundane and plodding present, alongside the often inaccessible but stubbornly recurring after-effects of the traumatic past.

Revising conventional understandings of trauma with a studious eye toward the present's material context and the future's untold promise, Cvetkovich's notion of everyday trauma resonates meaningfully with Hirsch's postmemory. Both theories supplement the logic of historical catastrophe's proximate psychic effects to account for heritable feelings of resonance, pain, or vague familiarity with historical trauma that do not matriculate to full identification with that past. But whereas post-memory holds a conceptual frame of familial insularity in place, queer theories of everyday trauma weaken that privatizing impulse, register-ing a more diverse and heterogeneous multiplicity of ways in which the interface of historical trauma and contemporary sociality is lived. In this regard, queer studies' intervention into trauma theory may mitigate some of prohibitive reading's most damning indictments of trauma's po-tential for myopic recursiveness. For, if what most rankles prohibitive reading's adherents is trauma's capacity to lure us away from the political through its aggressive imposition of private and privatizing memories, then Cvetkovich, too, resists such a trajectory in which injury can *only* devolve into impotent, anachronistic desire. Yet, unlike proponents of prohibitive reading, she encourages a perspective in which queer the-ories of everyday trauma amend (sometimes antagonistically), but do not disavow, event-based formulations of trauma that carry a deep in-vestment in generational time. How might we imagine the poly-vocal emplotment of these competing temporal frames—the traumatic and postmemorial time that interpellates African American subjectivity, the mundane, daily time of late modernity, and the ecstatic time of queer fantasy? How do they echo, consolidate, obscure, and renounce one an-other? How do their narrative inscriptions of trauma yield multiple, at times antagonistic, forms and objects of desire?

Published in 1989, Randall Kenan's *Visitation of Spirits* is a novel born of dissonant and competing temporalities.[60] Its protagonist, Horace Cross, is a modern teenager raised by his extended family among an aging community of North Carolina's rural black poor. Over the course of the novel, Horace grapples with his sense of obligation to a commu-nity forged through a legacy of racial injury, his ambivalent feelings of group belonging and dis-belonging, and his simultaneous desires to express and repress his emergent queer identity. Like the other texts examined in this chapter, *A Visitation of Spirits* is about historical trauma and its residual force, but Kenan is unique in the degree to which his engagement with history is relentlessly framed by the imperatives of the present. The postmemory of slavery, as depicted here, is potent but waning.

"A son of the community, more than most" (188), Horace is interpellated by both the old and the new. He is raised with the expectation that he will extend the Cross family tradition of theo-political race leadership against the dehumanizing legacies of the slave past, and to this end, his elders indoctrinate him with stories of a "terrible past they all had to remember" (71), in which "the evils of the world" appear "solidly and plainly" (89). But although their views take on a righteous and prescriptive rigidity, they are simultaneously watching their "way of life . . . [evaporate]" into a daunting and unknowable postmodernity (9).

In one of the novel's most poignant scenes, Horace's grandfather, Zeke, is flummoxed when he drives past the dilapidated remains of an antebellum slave market. He remembers "hearing his grandpappy telling tales of slave markets" and is bewildered by the idea of the unimaginable humiliation his ancestors suffered, but his psychic response is diverted, unconsummated. Throughout the rest of the day, he feels a heightened sensitivity to his own, smaller, seemingly unrelated "humiliations," but at the traffic stop where the slave market stands, he is unable to assimilate or make sense of his own felt injury. His stream of consciousness dissolves into traffic noise. "He didn't know what to think." He "wondered when his joints would begin to hurt again" (65).

In this way, the novel casts slavery as a wound whose infliction precedes the known world of the twentieth-century South, even as its pain and shame reverberate in passing thoughts, in the enduring and often mundane reproduction of socio-economic disparity, and in community members' calcified racial animus. Horace is heir to this stubborn but elusive psychic legacy, yet he is also a child of integration, technology, and 1980s popular culture. So while the past powerfully ascribes meaning to his embodiment as an African American in the rural South, its prescriptive lexicon falls short of apprehending the world's "new and hateful monsters that exacted a different price" (188).

*A Visitation of Spirits* is set largely in the present and near past, with much of its plot unfolding as a sequence of proximate memories of daily life: school science projects, church services, family meals, teenage crushes. The scale of traumatic time finds only one, compact articulation, though its singular instance is also the plot's most essential, pivotal scene. Late in the novel, Horace is confronted by a racial-religious vision of the history of slavery that intrudes aggressively and explicitly upon his lived present. It seizes and claims Horace, demanding of him an impossible, retroactive racial redemption. Overwhelming Horace like a traumatic memory, the vision reveals an unfinished, intergenerational narrative of African American suffering and yearning for redemption. He sees "men and women hunted by their own on the shores of a great land . . . shackled up and loaded onto ships like barrels of syrup and made to sit there crouched in chains." Many of them die; many of their lives are worse than death. The vision progresses through Emancipation, but legal freedom fails to produce a teleological triumph. Instead, "the sons of oppression are freed only to be bound up again and again, with invisible chains and ropes and painful snares." They endure "work, toil, endless, uphill." They "try to sing but find no voice." Looking to Horace, they ask, "Who will be the savior?" (232–234).

In a starkly dissonant juxtaposition, the historical vision is triggered by Horace's memory of a cast orgy, following the production of a community play called "Ride the Freedom Star."[61] Offering an opposite rendition of the shared referent of racial slavery, the play is loosely based on the dynastic rule of the white Crosses (the enslavers of Horace's ancestors) from the Revolution through the Civil War. Privately funded by family wealth accrued in large part through slave labor, "Ride the Freedom Star" is a garishly inaccurate nostalgia play written by the comically stupid "last male of the white Cross line" (212). The play is exceedingly bad: It is over-populated, "cliché-ridden," and "many of the historical facts were just plain wrong" (213). Furthermore, the play's narcissistic historical revisionism recasts black historical trauma as melodrama and slapstick. Throughout the play, black existence itself appears to be summoned for the purpose of white audience members' emotional release: "The blacks were mainly there for buffoonery and hijinks that brought laughs and chuckles from the audience, for the church scenes with their raw and dynamic singing, and for the minister's sermon, which was the most passionate, hell-raising moment in the entire play" (213–214).

Initially, the play works to underscore Horace's affective ambivalence toward the slave past. Knowing that it is "more than a little inaccurate," he is nevertheless curiously tentative and uncertain in his reaction to the play (224). He wonders what the actors think of it, and he is offended by their dismissiveness. He ventures, cautiously and not entirely convincingly, that the play makes him feel "proud" "to know how far we've gotten," though this vague and hackneyed assertion of racial progress unwittingly betrays the very limits of Horace's ability to imagine the generational redemption he is meant to bring (224).

Further complicating things, the set of "Ride the Freedom Star" provides Horace with his first glimpse of viable queer life. Its actors "were mostly gay, which haunted and taunted Horace, for to him they were physically beautiful" (216). They are irreverent, cosmopolitan, and casually seductive, but they are also the men who, with cynical detachment, enact the distortion and erasure of Horace's family history. Thus Phillip Cross's fantasy of slavery as a benign and blissful golden era of American history collides with Horace's fantasy of a queer lifeworld, envisioned as an undiscovered terrain that would allow him to "[understand] the truth behind the lure of the flesh" and, indeed, to "[touch] . . . ecstasy" (223). These ostensibly incongruent fantasies of nostalgic white supremacy and aspirational queer identification are uncomfortably juxtaposed in the space of the play but not made reducible to one another.

Horace's elders fear just such a collusion: They express concern that he will be emasculated by integration, turned into "some little girl" or "one of them perverts" by his ready acceptance of white socio-cultural mores (184). But while it is true that his affairs on the set of the play are at times characterized by racial insensitivity, the links between Horace's racial and sexual identifications and desires are not so transparently causal. Instead, they collide to produce a profoundly conflicted affective site, marked by the entanglement of shame and desire, anger and euphoria, identification and rejection.

At times, periodically and ephemerally surfacing throughout the book, queer sexuality offers Horace a fleeting glimpse of a different, utopian mode of being in time. Like Muñoz's time of queer ecstasy, this temporality is realized in moments of intense, transcendent pleasure that stand outside the recognizable rhythms of both daily life and generational time, although the disciplinary force of hetero-normative sociality repeatedly reins them in. For example, Horace describes his first gay sexual experience as follows:

> I remember finally touching a man, finally kissing him. I remember the surprise and shock of someone else's tongue in my mouth. I remember the taste of someone else's saliva. I remember actually feeling someone else's flesh, warm, smooth. I remember the texture of hair that was not mine, thighs that were not mine, a waist that was not mine. I remember the gamy smell of pubic hair. I remember being happy that I was taking a chance with my immortal soul, thinking that I would somehow win in the end and live still, feeling immortal in a mortal's arms. I remember then regretting that it was such a sin. I remember the feeling I got after we climaxed, feeling hollow and undone, wishing I were some kind of animal, a wolf or a bird or a dolphin, so I would not have to worry about wanting to do it again. (250–251)

In this passage, the "chance" that is opened up by the "feeling [of immortality] in a mortal's arms" interrupts the presumptive order of both daily life and redemptive (hetero-normative, theological, generational) time. Briefly inhabiting a hyper-presentist time of "surprise and shock," Horace forsakes the priorities of continuity and reproduction that inherited, historical trauma ostensibly demands. The proscriptive force of religion returns quickly—asserting itself in the very moment of climax—but it does not fully reinstall hetero-normative or generational time *at the level of desire*. For what Horace wants is not to be straight and holy, or to live in a straight and holy time of historical repair, but to find a technicality through which to elude castigation. The glimpse of a different way of being fuels his obsessions with the genres of science fiction and fantasy, his fascination with foreign cultures, and his post-coital wish that he "were some kind of animal, a wolf or a bird or a dolphin, so I would not have to worry about wanting to do it again." Such variations on knowledge and human or sentient possibility "all called to him, speaking to him of another, another, another . . . though he could never quite picture that other, the thing that called him so severely. Yet he labored and longed for it; as if his very life depended on knowing it; as if, somehow, he had to change his life" (88).

Horace's glimpse of the time of queer ecstasy becomes a vehicle through which the novel distinguishes itself from other postmemorial narratives of slavery, for it is through longing for this mode of being in time that he abnegates the reparative ideal of progressive, generational time. Bearing a kind of family resemblance to the literary structure I have called "traumatic time," *A Visitation of Spirits*'s moment of epiphany registers the psychic force of an unresolvable, irredeemable racial past, a past that accosts contemporary subjects unawares with its insatiable but always too late demands. But Horace turns away from the ancestral call. When summoned to redeem a panoramic view of traumatic racial history, he "saw clearly through a glass darkly and understood where he fit. Understood what was asked of him. Horace shook his head. No. He turned away. No. He turned his heart away. No" (234).

Horace turns away from what he perceives to be the rigid and voracious demands of the past, but his turning away does not toe the line of prohibitive reading: He does not turn away to embrace the future or to escape a fate of endless recrimination. Rather, he turns to resignation. Riven by the demands and desires born of competing temporal modalities whose assimilability he cannot imagine, Horace determines that "the rules were too hard for me to keep" (251). He thinks of the generational time of family, race, and religious community, which compels him to redeem a lost history of unimaginable horror, to become "somebody who's gone make us proud" (187). He thinks of the everyday time of queer black life, scattered with ordinary pleasures and pains, and the occasional, inassimilable encroachment of the traumatic. He thinks of the anticipatory time of sexual desire and fulfillment—the time outside of time where he is energized by the possibility of "taking a chance with [his] immortal soul" (250). Hoping to "exorcise his confusion," he "[writes] his autobiography" but finds no possibility for narrative cohesion outside of the tragic telos of death. "In the end, after reams and reams of paper and thousands of lines of scribble, he had found no answers" (239).

Does this final, tragic culmination suggest that the time of queer ecstasy is an ineffective product of trauma, a form of denial that provides temporary escapism but no real prospect of transformative change? Or might we read the novel's emplotment of the time of queer ecstasy as a modality of hope whose defeat need not be a condemnation of its value? The very concept of trauma, after all, is meant to make sense of psychic injury that does not allow for neat resolution or closure. By definition, trauma takes shape through its compulsive desire for the elusive and unattainable. Thus, its reparative gestures can only be partial, which is not the same thing as saying that its reparative gestures are futile or delusional. Judith Butler has written that the "critical promise of fantasy . . . is to challenge the contingent limits of what will and will not be called reality," and I would argue that this is precisely the labor of Kenan's novel.[62] Revising traditional models of trauma that depict a repetitive obeisance to the injurious event, *A Visitation of Spirits* represents an exploratory, inventive approach to past and present, interrupting normative patterns of sociality, trauma, and repair, to reveal the finitude of their reach.

2

# For Contradiction (On Masochism)

In the previous chapter, I identified one dimension of the problem of historical desire confronting the contemporary narrative of slavery: Its object is elusive, its resolution is impossible. Here is a second dimension: In the contemporary narrative of slavery, the desire for liberation is inextricably entwined with a desire for the reenactment of punishment and pain. This seeming contradiction occurs because the fantasy of liberation, of and from the slave past, is necessarily imagined as the telos of ancestral suffering. Thus, feeling historical pain is a requisite component of the fantasy of pain's alleviation. In a word, one finds a *masochistic* fantasy intrinsic to the contemporary narrative of slavery.

If prohibitive reading takes this premise of a psychic investment in pain as a self-evident rationale for discrediting the contemporary narrative of slavery, then therapeutic reading regards such pain as the vehicle for the genre's unique promise, to rescue the contemporary reader from repression or self-alienation. In this spirit, to offer one example, Keith Byerman frames his analyses of "remembering the past in contemporary African American fiction" with the advisement, "it is necessary to go through the shame and disruption of remembering in order to begin to forge relationships that can become communities that can make a difference."[1] Stepping back from the now-familiar refrain that it is important to remember in spite of pain, I aim to displace the critical pre-occupation with black historical fiction's assumed inculcation of the reader (for better or worse), to focus instead on how the literature may reveal the psychic economy of African American literature's historical desire. Put another way, my project here is to interpret therapeutic reading, with its constitutively masochistic form, not as a liberatory or constraining hermeneutic but as a literary figure and attendant narrative form that operates powerfully within African Americanist fantasies of historical return.

In what follows, I couple literary analysis with cross-disciplinary theories of masochism to generate an interpretive frame for reconceptualizing the desire to be punished that lives within the desire for reparative return. "Masochism" can help us to think through this conundrum on two levels. As a theory of desire—or more precisely, as an unwieldy body of theories of desire—it provides useful models for thinking about the contours and capacities of longing forged in the crucible of pain. As a theory about contradictory impulses (pleasure, pain) that is itself interpreted in myriad, often contradictory ways, the conceptual life of "masochism" gestures toward the possibility of a criticism detached from the presumptive imperatives of synthesis or closure. Finding precedent in the idea that masochism thrives precisely by deferring closure and dilating on contradiction held in tension, I chart a criticism of post–Civil Rights African American literature, particularly attentive to its treatments of historical desire, that lives in the thickness of complexity, turning a curious eye toward contradiction.

My analysis turns on two novels, Octavia Butler's *Kindred* (1979) and Gayl Jones's *Corregidora* (1975), in which painful fantasies of immersive historical return are extravagantly explored. In Butler's fantastical novel, a contemporary subject is seized from her Los Angeles home and mystically transported to an antebellum slave plantation. In Jones's novel, a modern blues singer is haunted and ultimately possessed by the racial-sexual trauma of her enslaved foremothers. Bracketing trauma fiction's obsessive (non-)revelation that the past is irretrievable, these novels set out to imagine what it would feel like, and what would happen next, if we proceeded with the fantasy of reparative return, anyway. Because both plots follow from the fictional "given" that pain is transformative and necessary, they allow us to ask: What narrative possibilities does masochism enable or foreclose? What pleasures, or systems of reward, are held out to inspire and sustain literary fantasies of historical return? How and where does power accrue in the (literary) masochistic scene, and what is the masochist's relationship to power?

As with each of the psychopathological idioms that structure the chapters in this book, "masochism" is a capacious concept that originated in a clinical context but quickly came to circulate as part of a larger cultural vocabulary. My use of the term is avowedly promiscuous and idiosyncratic, including but also expanding upon, transposing, and metaphorizing conventional understandings of masochism as pleasure in pain. To this effect, I begin with Freud's psychopathological model and a political allegorization of it, but over the course of the chapter, I also examine and apply counter-discourses emerging from feminist and queer theory that re-imagine masochism as a restorative practice. The present chapter proceeds from the belief that theories of masochism consolidate a rich interpretive tool for black literary studies, yet I would be remiss if I did not acknowledge the obvious counterpoint that "masochism" is also an analytic term accompanied by a lot of baggage. As a way of preliminarily positioning my readings within a broader discursive field, I offer a cursory sketch of some proscriptive and reclamatory approaches to masochism in contemporary African American studies.

One powerful strain of discursive and behavioral censorship that has militated against the development of sustained, African Americanist attention to the topic of masochism has been the normative ideal of "respectability"—an ideal that carries an ambivalent relationship to racial progressivism. Many scholars have charted respectability's emergence as a morally reproachful self-defense against vitriolic racial-sexual stereotypes.[2] As such, it articulates a sympathetic defense of black women (in particular) that is nevertheless enshrouded in praxis of social and sexual conservatism. Insofar as the guise of race-liberalism authorizes the performance of an anti-sexual sociality, respectability's rehabilitative efforts simultaneously work to restrain black sexual representation and practices. On these grounds, and noting in particular its recapitulation to sexist and homophobic ideals, a growing body of contemporary African Americanists working in feminist theory and black queer studies—including Aliyyah I. Abdur-Rahman, Brittney Cooper, Sharon Patricia Holland, Arlene Keizer, Susana Morris, Amber Musser, Jennifer C. Nash, Darieck Scott, and Christina Sharpe—have persuasively argued against the hegemony of respectability in black social and academic forums.[3]

Sharpe has been especially attentive to the ways in which masochistic desire and sadomasochistic (s/m) practices have been deemed uniquely taboo within the cross-disciplinary field of African American studies; even deliberately sex-positive projects have been reluctant to acknowledge explicit eroticizations of power and powerlessness within black culture. Sharpe hypothesizes that anti-masochistic censorship in black academic and social discourses likely results from s/m's unsettling rekindling of history: It unnerves us insofar as it "[makes] explicit the very master-slave configurations that haunt us, that make visible slavery within freedom and questions of consent."[4] Expanding upon her identification of the specters of racial slavery at the core of black censorial desire, I would venture that masochism disquiets because it disrupts important black political fictions of self-sovereignty; because it erodes the assumption of most progressive politics that the subjugated aspire, in uncomplicated ways, for freedom; and because it rejects cultural fantasies of progressive history in which the present or future finally and decisively triumphs over the injuries of the past.

Furthermore, enacting or even considering masochistic sexuality and desire may seem particularly unappealing at a moment when African Americans are increasingly cast as "unworthy" or insincere victims in political rhetoric, public policy, and civil society. For, to the degree that masochism requires one to claim desire of and as a victim, one might argue that it treads dangerously close to persistent conservative allegations of black subjects self-servingly "playing the victim." In *The Cult of True Victimhood*, Alyson M. Cole observes that "anti-victimist literature" has been on the rise since the early nineties, producing a conservative rhetoric in which "real" victims are defined by increasingly narrow, at times even impossible, standards of virtue, blamelessness, and measurable suffering.[5] It is hardly imaginative to hypothesize that this cultural milieu acts as a powerful deterrent to black intellectual and experiential engagements with masochistic desire.[6]

Indeed, African Americans' widespread aversion to the concept of masochism gains still another dimension when viewed through the prism of black cultural nationalism's enduring legacy. A radical cultural movement designed to upend Eurocentric discursive hegemonies that for centuries aligned blackness with ugliness, weakness, death, and malignancy, black cultural nationalism announced and articulated the counter-hegemonic ideals of black pride, black beauty, and black power. As countless post-nationalist critics and authors have demonstrated, black cultural nationalism was radical, creative, and liberatory but also rigidly prescriptive and intensely censorious. For better and for worse, the cultural nationalists' invention of a powerful new black subject hinged on the disavowal of various forms of black negativity, including all "elements of their history that could not pass through the ideological filter of black pride."[7]

But if, as the received wisdom holds, masochism signals unwieldy personal and political dangers, particularly for marginalized groups, then a growing body of literature and scholarship has alternatively identified masochism with a range of unique promises and pleasures. Consider, for example, Samuel Delany's densely theoretical science fiction novella, *The Game of Time and Pain*. Delany's protagonist, Gorgik, is a former slave turned liberator, now an elder statesman, whose sexual appetites attach to the slave collar he once, forcibly, wore. The slave collar is a prominent and versatile symbol in Gorgik's self-accounting, signaling at once the political crime of bondage and the sexual excitement of reclaiming that sign of social annihilation. As Gorgik puts it, "I knew, at least for me, that the power to remove the collar was wholly involved with the freedom to place it there when I wished. And, wanting it, I knew, for the first time . . . in my life—the self that want defined." In this figuration, the iron symbol and instrument of imprisonment is itself made vulnerable to radical reappropriation. In its second life, the collar becomes an accessory of choice, an unexpected sign of freedom and ecstatic unencumbrance. Reveling in this alchemical conversion of subjugation into agency, our hero tells us, history is "never inevitable, only more or less negotiable."[8]

Many theorizations of rehabilitative masochism demur from Delany's triumphalism but share his basic premise that masochism can work as an unexpected counter-force to historical powerlessness. For example, Keizer reads Delany's depictions of s/m as an analogue to the psychoanalytic logic of "working through" trauma through repetitious reenactment,[9] while the controversial visual artist Kara Walker draws on this kind of logic to explain her infamous silhouettes of slavery when she says, "In order to have a real connection with my history, I had to be somebody's slave. . . . But I was in control: that's the difference."[10] In each of these views, the compulsion to return to the traumatic past acts as both symptom and cure: Masochistic performance is a gesture that expresses traumatic irresolution while opening up a phantasmatic space for working through past pains. Still other articulations of masochism's value for critical and political discourse point to its embedded critique of the liberal ideal of self-sovereignty (Darieck Scott), or its attention to the sensory and affective pathways of power (Musser), or its capacity to illumine "the connection between contemporary labor, terrors, and desires, the labor and the excesses of chattel slavery, and power, sex, and identification" (Sharpe).[11] In the course of this chapter, I rehearse some of these, and other, orientations toward politicized theories of masochistic fantasy and desire.

Speaking candidly, my own orientation toward masochism is ambivalent and inconclusive. I am convinced that desire forged in the crucible of victimization is often propelled by a recursive energy that the trope of masochism may substantively illuminate. Moreover, I find enticing and at times persuasive queer and feminist claims that masochism may re-open for trans-historical re-imagination an unresolved and enduringly hurtful past. Understood in this way, masochism promises to salve the stubborn wound of historical trauma. It is, to my knowledge, the only form of historical engagement that contains such a radically reparative promise.

I remain dubious, however, about masochism's dramatic and demanding call for willful self-shattering, particularly when that call addresses subjects whose very socio-political existence is produced through an extreme and extended tradition of self-dispossession. My hopefulness about the revisionary potential of masochistic reenactment is, in substantive ways, dialed back by the inescapable truth that re-enactment necessarily and painfully reproduces scenes of injury, even as it makes conceivable alternative trajectories of event, desire, and identification. Masochism's "cost" of relinquishing the reparative psycho-political ideal of sovereignty is, I believe, an exorbitant one, even if sovereignty itself is not a tenable psychic or political status but a potent structure of fantasy in its own right.

Registering both the danger and the allure of masochistic fantasy, my aim in this chapter is neither to endorse nor to discredit masochism but simply to explore the contradictory truths it produces, and often refuses, to resolve. Through a double-voiced, thick description of masochistic fantasy in contemporary narratives of slavery, I depict masochism as a site of moral, affective, and political ambivalence *and* as a narrative infrastructure that resists resolution, holding in tension the perils of a painful and impossible love, on the one hand, and the redemptive possibilities of re-enactment-with-a-difference, on the other.

## Masochism as Political Allegory

The Austrian sexologist Richard von Krafft-Ebing is frequently credited for coining the diagnostic category "masochism," although this term is named not for its "discoverer" but for its prototypical subject: the eccentric, nineteenth-century writer, Leopold von Sacher-Masoch. In Krafft-Ebing's *Psychopathia Sexualis*, masochism is tautologically defined as the family of "perversions" obsessively described in Sacher-Masoch's fiction: "The individual affected is controlled in his sexual feeling and thought by the idea of being completely and unconditionally subject to the will of a person of the opposite sex; of being treated by this person as a master, humiliated and abused."[12] But Krafft-Ebing's contributions to the theoretical development of the concept consist primarily in descriptive work. For him, Gertrud Lenzer notes, "the symptoms of the disease constituted the disease itself."[13]

It was Freud who first sought to explain and sub-categorize the logic and economies of masochism—its developmental origins, its systems of reward, and its metapsychological import. In his influential essay "A Child Is Being Beaten," he identifies "the essence of masochism" as the "convergence" of an illicit, impossible love (the daughter's incestuous love for her father) and the guilt that is produced by that love.[14] Freud's clinical scenario begins with a daughter who covets exclusive access to her father's power and protection; she wishes to be the sole object and recipient of his love. Upon discovering the prohibitive taboo that makes such love unacceptable, she develops a repressed fantasy of being beaten by her father. Within the daughter's psychic economy, the fantasy serves two purposes: It functions simultaneously as substitute and punishment for her incestuous love. By disguising love as punishment, the daughter retains, in altered form, her original desire. At the same time, the fantasy of punishment works to expiate her guilt, which accrues around her sublimated yet enduring wish for a forbidden love. In brief, Freud proposes that masochistic desire arises as a maladaptive strategy for managing an illicit love.

Freud's exploration of masochistic desire is characteristically confined to the individual psyche and the private sphere of family drama. He reads the desire to be punished as emanating from universal, ahistorical, and primarily familial dynamics of jealousy, constraint, identification, and love. But we may alternatively read Freud's essay as a political allegory, in which the familial saga illuminates specifically historicized, social relations of power, prohibition, political fantasy, and politicized identity. This is a project the political philosopher Wendy Brown undertakes in *Politics out of History*, where she repurposes Freudian masochism to speculate about how histories of marginalization may produce unexpected, self-injurious forms of political desire. I propose that the theorization of political masochism provides one suggestive model for understanding the fantasy structure that powers contemporary narratives of slavery.

The re-worked plot of political masochism goes something like this: Subjects born into late modern democracy harbor an early, formative desire for the protection and positive recognition (in Freud's term, the "love") of the powerful ("paternal") state. However, for certain marked and marginalized populations, such as racial minorities, women, and sexual minorities, the possibility of such positive regard is foreclosed by the "punitive social acts" of "racism, sexism, and heterosexism." These punishments at once pre-exist the individual and constitute the individual's abjected social identity through repeated acts of exclusion. Through them, the marginalized subject quickly comes to see her desire for full enfranchisement and positive recognition as impossible or unacceptable. She becomes "humiliated [by her] attachment"[15] and turns back on herself, as if to say, "I should not have desired recognition," or "I now know my desire to be illicit."

As with the Freudian drama, however, the prohibition of desire does not quell its drive. The disenfranchised subject continues to long for recognition despite the apparent foreclosure of its possibility. Like Freud's masochist, she develops an obsessive fixation, returning incessantly to a symbolic site of foreclosure (the parental beating/the scene of social exclusion) in hopes of forestalling or denying the loss of the idealized social order from which she once sought recognition (the patriarchal family, the racist state). Yet this repetition is futile, for the "pejoratively marked subject" has already fallen "from membership in a universal citizenry, from formal equality, from liberal personhood," and what is more, this fall is precisely "the site of such an identity's creation." Thus, the most that can be salvaged is the repetition of the fall, as masochistic "repetition [comes to gratify] an injured love by reaffirming the existence of the order that carried both the love and the injury."[16]

Reminiscent of this cycle of punishment and unrequited desire, Butler's *Kindred*—the author's best known novel and a massive commercial success—takes shape through a repeated and escalating pattern of abuse, staged between a powerful white father figure and a compulsively returning black daughter. *Kindred*'s trans-historical encounters between its black protagonist and her white ancestor are made possible through the fantasy device of time travel. In the novel, Dana's spatio-temporal migration responds to the sporadic, unpredictable calls of Rufus Weylin, a white heir to a slave planter whom Dana quickly identifies as her "several times great grandfather."[17] In a literal, or genetic, way then, Rufus corresponds to the class of fathers that Freud identifies as the categorical love objects of masochistic fantasy. Still more suggestively, as a slaveholder in the antebellum South, Rufus figures within the text as the Historical Father, an avatar for white masculine traditions of power through which Dana's racialized and sexualized occlusion from full citizenship was pre-emptively secured.

Whereas in the Freudian story beating fantasies follow the daughter's apprehension of the incest taboo, in *Kindred*, Dana's compulsive returns to a historical site of punishment follow a series of symbolic rejections that mark the impossibility of her desire for full citizenship. Several months before she is first abducted by the past, friends and family protest Dana's interracial marriage, and the ceremony takes place without witnesses. Although Dana and Kevin attain in name the legal status and protections that accompany marriage, their union remains unrecognized, and more: It is aggressively disavowed by both of their families, in the workplace, and in various public spaces. Certainly, the degree to which one's marriage is regarded as socially legitimate is not the sole or primary index of enfranchisement, but neither is this textual event arbitrary or accidental.[18] Particularly in the context of African American history, the rite of marriage has long been regarded as a telos of enfranchisement. Thus, for example, Houston A. Baker has read Frederick Douglass's marriage certificate as "the inscribed document that effectively marks Douglass's liberation."[19]

Moreover, Dana's exclusion from civil society's standards of marital legitimacy occurs in the year of the American bicentennial—a year oversaturated with commemorative events and patriotic rhetoric, and a year notorious for its selective amnesia regarding the different historical legacies of the Revolution for African Americans. As the historian Leon Litwack has argued, the widespread, uncomplicated, and laudatory representations of the American past that characterized 1976 were made possible only through a sustained refusal to recognize the African American presence as part of national history.[20] The bicentennial's celebratory ethos of patriotic nostalgia thus re-inscribed African American exclusion from the parameters of recognizable American citizenship. *Kindred* gestures toward this contemporary site of black exclusion—though it does not linger there—by sending Dana on her culminating trip to the punitive past on July 4, 1976. Indeed, the contemporary scenes within Butler's novel assemble myriad, often mundane acts of exclusion as assertions of social taboo, renouncing and prohibiting Dana's desire, as an African American woman, for state recognition.

Like political masochism's compulsive re-stagings of exclusion from liberal personhood, *Kindred*'s plot subsequently unfolds through Dana's repeated returns to the historical site at which the possibility for her full enfranchisement was originally, categorically foreclosed—the site of enslavement. Her desire for recognition persists but is now re-formulated as the impossible desire to return to and revise a bygone past. To be sure, Dana adamantly denies the force of her own desire in her recurrent abductions by the past, but this denial is diluted, if not contradicted, by her ready concession that she is *invested* in her white forefather's survival, though his persistence in his being hinges on her own, enduring subjugation. As early as her second visit to the past, she postulates, "Was that why I was here? Not only to insure the survival of one accident-prone small boy, but to insure my family's survival, my own birth. . . . If I was to live, if others were to live, he [Rufus] must live. I didn't dare test the paradox" (29).

Dana's logic meshes with a line of reasoning common to time travel fiction: She believes that in order to sustain her life in the present (i.e., to ensure her birth), she must uphold the meeting and mating patterns of the past. Having learned from an inherited family Bible that Rufus, together with a black woman named Alice Greenwood, will conceive Hagar, Dana's mixed-race great-great-grandmother, Dana becomes convinced that she must help to sustain Rufus's life, at least until Hagar is born, in order to provide for the terms of her own existence. Yet predictably, given the dominant racial ideologies of Rufus's time and class, as well as his social position as heir to a slave plantation, Dana's vested interest in sustaining his life comes into conflict with her politically and historically informed desires to resist or fight the slave economy and to protect and enrich the lives of the Weylin's human property. Her desire for racial justice—an ethics that would enable a life of greater freedom for herself as a black woman and, more broadly, for black people as her "kindred"—is thus complicated by her discovery that her very existence depends upon a history of racial subjugation. In other words, and following the pattern of political masochism, the "I" for whom Dana desires freedom is itself produced in part through a history of slavery. Understood in this way, Dana's project of self-preservation must also contain gestures of submission and self-compromise.

Here, we find the contradiction in desire that is the signature of therapeutic reading. On the one hand, Dana's relationship to the past is marked by a paradoxical investment in oppressive, racialized power. On the other hand, a powerful current of reparative desire propels it. If, following Brown, we read Dana's desire for rights and recognition in the present as an illicit political desire, already foreclosed by national traditions of slavery and racism, it follows that Dana's returns to the past constitute the fantasy structure that enables her (impossible) appeals to the Historical Father. Embedded within these returns/appeals is a trajectory of desire that says, "If I can reach the Father before he rejected me, I can set things aright." Or, as Dana justifies her efforts to endear herself to a young Rufus: "He'll probably be old enough to have some authority when I come again. Old enough to help me. I want him to have as many good memories of me as I can give him now" (83). Much like psychoanalytic and political variants of masochism, Dana's fantasy of returning to an abusive past is a fantasy of subjugation (of returning to slavery) that masks a stubborn desire for recognition or love (the desire to appease the Historical Father, to win over a foreclosed and abusive past).

Thus we may map the plot of *Kindred* onto a theory of political masochism through a series of direct and transparent correspondences. Both imagine a painful current of reparative desire that tethers a contemporary subject to a haunting site of historical exclusion, and in both instances, this circuit of desire and punishment is seductive, but also injurious and irresolvable. The longed for, retroactive recognition does not—cannot—materialize, and a repetitious wounding, more hurtful for its predictability, transpires instead. In this reading, *Kindred* adopts the form of political masochism, unfolding as a cautionary tale that warns against the destructive consequences of casting political desire backward. Adding force to the warning, the novel's culminating scene tethers Dana's salvation to her triumph over the cycle of punitive, historical return. When she finally apprehends the danger Rufus poses, as well as the limits of her love, Dana plunges a knife into the slaveholder's side and shatters the antebellum fantasy-scape. Her murder of the treacherous yet seductive Father signals a psychoanalytic "recovery," for this is the act that allows her to replace the illicit fantasy structure with socially sanctioned forms of love and desire. The trans-historical circuit of painful, bodily return that makes up most of the book is supplanted by a research trip to Maryland, where Dana looks for documentary traces of Rufus's existence. On this trip, both she and Kevin articulate their committed disengagement from the masochistic fantasy. "It's over," Kevin assures her. "There's nothing you can do to change any of it now." Dana soberly replies, "I know" (264).

Yet even as *Kindred* may be shown to map neatly onto a prescriptive, anti-masochistic critique, it is also the case that the novel fails to achieve vindication or closure, ending with the explicit non-ending of Dana's enduring search for Rufus. "You'd think I would have had enough of the past," Dana muses, but still, *Kindred*'s final pages show her seeking out Rufus's grave, scouring the records of the Maryland Historical Society, and questioning the locals about his life and death (264). In short, Dana's murderous destruction of her masochistic fantasy does not produce psychic resolution or a more peaceable relationship to the past. On the contrary, it leaves her with persistent and irresolvable losses, both embodied and psychological: "I lost an arm on my last trip home," she recounts. "And I lost about a year of my life and much of the comfort and security I had not valued until it was gone" (9). And again: "I don't have a name for the thing that happened to me, but I don't feel safe anymore" (17).

How shall we make sense of this final conundrum, in which Dana's seemingly insatiable quest to earn Rufus's recognition so robustly survives his death? In Brown's accounting, the problem of political masochism is largely a problem of excess—of leftover feelings and wants with no viable place in the present. But in *Kindred*, the excision of masochistic fantasy does not solve the problem of excess. Dana's potent historical feelings continue to press into her life, overriding her efforts to live in the present. Even after the time travel sequence ends, Dana feels powerfully compelled to seek out the past, to pore over it. She is still made vulnerable and insecure by it. What, then, does the prescriptive renunciation of masochism as such achieve? And more, why does Dana's termination of the circuit of masochistic fantasy/time travel compound rather than eradicate or ameliorate her losses?

Perhaps political masochism offers a cogent analysis of the structure and mechanics of self-injurious desire, but it falls short as an aid to imagining the full scope of what masochism might mean for subjects who come into social being as constitutively disempowered. For political masochism—constrained, perhaps, by the original valences of the Freudian narrative—assumes in some measure that the "perversion" of masochistic fantasy is self-evident, that the masochist's delusional system of identification and desire disqualifies her from credible self-representation, and that relinquishing masochistic fantasy will invariably yield improvement. Its tacit promise is this: We will interrupt a cycle of unnecessary pain, we will better understand the terms of political possibility, and we will become better citizens, if only we let go of our impossible desires.

In addition, the allegorical form of political masochism brings about a dubious censure of Freud's original, erotic register. A system of symbolic representation, allegory operates through an economy of substitution; one thing stands in for another. In political masochism, the illicit sexual desire of the Freudian masochist represents the political desire of marginalized subjects. This comparison yields a rich and largely compelling description of the mechanics of political desire against ostensible self-interest. Yet the genre of allegory forces Brown to elide considerations of the erotic *within* the domain of politics.[21] By *replacing* the eroticism of Freud's story with a strictly circumscribed notion of political desire, political masochism effectively neuters the political, foreclosing explorations of how the erotic may not in fact run parallel to the political but may infuse and inform it. As I will show, *Kindred* reproduces this discursive censorship of the sexual but also critiques the notion that political desire may be assessed as something asexual, or wholly separable, from other human drives.

My point is not to discount political masochism but to identify and tend to some promising interpretations of pain and its psychic uses that this orientation toward masochism overlooks. How might we challenge and complicate this theoretical frame if we reject the premise that political and libidinal desires may be theoretically extricated from one another, and if we do away with the commonsense idea that pathology is inherent to pain's pursuit? This approach characterizes the work of a number of late twentieth- and early twenty-first-century feminist and queer theorists who conceptualize masochism as an explicitly sexual psychic drive bearing unique potential for psychic healing. On this view, masochistic fantasy operates, not as impotent delusion, but as an agency that allows us to imagine ourselves and the social world otherwise. Ann Cvetkovich, for example, proposes that enacting masochistic fantasy through "repeated, and especially ritualized violence" may bear a unique, if ambivalent, power "to heal and/or perpetuate an original trauma."[22] Similarly, Elizabeth Freeman describes lesbian s/m in particular as the erotic production of a "temporal Möbius strip" that allows the masochist "a consensual might-have- been triumphing over a personal history of being victimized."[23] (On another occasion, apropos of *Kindred* as the present chapter's case study, Freeman calls s/m an "erotic time machine.")[24] What would it look like to read *Kindred* in this way, taking note of how masochistic fantasy operates not (only) as the guilty vehicle of a pathological love but as a privileged conveyance that uniquely enables access to potent and unresolved forms of historical desire?

## Masochism as Historiography

In *Time Binds: Queer Temporalities, Queer Histories*, Elizabeth Freeman develops a new theoretical model for thinking through some of the therapeutic and epistemological potentialities of masochism. Against psychoanalytic and political models that regard masochism as a structure of inappropriate feelings that are intrinsically inimical to personal or social thriving, Freeman makes creative use of the concept of masochism to re-imagine the genre of history. Describing masochism as a way of feeling that exceeds "appropriate" forms of knowledge and "bourgeois-sentimental, emotional reactions to historical events,"[25] she positions it as the repressed other of historiographical knowledge *and* a form of active resistance to such repression. At its best, she says, masochism enables a bodily epistemology that can desublimate disciplinarily and culturally censored forms of historical affect.

For Butler as for Freeman, the repression of "historical feeling" amounts to an incomplete and restrictive form of historical understanding. Moreover, she concurs that the corrective task of recuperating a more comprehensive, affectively engaged historical understanding requires a turn to masochistic fantasy. Butler endorses this logic most explicitly when, in several interviews, she traces *Kindred*'s origins to an ideological confrontation with a black nationalist college peer, regarding the status of the African American slave past. "Even though he knew a *lot* more than I did about Black history," she recounts, "it was all cerebral. He wasn't feeling any of it."[26] The author goes on to align her friend's exclusively "cerebral" historical knowledge with a failure of empathy, a false sense of self-sovereignty, and a troubling commitment to historical detachment. She claims that, although her friend ostensibly "knew" the facts of historical oppression, he "apparently never made the connection" whereby ancestral sacrifices of dignity enabled his own existence. "He was still blaming [his parents] for their humility and their acceptance of disgusting behavior on the part of employers and other people," Butler laments. "I wanted to take a character, when I did *Kindred*, back in time to some of the things that our ancestors had to go through, to see if that character survived so very well with the knowledge of the present in her head."[27]

Anticipating Freeman's argument, Butler regards "cerebral" historical knowledge as flawed by its constitutive excision of "feeling"—and more precisely, by its excision of *identificatory* feelings toward history's victims. As Butler recalls, the thing that catalyzes her masochistic fantasy (though she never names it as such) is her friend's ungenerous disavowal of ancestral suffering. She wishes, with *Kindred*, to rehabilitate the repudiated ancestral slave as a symbol of resilience, rather than defeat, and as the avatar of a more expansive, nuanced vision of heroic black identity. "I realized that he didn't know what heroism was," she says of her nationalist interlocutor. "That's what I want to write about."[28] A literarily transcribed masochistic fantasy thus emerges as Butler's template for the hermeneutical practice I am calling "therapeutic reading." Her story of a contemporary subject who endures the suffering of her ancestors represents an affective pedagogy, a strategy through which she seeks to teach empathic (and indeed, loving) feeling to a resistant, "cerebral" other. "I was trying to get people to *feel slavery*," she explains, when asked about her approach to history in *Kindred*. "I was trying to get across the kind of emotional and psychological stones that slavery threw at people."[29] If conventional historiographical study yielded, for Butler's friend, antipathy toward the slave past, then it is through the fantasy of shared, identitarian suffering that the author imagines the possibility of mitigating his bad feelings toward his ancestors and, perhaps, of producing a historically situated ethics of African American self-compassion.

Through her repetition of this anecdote in various venues, Butler encourages a critical investment in the possibility of therapeutic reading. Much as Morrison describes her authorial desire to "kidnap" the reader, "[throwing her] ruthlessly into an alien environment as the first step into a shared experience with the book's population," Butler revels in the fantasy of literature's exaggerated agency in producing and shaping the reader's experience.[30] My interest, however, lies less in the credibility of Butler or Morrison's statements of intent than in the narrative forms that refract their investment in the fantasy of therapeutic reading. Put another way, my guiding question is not, "Does Butler succeed in teaching the reader the ropes of therapeutic reading?" but "What narrative forms, psychic logics, and structures of desire are called upon to tell the story of transformative historical return?" Freeman's theorization of s/m as the foundation for an epistemology of transformative historical encounter proves useful here, for unlike theories of political masochism, it holds out hope that reclaiming historical pain may be purposeful and effective.

Freeman coins the term "erotohistoriography" to describe a bodily epistemology whose specific iterations include masochism as well as other, conspicuously temporalized forms of queer desire. Erotohistoriography "[treats] the present as temporally hybrid" and "uses the body as a tool to effect, figure, or perform" trans-historical encounters. Whereas the conventional historian may measure his or her research by the standard of "objective and disinterested analysis," the erotohistoriographer is a sensuous time traveler, for whom the past appears not as a sequence of discrete and knowable events but as a dynamic, porous, and permeable context for apprehending—variously, not conclusively—possible configurations of the self-in-history. (Freeman's archetypal model for her theory of erotohistoriography is Frankenstein's monster—a fictional figure whose body is literally pieced together from the remains of the dead, who "[wears] and [performs] anachronistic behaviors in the literal form of mismatched body parts" and who, in so doing, "learns virtue from precedent.")[31]

According to Freeman, whose work builds on an oeuvre of lesbian/ queer writing on masochism, erotohistoriography's value consists not only in its presentation of an alternative way of "doing" history but also in the rehabilitative potential it offers up by enabling a dynamic re-visioning of the self in dialogue with traumatic, unresolved pasts. For example, an erotohistoriographical reading of *Kindred* might posit that by identifying with and against various ancestral figures— from her lookalike, an enslaved concubine named Alice; to Rufus, the white slave master; to Sarah, a seemingly complicitous black "mammy" figure—Dana is compelled to dismantle her original, anti-historical and monadic sense of self and to re-imagine herself in terms of multiple af- fective connections to a complicated past. Energized by the hope that "liberatory rather than random or reactionary difference might appear in the nonidentical repetitions that constitute identity,"[32] erotohistoriog- raphy re-maps the possibilities of "history," "identity," and the relation between these categories.

So whereas political masochism illustrates the futility of repetitious, punitive cycles that produce "injured identity," erotohistoriography pos- its that re-enactments of identitarian trauma may in fact constitute the very site at which reparative revision becomes imaginable. Masochism, in the latter frame, is not the symptom of a "bad" or malignant identity but an unwieldy modality of historical encounter through which con- temporary identifications and desires might be productively negotiated and reconstituted.

As we might anticipate from Butler's anecdote about *Kindred*'s gen- esis, much of the novel's plot follows the erosion of Dana's uncompro- mising will to self-determination. Inversely, Dana's growing sense of her own vulnerability—apprehended through identification with his- torical victims—corroborates the novel's critique of historiography as book knowledge and enables the protagonist's evolving commitment to a kind of trans-historical intersubjectivity. Early in the novel's chronology, Dana portrays the terms of racial history as "degrading nonsense" and expresses a willingness to die sooner than to accept certain compromising terms of existence. But as the plot advances, her anger and militancy are progressively worn down (127). By learning firsthand the radically circumscribed possibilities for black agency in the antebellum South, Dana develops a profound critique of her initial "moral superiority," which she comes to associate with the "contemptuous" retrospect of "the militant nineteen sixties" (145).

Mirroring the critique of black cultural nationalism that she offers in interviews, Butler is explicit in her intention to distinguish Dana's intensifying attachment to the past from a growing passion for any conventional conception of historical knowledge. Indeed, one of the most important "lessons" of Dana's repeated historical abductions has to do with the limitations of book knowledge and sanctioned forms of historical narration. Dana finds little use for her reference books and historical documents when she is confronted with the visceral immediacy of historical oppression, and although she is a professional writer, she finds that she is unable to give shape to her own experiences of historical feeling in socially intelligible ways. "I had tried and tried [to write about Rufus]," she recalls, "and only managed to fill my wastebasket" (194). What Dana discovers in the history of slavery is an affective density that resists *telling*—or narrative apprehension—that is retrievable only through performative re-encounters with the past that etch their meaning on the body and mind through the sensory register of pain. And while the novel provides innumerable examples of what Dana cannot say or know, one is struck by her seemingly inexhaustible capacity to absorb the *feeling* of historical suffering.[33] In the sting of the descending whip, the violent fists of a rapacious patroller, and the magically re-inhabited body of the wounded, aching slave, Butler figures a "stark, powerful reality that the gentle conveniences and luxuries of [Dana's Los Angeles home], of *now*, could not touch" (191, Butler's italics).

In this sense, Dana's abduction by a brutalizing past transparently performs the critique that Butler offers in her description of the book's political project, but Dana's narrative also exceeds the terms that Butler avows. For in addition to *Kindred*'s corrective pedagogy of affective historiography, Butler emplots a queer, trans-historical *desire* routed through bodily identification with the suffering of one's ancestors. In other words, Dana's abductions are also *seductions*. To her own surprise, Dana develops a curious loyalty to Rufus, which unfolds in a far more intricate pattern than any simple, causal logic of power and obeisance. "I hadn't expected to care about him except for my own and my family's sake," Dana remarks on one occasion (203). But "however little sense it made, I cared. I must have. I kept forgiving him for things" (180). Although she is made anxious and abused by her relationship to him, Rufus nevertheless holds out to Dana the promise of an important and elusive recognition. The more time she spends in the past, the more Dana experiences the present as a site of de-contextualization and anonymity (her family disowns her, no one at work knows her name). By contrast, she describes her compulsive returns to Rufus's time as "so much like coming home that it scare[s] me" (192).

This complex, affective web of time, pain, and desire at once supplements *Kindred*'s critique of detached historiographical methods and reveals Butler's specific investment in masochistic fantasy as a preferred mode of critique. Indeed, we may find within *Kindred* at least three plausible readings that locate reparative power in Dana's acts of painful, historical return. The first reading foregrounds Dana's relationship to Rufus (the Historical Father) as a site of negotiation, which allows Dana to constructively re-imagine her relationship to the slave past. In essence, it would say, in spite of her insistence that she "[has] no control at all over anything," and in spite of her dramatically restricted power as a black woman on an antebellum plantation, that masochistic time travel ironically allows Dana a kind of historical agency that was previously unimaginable (113). A once inaccessible, deterministic past is reopened to receive her threats, appeals, and other attentions; she discovers firsthand, as she repeatedly saves Rufus's life, the Hegelian truth of the interdependence of master and slave, and although the full and enfranchising socio-historical recognition that Dana longs for is foreclosed by a chronological order that remains irreversible, Rufus *does* offer, in lieu of historical recognition, something like historical hospitality. He actively welcomes Dana to the past, offering a sincerely meant (if false) reassurance of belonging: "You'll be alright here," he tells her. "You're home" (143). In this reading, we might infer that Dana's re-vivified enmeshment with a slaveholding patriarch allows her a kind of recuperative agency and that the re-vivified scene of the antebellum past unexpectedly provides "a space in which conflict and anger can emerge as a necessary component of psychic resolution."[34]

An alternate erotohistoriographical reading of the novel would foreground the "non-identical [historical] repetitions" produced through Dana's identificatory encounter with Alice Greenwood, Rufus's concubine and Dana's great-grandmother several times removed, who surfaces in the context of Dana's time travel as both an ancestor and a historical alter ego. Dana's identification with Alice is ambivalent and partial but also irrefutable. Nearly every character in the book, including Dana and Alice themselves, remarks upon the two women's striking physical resemblance, as well as their mirrored status on the plantation as "Rufus's women." Still more explicitly, Rufus insists that the two are, in fact, the same. "You're so much like her [Alice], I can hardly stand it," he says to Dana. And then, "You were one woman. . . . You and her. One woman. Two halves of a whole" (257). To the degree that we credit Rufus's claim, we might interpret Dana's relationship to Alice not (only) as one of inter-generational, familial resemblance but (also) as one of revisionary repetition. When the white Historical Father attempts to subdue Dana through the same rhetorical and physical deployments of power that he used against Alice, Dana becomes an alternative version of her foremother, emboldened by a vindicating knowledge of the future (symbolized by a knife she's brought from 1976) to imagine as otherwise a formative scenario of traumatic racial-sexual origins. Although Dana's ancestor and historical double suffers non-recognition and obscure death, Dana returns to bear witness to Alice and to re-construe the historical scenario by confronting it with her belated, twentieth-century sense of entitlement and agency. Plunging the knife into Rufus's side, Dana survives what Alice could not endure: the insatiable, brutalizing, corrupting, and intermittently seductive power of the Historical Father. The point here is not that Dana changes history or replaces the fact of Alice's death with that of her own survival; neither of these claims are true to Butler's narrative. Nevertheless, one might convincingly argue that Dana's masochistic return to the past functions as a therapeutic phenomenon, insofar as it dilutes the singular grasp of an intransigent, oppressive historical narrative by casting that story alongside alternate scenarios of what might have been.

We can read Dana's relationship with Alice in yet another way. In addition to enabling a multiplicative revision of historical possibility, Dana's masochistic fantasy makes possible her reparative re-encounter with the abject figure of the ancestral slave. Traveling back in time, Dana is presented with an uncanny doppelgänger with whom she cannot help but identify. Like Dana, Alice is born free but subsequently made a slave through Rufus's coercive force. Enslaved as punishment for asserting her freedom, Alice lives the disciplinary consequences of an antebellum, proto–black pride, enduring beatings, rape, and sustained and forceful opposition to her assertions and enactments of individual will. Over the course of her repeated returns to the past, Dana bears sympathetic witness to Alice's progressive degradation. When Alice is ravaged by slave catchers and their dogs, Dana bandages and feeds her, nursing her to health. When Alice lashes out in impotent rage, Dana cajoles and reasons with her, urging her to act in the long-term interest of self-preservation. And when Alice finally succumbs to nihilistic despair and hangs herself from a barn roof, Dana dismounts the dead body, grieves her loss, and tends to Alice's surviving children. Through this vicariously masochistic narrative trajectory, Butler engineers an opportunity for her contemporary protagonist to embrace—retroactively, yet still with tactile immediacy—a pained and once-forsaken historical victim. Read as erotohistoriography, masochistic fantasy here repeats history with the critical difference of sympathetic recognition by the morally adjudicating gaze of the future.

Yet there is a case to be made against an erotohistoriographic reading of *Kindred*—a case that turns on Dana's firmly bounded resistance to thinking through the erotic dimensions of masochistic fantasy. When theorized as a de-repressive, transformative performance, masochism's power hinges on the mystical economy of the erotic. Masochistic fantasy works by exploiting a specifically sexual power that can break apart both the subject and her present, allowing the masochist to feel at once the contingency of her known world and the "fragments of times that may not be [her] own." Through these temporal and subjective disruptions intrinsic to sexuality, s/m "becomes a form of writing history with the body in which the linearity of history may be called into question, but, crucially, the past does not thereby cease to exist."[35]

True, Butler is similarly invested in a kind of de-repressive unmaking of her protagonist by way of sensate contact with dominative "times . . . not [her] own." However, for Dana, the erotic comes into view, not as the overt conduit for time travel, but as an aggressively repressed facet of her relationship to Rufus and her past. Kevin seems to know this better than Dana; he repeatedly, if unsympathetically, interrogates her about the sexual content of her trans-historical abductions. But for Dana, the erotic undercurrent of the force that pulls her to Rufus is unthinkable until it is irrefutable. In the moment that Rufus announces his power and desire *as sexual*, Dana aborts the fantasy structure entirely. Framing his sexual proposition as an encroachment on "what he knew I could not give" (257), she responds with murder, "[raising] the knife, [driving] it into the flesh I had saved so many times" (260). Thus in *Kindred* erotic apprehension signals not the opening but the closing of temporal "passageways." Dana returns to the present, not to return to the past, and the past once again recedes to a distant and irretrievable site of historical irresolution.

Understandably, many critics have applauded Butler for the novel's culmination in Dana's courageous act of self-defense. After all, Rufus's murder represents her most assertive and impactful act of agency against a dominative past. By killing Rufus, Dana reclaims ownership of her body and ends the brutalizing cycle of temporal abduction through which she was made to feel that she "had no control at all over anything" (113). In Angelyn Mitchell's reading, it is this act of severance that makes *Kindred* a "liberatory narrative," which matriculates to the "enslaved protagonist's . . . conception and articulation of herself as a free and self-authored agent."[36] I would similarly contend that Dana's retaliation against Rufus flickers as a moment of triumphant self-reclamation, yet at the same time, I wish to complicate this kind of utopian reading by noting that to the degree that we understand masochistic fantasy in *Kindred* as *the* revisionary and reparative modality through which Dana accesses, opens, and explores her past, we must also consider an interpretation of Rufus's murder as a refusal of erotohistoriographic subjectivity, a return to repression, a rejection of a life that touches and is touched by the past. Moreover, if the transformative possibilities opened up by masochism consist in large measure in the lesson that we have survived, and that we can survive again (and again), then surely this potential is imperiled by

Dana's abrupt foreclosure of the fantasy structure, prior to survival, in lieu of survival.

By killing Rufus, Dana successfully fends off the imminent threat of sexual assault, but she does so at the cost of continued exploration of her vital connection to the past. Indeed, and in spite of the narrative satisfaction that Dana's retributive triumph provides, this scene proves profoundly incommensurate with Butler's self-proclaimed logic of empathic and identificatory historical consciousness. Butler purports to write *Kindred* as a chastisement of a peer's limited capacity to put himself in the place of his forebears, yet she herself seems to establish black women's sexual subjection as beyond the limit of what can or should be phantasmatically re-encountered. In Dana's six returns to the slave past, she *never* experiences, and only superficially and dismissively imagines, herself as the object of enslaved black women's categorical vulnerability to racialized sexual violence. By some mystical power of time travel, she escapes back to 1976 before a patroller is able to rape her; on a subsequent return to the past, Kevin poses as her master and shields her from the advances of antebellum white men; until the end, she represses the increasingly erotic charge of Rufus's attachment to her; and, dressed in the casual garb of the late twentieth-century, she is not even wholly recognizable to her ancestors as a woman in the first place. ("[You wear] pants like a man," various characters tell her, confusedly and ad nauseam; 22, 71, 165, 199.) In these various ways—through magic, chance, repression, and disguise—Dana evades identification with the enslaved women she encounters, holding on to a sense of sexual self-sovereignty that she contrasts against their status as "thing[s] passed around like the whiskey jug at a husking" (260). The figure of the female slave-as-sex-object thus emerges as the limit of Dana's capacity for trans-historical identification and desire, and as the limit against which Butler recoils, no longer open to the transformative potential of masochistic fantasy.

Sex thus marks the boundary of Butler's critique of detached historiographical methods. The masochistic repetition that constitutes the novel's plot and that produces its intended lesson ultimately becomes untenable because Butler aggressively censors representations of the erotics of racial domination. Certainly, Butler's antebellum women characters can and do suffer as women, but these forms of suffering remain beyond the reach of the contemporary imagination. Rather than envisioning herself in their place or re-experiencing the particular modalities of their pain, Dana defines herself *against* the sexual abjection that women like Alice and another slave, Tess, endure. As such, their gendered experiences of enslavement are not re-inhabited and negotiated through an identificatory fantasy of historical return; rather, they remain fixed, "past," staved off, and enshrouded in shame.

## "It Had to Be Sexual": Masochistic Fantasy in *Corregidora*

Whereas Octavia Butler imagines eroticism as a terminus for thinking through the transformative potential of masochistic fantasy, her contemporary Gayl Jones conceives of the sexual as indispensable to a historically contextualized understanding of African American identification and desire. As we have seen, Butler's Dana encounters the sexual as the limit to her open relationship to the past: sex is the thing that she "could not give" (257), the thing over which she chooses murder and psychic irresolution. By contrast, the protagonist of Jones's 1975 novel *Corregidora* discovers that a masochistic reworking of the inherited traumas of racial slavery *must* begin with the erotic: To borrow her phrase, "it had to be sexual."[37] *Corregidora* performs the identificatory sexual re-enactment with slave ancestors that *Kindred* forecloses, casting it as the very structure of fantasy and desire at the heart of contemporary narratives of slavery.

In *Kindred*, black women's sexuality is a family secret, the apprehension of which compels its discursive foreclosure. In *Corregidora*, black women's sexuality is again cast as a family secret, but it is a secret that Jones's protagonist comes to doggedly pursue.[38] In the novel, Great Gram, the prized slave of "old man Corregidora, the Portuguese slave breeder and whoremonger," commits a secret act on the master that compels and powers her fugitive escape (8–9). This unspoken event of circumscribed yet impactful agency is subsequently buried under Great Gram's compulsive memories of the myriad forms of sexual, physical, and psychological abuse she endured as a slave. Never speaking of the terms of her escape, Great Gram spends the rest of her life narratively reconstructing scenes of her suffering and transmitting these stories to the matrilineal family she establishes in the United States. ("She told the same story over and over again"; 11.) The duty of her descendants, she decrees, is to "make generations" to mimetically repeat and preserve the story of her wrongful tribulation and to hold this testimony up against the power of a hegemonic cultural will to forget.

Ironically, this attempt at belated self-preservation works to radically confine the autonomy of Great Gram's descendants—Gram, Mama, and Ursa—who become trapped in a version of the past they can neither fully access nor act upon. Great Gram's story, its embedded mystery, and its rigid moral lens are asserted and re-iterated with such force that they occlude all other frames of interpretation, identification, and desire for three subsequent generations of "Corregidora women." Thus Ursa, the protagonist and final daughter, expresses an inability to know her own desire beyond the strict parameters of "what all us Corregidora women want. Have been taught to want. To make generations" (22).

With its ritualistic repetition and its obsessive fixation on violence and retribution, the structure of identification with which *Corregidora* begins suggestively enacts the pattern of political masochism. For Great Gram's demand of her unlucky heiresses is not simply that they retain the information she relays but, more comprehensively, that they re-experience—and in so doing, validate, and keep alive—the truth of her suffering. The injury that Great Gram endured/endures is twofold: It consists, most obviously, in her extended brutalization as a child and young woman but also in the devastatingly re-iterated non-recognition of her pain. This non-recognition takes various forms, both public and private, ranging from Old Man Corregidora's blindness to her sexual non-consent, to the Brazilian government's brazen destruction of slavery's paper trail in the immediate aftermath of abolition, to the barbed questions of her granddaughter's African American suitor in twentieth-century Kentucky. He asks, "How much was hate for Corregidora and how much was love?" (131). Against this ever-expanding array of dismissals, Great Gram imagines a form of martyrdom—an inter-generational life of suffering—that will achieve the vindication she is denied. "The important thing is making generations," she tells Ursa. "They can burn the papers but they can't burn conscious, Ursa. And that what makes the evidence. And that's what makes the verdict" (22).

Here, Great Gram's moral logic of identitarian "evidence" recalls Wendy Brown's formulation of political masochism, in which the desire for recognition compels the re-vivification of both historical injury and the redundant insult of that injury's dismissal. Brown writes: "To make [the survival of a traumatic past] into an identity, to make the past into the subjective and objective present, one has to reiterate the injury discursively, emotionally, as bodily and psychic trauma in the present. One has to establish that injury lives, that the trauma is repeated not only through the subject's psychic and bodily distresses but also through its denials and dismissals by others."[39] This Janus-faced desire, which simultaneously speaks in the idioms of self-preservation and self-destruction, would appear to form the core of Great Gram's legacy. "We got to burn out what they put in our minds," she tells Ursa, with resolve. Yet, she continues, "Except we got to keep what we need to bear witness. That scar that's left to bear witness. We got to keep it as visible as our blood" (72).[40]

In the case of political masochism, injurious repetition is symptomatically inflexible—"a source of political paralysis" and "a constraint on a subject's willingness to surrender [her maladaptive] investment."[41] Likewise, Great Gram's prescriptive repetitions are experienced by her descendants as painfully restrictive and even self-obliterating. But even as Jones dramatizes the extraordinary destructive potential of masochistic repetition ("How many generations had to bow to his [Old Man Corregidora's] genital fantasies?"), she also explores the possibility that masochistic repetition *cannot* maintain an absolute standard of rigid inflexibility because, like all citational performances, it invariably recurs with a difference (59). In this difference, she fantasizes the possibility of therapeutic, agential change. Indeed, according to Ashraf H. A. Rushdy, *Corregidora*'s discourse of memorial inheritance, especially as embodied by Gram and Ursa, is at least as much about "the difficulty of recollection, the fluid quality of experience, [and] the changing nature of feelings" as it is about the intransigent, imploring impotence of the victim.[42] If this is so, then how might erotohistoriography, with its emphasis on non-identical repetition and trans-historical feeling, illuminate our reading of the novel?

*Corregidora* starts with a fall: Ursa suffers a miscarriage and consequent hysterectomy after an argument with her abusive first husband, Mutt Thomas, culminates in her tumbling down the stairs. The fall is both literal and metaphoric, for by becoming infertile, Ursa is necessarily cast out of the eternal, traumatic time of "making generations" that her foremothers so assiduously cultivate and guard. And as in the Genesis story, Ursa's fall corresponds with her apprehension of her own capacity for desire. "I *am* different now," she reflects. "I have everything they had, except the generations. I can't make generations. And even if I still had my womb, even if the first baby *had* come—what would I have done then? Would I have kept it up? Would I have been like *her*, or *them*?" (60, Jones's italics). Severed from her destiny to sublimate identity through reproduction but still powerfully interpellated by Great Gram's moral-historical demands on her future, Ursa struggles to imagine new terms for her sexual and social subjectivity that will accommodate both her profound sense of familial enmeshment and her emergent sense of individual difference and desire.

Whereas in *Kindred*, masochistic fantasy takes the magical form of time travel, *Corregidora* is a realist novel whose exploration of masochism is routed through Ursa's chosen art and profession: the blues. The protagonist's painful pursuit of individuation—what she calls "singing back"—takes the blues form of repetition with a difference (103). Ruminative, ambivalent, and profoundly sexual, Ursa's blues suggestively recall the erotohistoriographical ideal, in which "liberatory rather than random or reactionary difference might appear in the nonidentical repetitions that constitute identity."[43]

Crucially, despite her avowed difference, Ursa's contestation of Great Gram's psychic and identitarian regime does not hinge on the eschewal of her foremother's traumatic testimony. Instead, it is energized by her immersive re-imagination of the victim's history as a site of affective vitality and dynamism. She returns to the historical scenes that Great Gram and Gram obsessively described, but in doing so, she displaces their juridical preoccupation with "evidence" to foreground instead the obfuscated yet still potent domain of historical *feelings*. Entering her family history by attempting to rewrite it in and as the blues, Ursa wonders, "What did they [Great Gram and Gram] feel?" (102).

In the blues, Jones finds something like an indigenous idiom of reparative masochism—a painful yet pleasurable modality of sensate, affectively suffused, performative repetition. Recalling Freeman's optimistic faith in erotohistoriography's non-identical repetitions, the blues form characteristically and self-consciously proceeds through improvisational repetition, disallowing the certain and stagnant brand of historical knowledge that Great Gram requires. Instead, the blues approach history as an asynchronous "process of accumulation and variation,"[44] allowing Ursa to encounter historical feelings as accessible, porous, and motile. In contradistinction to Great Gram's prescription for narrative sameness ("I know I said it, and I'm going to keep saying it"; 41), Ursa adopts a mantra that more closely approximates the ethos of a nimble, reparative masochist: "Everything said in the beginning must be said better than in the beginning" (54).

Furthermore, Jones is adamant in her characterization of the blues as a narrative mode that constitutively entails a kind of sexual performativity. Ursa is a lyricist and songwriter, but she is also a performer who sings "out of [her] whole body" (46), who "[opens her] door and [sings] with [her] thighs" (67). That she talks forcefully about sexual trauma is to be expected, for she is indoctrinated by generations of women who sought, through speech, to make their past pains her own. But unlike the performative speech of her foremothers, which is issued to reproduce in the listener the exact and uninterrupted experience of the speaker, Ursa's blues are dialogic, acknowledging and engaging the otherness of the audience. Accordingly, Jones's descriptions of Ursa's craft recurrently invoke images of receptivity: an opening door, beckoning thighs, the fantasy of an audience that "could see my feelings somewhere in the bottom of my eyes" (51). If Great Gram's guiding desire is to make her trauma visible to the juridical eye of a divine future, then Ursa's corresponding wish is to become an agential and recognizable constituent of the present—one who "[feels] satisfied, alone, and satisfied that I could have loved" (103).

To claim this subjectivity in the present, while also recognizing the formative force of her ancestral past, Ursa fantasizes "a song branded with the new world" that would at once affirm the anguish of "the girl who had to sleep with her master and mistress" and make room for the proscribed curiosity—the closeness *and* the distance—of the victim's descendants. "I wanted a song that would touch me," she says, "touch my life *and* theirs" (59, Jones's italics). Imagining the blues as a conduit for tactile intimacy with the past, Ursa explores the censored, affective dimensions of her foremothers' history ("What did they feel?"). At the same time, she seeks to discover and uphold her own, temporally proximate feelings that exceed her inheritance, extending beyond what has already happened and what has already been felt. Placing her own catalog of experience and emotion alongside the story of ancestral suffering that she is compelled to retell, Ursa's "new world song" envisions the assimilation of her sympathetic grief for her foremothers, who were brutalized, "sacrificed," and forced to bear the master's children (59), with her own, isolating anguish of abuse and infertility, the "broken . . . string of my banjo belly." This assimilation consists, not in comparison or equation, but in a profound, ambivalent, pre-cognitive intimacy: "My veins are centuries meeting," Ursa explains. "Every time I ever want to cry, I sing the blues" (46). Conceived of as such, the "song that would touch my life *and* theirs" proceeds neither through logic nor compensation but by way of a sensate, trans-historical bridge that reactivates the dynamic possibilities of feeling—of touching and being touched in and by the past (59).

But if Jones uses the blues as an aesthetic device to hold together several, irresolvable sets of "private memories" (101), compulsions, and desires, then it should not be mistaken for a utopian figure of harmoniousness. To the contrary, Ursa's singing is famously violent and abrasive. Her "spirit" is described as "knives dancing" (46); her voice is "like callused hands" that seduce in spite of their hardness, "the kind of voice that can hurt you . . . and make you still want to listen" (96). Operating throughout the novel as a metonym for a particularly gritty subset of the sexual, Ursa's blues exploit and enjoy affective ambivalence. They rework complex sites of irrefutable pain to seize from them an unseemly, excessive, and avowedly erotic pleasure.

What can it mean to find erotic pleasure and desire in, and in spite of, a history of radical self-dispossession? This is the question that *Kindred* will not ask. Though *Corregidora* boldly approaches the subject, here, too, the question is inherently illicit, not only because it gestures toward the sexual but also because it rewrites the history of Old Man Corregidora's crimes in a register that exceeds Great Gram's totalizing frame of moral condemnation. It reimagines sex—curiously, inconclusively—as potentially *more than* the mechanism of the master's dominative power or the sign of his slaves' utter objectification. To be sure, the point of Ursa's curiosity, and of her masochistic re-imaginings of the past, is not that trauma was absent or that consent was tacitly present in the prolonged psycho-sexual torture of her great-grandmother and grandmother. Nor is it that the blues or masochistic re-enactment can wholly redeem one's haunting memories of brutal experience. Rather, Jones turns to idioms of "the pleasure mixed in the pain" to suggest that the survival of sexual trauma may require a semi-flexible re-circulation of sexual feelings, as well as a more fundamental re-framing of sexual affects as potentially inconstant, contradictory, and motile (50). Here again, one finds a suggestive parallel to erotohistoriography, for according to Freeman, s/m's reparative power consists precisely in its capacity to "[take] up the materials of a traumatic past and [remix] them in the interests of new possibilities for being and knowing."[45]

Consider: Sex is the site of the Corregidora women's original and re-iterative injuries, but it is also the drive and desire that exceeds the master's control and, later, a performative mode that holds out the promise of reparative change. On the one hand, Jones shows through Great Gram's testimony how the expropriation of black women's sexuality under slavery consolidated convictions about the master's absolute power to name and adjudicate reality. As a slave owner and brothel proprietor acting with the backing of the law, Old Man Corregidora not only exploits the labor of his human property but also sets the terms of their most intimate engagements, determining what constitutes sex, what sex can look like, who can participate in it, and how. ("Any of them, even them he had out in the fields, if he wonted them, he just ship their own husbands out of bed and get in there with them"; 125) But, on the other hand, and in spite of the master's certain and extreme sexualized power, the domain of the sexual harbors an unpredictable and unwieldy interiority that remains inaccessible to Old Man Corregidora. When Ursa wonders, "What did they feel?" she seeks to know and name the terms of her foremothers' unspoken yet inextinguishable self-persistence. In the contours of "*their* desire," she imagines the limits of Old Man Corregidora's dominion (102, my italics). Thus, her "new world song" asks the women who came before her, "When did you begin to feel yourself in your nostrils? . . . When did you smell your body with your hands?" (59).

Rushdy rightly notes that it is Gram, the other blues-loving Corregidora woman, who anticipates and inspires her granddaughter's "new world song." Her oblique pretext to Ursa's blues takes the form of a riddle that displaces Great Gram's exclusive fixation on scenes of disempowerment to consider as well the unspoken conditions of her escape. According to Gram, "Up till today she [Great Gram] still won't tell me what it was she did," but some mysterious act of radical transgression emboldened her to escape the seemingly intractable grasp of slavery. "He would've killed her . . . if she hadn't gone. . . . What is it a woman can do to a man to make him hate her so bad he wont to kill her one minute and keep thinking about her and can't get her out of his mind the next?" (172–173).

Rather than affixing to the story of escape itself, Gram's curiosity (which in turn guides Ursa's) focuses on a story of insurrectionary violence that precedes and necessitates Great Gram's subsequent death or departure. Her provocative wording—"what is it *a woman can do to a man* . . ."—recuperates for the enslaved not only the possibility of an interiority that resists total domination but, more, the possibility of the victim's actionable will, circumscribed but present. Bearing the cryptic promise of a legacy of black women's agency that emerges from and subverts conditions of extreme constraint, Gram's riddle tenaciously invades Ursa's dreamscapes, romantic life, and sexual fantasies. As it does so, it complicates the presumptively singular and over-determining claim of the Corregidora curse on Ursa's libidinal imagination. For whereas Great Gram's ritualistic repetition aggressively disallows the recognition of any agential actor but Old Man Corregidora, Gram's riddle makes fathomable the disavowed power of the powerless. Thus contested and reframed, Great Gram's story is no longer simply a hardened didacticism enacted upon her descendants but a seductive site of curiosity that activates Ursa's exploration of her own dynamic relation to the past.

In the novel's culminating scene, Jones mobilizes Gram's riddle to approach in a new way both Ursa's own experiences of sexual trauma and the ancestral stories of racial-sexual trauma that are her inheritance. Twenty-two years after her fall, she and Mutt meet again and warily consider reconciliation. In the cathected sexual encounter that follows, Ursa's narrative present is spliced with the near and distant past, re-iterating history as both the same and different: "It wasn't the same room, but the same place. The same feel of the place." As she prepares to perform fellatio on Mutt, Ursa is reminded of Gram's riddle and is consumed by a powerful identification with Great Gram. In the process, she spontaneously apprehends an answer to the riddle:

It had to be sexual, I was thinking, it had to be something sexual that Great Gram did to Corregidora. I knew it had to be sexual: "What is it a woman can do to a man that make him hate her so bad he wont to kill her one minute and keep thinking about her and can't get her out of his mind the next?" In a split second I knew what it was, in a split second of hate and love I knew what it was, and I think he might have known too. A moment of pleasure and excruciating pain at the same time, a moment of broken skin but not sexlessness, a moment just before sexlessness, a moment that stops just before sexlessness, a moment that stops before it breaks the skin: "I could kill you."

I held his ankles. It was like I didn't know how much was me and Mutt and how much was Great Gram and Corregidora—like Mama when she had started talking like Great Gram . . . .

"I could kill you."

He came and I swallowed. He leaned back, pulling me up by the shoulders. (184–185)

In this extended passage, Jones locates in the sexual a constitutive human vulnerability *and* a constitutive human capacity for violence. The thing that Great Gram did to Corregidora, that a woman can do to a man, that a slave can do to a master, "had to be sexual" because sex is the unique site at which power and powerlessness, self-aggrandizement and self-disaggregation, may be profoundly and (con)fusingly collapsed. In "a moment of broken skin but not sexlessness," the swollen and erect phallus—that singular icon of masculine power—is humiliated in its desire, subordinated to the will of the feminine object/abject. "I could kill you." This excess of masculine desire ephemerally appears as the flaw in the master's aspiration to absolute power. "I could kill you," Ursa/Great Gram says, and this is the phrase that propels self-liberation.

Alternatively, we can interpret the line "it had to be sexual" to mean that Ursa's trans-historical apprehension can only happen through sex. That is, sex is the unique register that enables Ursa's revelatory and potentially reparative time travel. It makes possible and ushers in different ways of being in time: the "split second," the anticipatory pause, the momentary dissolution of time and self. According to Freeman, it is s/m's unique capacity to manipulate the normatively bounded experiences of time and subjectivity that affords its epistemological value and its transformative potential. By "[using] physical sensation to break apart one's present into fragments of times that may not be one's own," masochistic re-enactment can yield flickering moments of identificatory recognition across time—"not displacement but a certain condensation" of trans-historical subjectivities.[46] Ursa says something similar in her description of the moment in which her sex act with Mutt spontaneously becomes a re-enactment of slave sexuality. In the phrase, "I didn't know how much was me and Mutt and how much was Great Gram and Corregidora," she identifies an erotic scene of historical density that crystallizes a previously inaccessible historical knowledge: "In a split second, I knew what it was."

The precise mechanism through which sex distills trans-historical understanding or identification cannot be articulated, for the very thing that gives sex its mystical power is its elusive relation to language and logic. We might conjecture, nevertheless, that the possibility of deep, erotohistoriographic connection has something to do with the orgasmic shattering of the ego-in-time, the unmaking of bounded self-certainty, and the involuntary subordination of cognition and its attendant structures to a suffusive experience of affect and sensation.[47] Furthermore, *Corregidora*'s climactic scene suggests that sex can uniquely make possible certain stagings of trans-historical rapprochement because of its capacity to hold contradictory truths: "a split second of hate and love," "a moment of pleasure and excruciating pain at the same time." Like the blues—and, indeed, often manifested *as* the blues—sex in *Corregidora* is a volatile yet pleasurable, formal container for ambivalent, inarticulate, and excessive feelings—what Ursa calls "my feeling ways" (50). Preempting the impossible compulsion to explain or repair past trauma, Ursa's bluesy sex (and her sexy blues) instead holds out the promise of an ephemeral, extra-cognitive recognition. Through this visceral epistemology of self and other, past and present, Ursa achieves, not resolution, but a kind of sustenance, an inspiriting hope for alternative ways of living with history. In the final lines of the novel, she finally articulates, albeit in the negative, the terms of her own, previously unspeakable desire: "I don't want a kind of man that'll hurt me neither," she says to Mutt. Although he cannot (yet?) comply, he absorbs her request; "he held me tight" (185).

The logical conclusion to my juxtaposition of *Kindred* and *Corregidora* is that Jones achieves a kind of hopefulness Butler cannot because she finds narrative figures (the blues, sex) that can tolerate ambivalence and even extract novel pleasures from it. As a result, one might argue that *Corregidora*'s trans-historical encounters take on a dynamic, propulsive energy, defying the warning political masochism issues, that returning to scenes of historical suffering will only further entrench past pains. By contrast, Butler's foreclosure of the sexual results in the termination of Dana's trans-historical circuit, leaving Dana stuck in the present while still burdened by an unchanging and unchangeable historical record. The varied consequences of Butler's and Jones's respective treatments of masochistic, historical re-encounter are perhaps nowhere more dramatic than in the respective endings of their plots: *Kindred* ends with murder and the ravaged body of the survivor ("I lost an arm on my last trip home"; 9), while *Corregidora* ends with an embrace among the living ("he held me tight"; 185). Indeed, even if we read Dana's act of violence as a forceful triumph against her oppressive past, we must still grapple with the powerful specter of futility at the novel's end: What can it mean to kill someone who is already long dead? There is no public record or recognition of Dana's time-traveling insurgency. Its trace is registered only as her own injury, the permanent battle wound of her lost limb.

And yet I feel a measure of resistance to this reading of *Corregidora* as the fulfillment of *Kindred*'s botched task, for while *Corregidora*'s ending offers profound aesthetic satisfaction and beautiful formal rapprochement, the ending must also be read as inconclusive and, indeed, as harboring its own unwieldy danger. Although Ursa finally speaks her desire and Mutt "[holds] her tight," this is ultimately something of a hollow gesture, which hardly encourages robust confidence in the couple's future or even in the restorative potential of Ursa's dynamic current of repetition-with-change. Seeing Mutt for the first time in over two decades, Ursa describes the powerful persistence of her hatred for him, "Like an odor still in a room when you come back to it, and it's your own" (183). Moreover, if what Ursa does not want is "a kind of man that'll hurt me," then surely that "kind of man" is Mutt—a perpetrator of verbal and physical abuse whose final embrace may be at least as ominous as it is hopeful. To cast *Corregidora* as a narrative instance of reparative masochism requires the radical suppression of what we know about Mutt; it requires us to over-invest our faith in the transformative capacities of the blues *form*, to hope against the content of history that the protagonist's citational variations on the past will soothe, rather than compound, her suffering.

This kind of wager is precisely what Brown warns against when she maintains that repetition-with-difference is no anodyne against the pernicious force of masochistic desire. According to her account, the inevitable variations among masochistic repetitions are absorbed as the multi-vocal corroboration of a grand narrative of wounding and moral vengeance. The "political-psychic economy" of masochism not only tolerates but also requires "a surplus of scenes of victimization."[48] Viewed through this lens, Ursa's recitations and re-enactment of her foremothers' pasts may be less notable for their flexible re-working of historical affect than for the ways in which they reconsolidate inherited experiences and convictions about victimhood, powerlessness, and a negative relationship to sexual agency. Even in the novel's final scene, Ursa's momentary apprehension of power ("I could kill you") is quickly subsumed by Mutt's orgasm ("He came and I swallowed") and incorporated into a scene of masculine power ("He shook me til I fell against him crying"; 185). As Madhu Dubey bleakly notes, "On a thematic level, the novel's end does not mark a progression from the beginning; Ursa's and Mutt's desires are as incompatible at the end as they were at the beginning."[49]

By contrast, and in spite of its futility, there is something irrefutably satisfying in Dana's flickering extraction of revenge. In a fleeting moment, she breaks free from Brown's descriptive paradigm of political masochism, re-encountering the Father not to stage another, inevitable submission but to "[raise] the knife" and "[sink] it into his side" (260). Whatever its inassimilability with Butler's masochistic pedagogy of historical empathy, perhaps there is something to be said for the author's ultimate decision to preserve the fantasy of a heroically self-sovereign, black, female avenger. At least for this reader, Rufus's "long" and final "shuddering sigh" before "his body went limp and leaden across me" (260) provides a narrative pleasure that Mutt's detumescence ("he came and I swallowed") cannot rival.[50]

## Masochism's Uses

Earlier, I noted that a fundamental gap in the idea of political masochism consists in its inability to think about sex and politics together.

Rhetorically dividing these terms through the use of allegory, political masochism constitutes "politics" as a problem apart from the sexual. Now I wish to return to this criticism from the ostensibly opposite direction, to consider whether the limits of reparative masochism may consist in their implicit aversion to the register of politics. Can fantasies of reparative masochism speak in a register that is legible to politics, and if not, does this misalignment unavoidably suggest the uselessness of masochism?

In recent years, scholars including Judith Halberstam, Darieck Scott, and Kathryn Bond Stockton have suggested otherwise, proposing that masochism and a cluster of related terms may wield a subversive political power that counter-intuitively inheres in the repudiation of presently recognizable terms of political subjectivity and desire. In this vein, Halberstam describes masochism as a key modality within a "shadow archive of resistance, one that does not speak the language of action and momentum."[51] He pushes us to see masochism as "an antiliberal act, a revolutionary statement of pure opposition that does not rely upon the liberal gesture of defiance but accesses another lexicon of power and speaks another language of refusal."[52]

Scott performs a similar analytic maneuver with the keyword "abjection," through which he seeks to expose an as yet unrealized power in racial-sexual negativity—"*some* kind of power" within "that which is *not*-power according to the ego-dependent, ego-centric (and masculine and white) 'I' definitions we have of power" (Scott's italics).[53] Like Halberstam, Scott is concerned that the hegemonic political ideals of agency and self-sovereignty tacitly carry the legacy of white enfranchisement and black objectification. Rather than pursue the impossible emulation of white citizenship, he endorses a queerly revised, Fanonian turn: revolutionary, cleansing violence in the form of desirous, African American sexual abjection. In something akin to the masochistic climax of liberatory self-shattering, Scott identifies a model for radical divestment from the pursuit of self-aggrandizing power. He adopts the general pattern of reparative masochism insofar as he imagines the recursive possibilities opened up by sexual re-enactment as opportunities to negotiate the terms of coming into subjectivity. But he also moves beyond such claims, delineating "extravagant abjection" as a prescription for a new and liberatory *politics* of a subversively reimagined "black power."[54]

Allow me to underscore the stakes of this bold theoretical move: For Scott, divestment from the pursuit of self-sovereignty does not amount to a withdrawal from politics. Instead, he regards this divestment as a means of razing and radically re-inventing the existing political frame. Through the idiom and experience of abjection, he proposes, we can challenge and re-cast contemporary politics' dependence on the fictions of the defensive, monadic ego, intractable linear time, and the conceptual tethering of mastery and pleasure. Anticipating the inevitable critique, Scott contends that his fantasy of reinventing the political is neither escapist nor unrealistic. Following Fanon, he counters that colonial history is itself the indisputable proof that a people can unmake the world-as-it-was while performatively interpellating a so-called New World. "The possibility of radical difference," he insists, "is after all a *proven* possibility because colonialism was established and reorganized the world in precisely the manner of the introduction of a radical difference."[55] Scott thus maintains that contemporary formulations of citizenship and subjectivity are imperfect *and eradicable*. He turns to "extravagant abjection"—a capacious category that includes and exceeds masochism—as the first step toward reinventing political reality.[56]

There is much that I find exciting in Scott's theorization—most of all, the skill with which he weaves together Fanonian political militancy with a Leo Bersani–inspired ideal of queer sexual liberation. His faith in the possibility of a sexual politics of reinvention is grounded in an unexpected theoretical synthesis that itself breaks the frame of received thought on the topics of race, sexuality, and "black power." Yet even as I am lured by Scott's promise to "meet the challenge of the defeat already imposed on us . . . by the problem of history," I continue to find something stubbornly discomfiting in his politicized gesture of renouncing the desire for sovereignty. For Scott, the promise of untapped creative potential is bound up with the acceptance—indeed, the pursuit—of self-destruction. It is in the throes of profound, self-obliterating sexual abjection that he finds the germ of his politics, "an inchoate, churning, as-yet-unshaped resistance that is characterized by intense, even extravagant meaning-making."[57] Perhaps this is so, yet perhaps some perilous risk also inheres in African American repudiations of the will to a boundaried and self-possessed "self."

In part, my hesitation is precisely what Scott anticipates and pre-emptively discounts: a politically cautious and perhaps sexually prud-ish concern that risk will outweigh reward, that the pursuit of abjection may too often approximate "a confirmation of the defeat with which abjection works rather than the complication of it."[58] But in addition, my resistance to Scott's formulation stems from my sense that the desire for self-sovereignty *cannot* be fully and sincerely renounced, that it per-sists as an inextinguishable trace of what has been lost in the past—even within the ostensibly obliterating space of "extravagant abjection." To illustrate my divergence from Scott's theory and to articulate more suc-cinctly my own, ambivalent take on masochism and the contemporary narrative of slavery, I conclude this chapter by engaging with Scott's brief interpretation of *Corregidora*, in which he identifies Great Gram as an illustrative agent of his theory of black power in abjection.

In the conclusion to *Extravagant Abjection*, Scott references a well-known scene from Jones's novel, in which Old Man Corregidora rapes Great Gram while slave catchers pursue her friend, a fellow slave from Corregidora's plantation. Thinking of her friend while being raped by her master, she concocts a masochistic fantasy that fuses her vicarious desire for freedom with the forcibly imposed conditions of her sexual subjugation: "While he [Corregidora] was up there jumping up and down between my legs they was out there with them hounds after that boy. . . . And then somehow it got in my mind that each time he kept going down in me would be that boys' feets running. And then when he come, it mean they caught him" (127–128). In Scott's reading, this scene counter-intuitively crystallizes Great Gram's potential for creative power, for in her resort to "magical thinking," he locates a capacity to "sexualize and eroticize everything in her world," to radically remake the meanings of the constraints that are forced upon her.[59]

Like Scott, I am inclined to see a certain adaptive resourcefulness in Great Gram's production of masochistic fantasy. But whereas Scott locates the empowering promise of this scene in the dissolution of Great Gram's coherent and defended "self," I value Great Gram's fan-tasy primarily for its capacity to enable her continuing desire for self-persistence. Unlike Scott, I carry deep reservations about imagining this "magical thinking" as a desirable model for power, let alone one that we might abstract into a politics. After all, this is *not* a scene that ends with

Great Gram's escape or with a challenge to the master's authority that is in any sense perceptible to him. Instead, it is a scene that ends with unacknowledged rape and with the dead body of the fugitive, returned to the plantation he sought to escape.

More fundamentally, I want to trouble Scott's claim that Great Gram's power-in-abjection inheres in her relinquishment of a boundaried, self-aggrandizing ego. For it seems to me that Great Gram's "power" in the scene of abjection materializes precisely through a fantasy *of* consolidated and agential power. Whereas Scott has shown how, in this scene, the foremother (de-)constitutes herself through gestures of self-sacrifice and even self-effacement, I wish to illumine how, in the same moment, Great Gram is producing the coherent and self-consolidating Gestalt of the martyr.

Great Gram's masochistic fantasy operates by replacing the truth of her political impotence—her powerlessness to protect the young man from racist violence and murder—with an explanatory narrative in which her own suffering harbors the efforts of the fugitive running toward freedom. In her fantasy, the physiological and psychic injuries of rape are alchemically converted into a fugitive agency; they "*would be* that boy's feets running" (128, my italics). But Great Gram's fantasy is not only a prayer for the boy she cannot rescue. It is also a structure of identification that gives her access to a sense of social relevance within the annihilative matrix of slavery's power relations. Corregidora would make of her a dehumanized object for sexual use, so severed from human capacities for will or consent that her abuse is legible only as his pleasure. But the fantasy erects a different economy of desire into which Great Gram can enter, even as she feels (indeed, precisely as she feels) the immediate physical pain of her own violation and the sympathetic, psychic pain attending her friend's certain death. It provides her with identitarian coherence and moral standing; it steels her against the obliterating force of the slave master's psychosexual tyranny. In short, Great Gram's masochistic fantasy produces an inhabitable "self"—the self as heroic martyr, the self as incubator of a productive, emancipatory pain—in whose name survival becomes not only possible but a moral necessity. So whereas Scott reads this scene as a moment of political rebirth, in which Great Gram's abjection makes possible the imagining of an identity without ego and an attendant form of black solidarity, I am compelled to read this scene as an illustration of how the longing for a coherent and legible subjectivity persists in the masochistic imagination, even as it is sublimated or subordinated to a narrative of self-sacrifice. In a similar vein, in *Kindred*, the will to self-sovereignty persists in the form of the concealed knife that Dana carries into her own masochistic fantasy, and elsewhere in *Corregidora*, Ursa experiences a like desire in her urge to reclaim the power to kill.

How shall we make sense of this curious fact, that both novels simultaneously emplot a masochistic narrative structure of identification and desire *and* a stubborn will for the power of self-possession? In lieu of synthesis, I would venture that these are novels in which the ending is not the most concentrated repository of meaning. "The end is in principle excluded—the text demands continuation." Taken not as a hermeneutic but as a literary figure and form structured by masochism, therapeutic reading may materialize precisely as an instance of this kind of plot—a plot that "like life itself, resists being pigeonholed because it never comes to an end."[60] After all, isn't a forestalled ending a crucial requirement of masochism's most compelling promises? That we can live with inassimilable forms of desire, that we can hold together our longing for historical return and explorative futurity, and that doing so may even bring us profound and unexpected pleasures? Put another way, perhaps what masochism most usefully models for politics is not the possibility of post-sovereign subjectivity but, more modestly, the possibility of living with contradiction.

# 3

# The Missing Archive (On Depression)

In the opening chapter of Andrea Lee's 1984 novella, *Sarah Phillips*, the eponymous protagonist describes a hostile, semi-public exchange with her French lover, Henri Durier. While dining with Sarah and two of his childhood friends at a "small inn near the outskirts of Rouen," Henri is suddenly possessed by a fit of meanness. Giggling as he grabs Sarah's "frizzy ponytail," he declares his African American girlfriend "a savage from the shores of the Mississippi" and proceeds to spin an absurdly racist story about Sarah's alleged "pedigree." In fact, Sarah is a product of suburban privilege: Her parents are esteemed members of the Philadelphia-area black bourgeoisie, and at the time of Henri's attack, she occupies the elite position of a Harvard-educated American expatriate, traveling to Europe to pursue literary ambitions. Yet in Henri's bizarre and aggressively anti-historical account, Sarah is recast as the accidental progeny of a "part Jew" "Irishwoman" and a rapacious black "monkey." "It's a very American tale," he elaborates. "One day this *Irlandaise* was walking through the jungle near New Orleans, when she was raped by a jazz musician as big and black as King Kong, with sexual equipment to match. And from this agreeable encounter was born our little Sarah, *notre Négresse pasteurisée*."[1]

Sarah is bewildered, first, by Henri's undue cruelty and, subsequently, by the unexpected potency with which his defamatory story affects her; "The story of the mongrel Irishwoman and the gorilla jazzman" dispenses an affective force that cuts through the narrative's conspicuous untruth, even as she remains unable to name the feelings that so powerfully claim her. Escaping to the bathroom, Sarah crouches inside a stall, "breathing soberly and carefully as [she tries] to control the blood pounding in [her] head." "His silly tall tale had done something far more drastic than wound me," she reflects. "[It] had summed me up with weird accuracy, as an absurd political joke can sum up a regime, and I felt furious and betrayed by the intensity of nameless emotion it had called forth in me" (12).

To the consternation of many of the novella's critics, this "intense and nameless" bad feeling does not matriculate to confrontation, historical critique, or politicizing epiphany. Sarah rejoins the group reporting a vague sense of loss, but shortly thereafter, she resumes her relationship with Henri, tacitly accepting his tepid apology. Thus Lee's depiction of anti-climactic irresolution that ensues from a scene of biting, everyday racism stands in stark contrast to many of the literary texts I have examined so far, in which the bad feelings that attend contemporary racism are meant to trigger dramatic, trans-historical revelations about race, racism, and identity formation. (One can picture Octavia Butler fantasizing Sarah's abduction to a painful slave past!) In the latter tradition, time travel, possession, and other mystical technologies connect banal scenes of racism and racial alienation in the present to the revitalized moral claims of an unredeemed past. Fantasizing a present that opens backward into a traumatic past, these novels actively long for a historicized racial heroism, even when they cannot imagine its accomplishment. But *Sarah Phillips* refuses these common objects of racial desire, remaining insistently anchored in the present and near past, turning a cynical eye toward racial heroics, and refusing to broach the distant and sensational "there" of historical trauma that so many of Lee's contemporaries foreground.

In the estimation of many readers, *Sarah Phillips* thus materializes as a text that skims the affective surface of black life, compulsively pulling away from the painful intricacies and inter-generational depths of bad feelings about race and racism.[2] Sarah occasionally and temporarily feels bad—even acutely so—but she resolutely declines to give social or historical context to her bad feelings. As Valerie Smith notes, Sarah's "responses to the muted manifestations of racism and sexism that she faces take the forms of studied nonchalance about her privilege, gratuitous rebelliousness, ambivalence about her familial and cultural roots, confusion about the direction her life should take, and uncertainty about where to place her loyalties."[3] Articulating her displeasure more explicitly, Mary Helen Washington demands to know, "Why isn't Sarah angry at this [Henri's] insult? Why does the narrator offer intellectual explanations and refuse to identify her feelings?"[4]

In fact, Sarah *is* angry at Henri's insult. She is, by her own account, "furious," and before she exits the dining room for the privacy of the bathroom, her immediate response is a reproach. "Leave me alone!" she says, withdrawing her head from Henri's menacing grip. "I think that is the stupidest thing I have ever heard" (11). Washington's critique thus bears a factual error—she claims that Sarah is not angry when in fact she is—but this error itself is telling. Eliding the scene of Sarah's anger to focus instead on her subsequent impotence and affective impasse, Washington uncannily repeats Sarah's own experience, in which focused counter-aggression unravels into something less actionable or identifiable, the terrible reign of some unharnessable, "nameless emotion" that overpowers other registers of feeling.

My intention here is not to emerge as Sarah's champion but to propose a different interpretive pathway from those that have dominated discussions of *Sarah Phillips* to date.[5] Read against African American literature's historical turn, I am intrigued by Lee's tacit yet insistent aversion to the dramatic register of trauma, as well as her implicit rejection of the notion that literature's work is to effect prescriptive psychic change. I am fascinated, too, by her unexpected representations of African American history, which she casts alternatively as an absurd yet potent lie, something lost to the realist register of consciousness, or the irretrievable crucible of an amorphous, affective force. Might we approach *Sarah Phillips*, not as a novella about the emotional bereftness that attends racial alienation, but as a text that boldly insists upon an index other than intergenerational trauma for measuring contemporary black experiences of racial formation and discrimination? What if we begin with the assumption that Sarah's inarticulate bad feelings represent a unique, essential, and overlooked substratum of post–Civil Rights African American psychic life? In this spirit, the present chapter shifts focus from direct literary engagements with unresolved atrocities of the slave past to texts that carry a much more ambiguous relationship to African American history.

*Sarah Phillips*, with its iconoclastic and, for many, unlikeable protagonist, is not a singular outlier within the corpus of late modern black fiction. Instead, I argue, it is an exemplary text within an extra-canonical counter-tradition—a missing archive—of contemporary African American literature. This under-studied body of work is marked, not by dramatic aspiration to an ideal of trans-historical rapprochement, but by stubbornly presentist, anti-cathartic, everyday experiences of race and racism. Here, when the history of slavery appears at all, it is ephemeral, hyper-mediated, or otherwise beyond reach. Contemporary characters are stymied or relieved by the racial past's psycho-affective irretrievability, and they grow cynical about cultural investments in the (already failed) redemptive promise of inter-generational memory. As the narrator of James Alan McPherson's short story, "Elbow Room," puts it, "The old stories were still being told, but their tellers seemed to lack confidence in them. Words seemed to have become detached from emotion. . . . Everywhere there was this feeling of grotesque sadness, far, far past honest tears."[6]

The purpose of this chapter is to chart the constitutive psychic structures and affective manifestations that animate anti-historical black fiction from the post–Civil Rights period. In addition to *Sarah Phillips* (1984), I take up two other acclaimed but critically under-examined texts—James Alan McPherson's "Elbow Room" (1977) and Alice Randall's *Rebel Yell* (2009)—to make a case for "depression" as a descriptive and explanatory rubric to enhance our understanding of contemporary black literary production.

Drawing on psychoanalysis and affect theory, I invoke "depression" as an umbrella term that prominently includes but also extends beyond Freudian melancholia. Melancholia provides a theory of how identity takes shape in relation to history, love, and loss; depression attends to this structural formation and also attempts to make sense of the texture and intensity of a range of extra-melancholic bad feelings, such as (externalized) rage, shame, boredom, and aimlessness. If the narrative structures of trauma and masochism in contemporary African American literature tend to reify the idea of a historically resonant psychic injury that compels a fantasy of return and repair across an inter-generational expanse, then depression suggests a different timing of loss and desire while bringing a contemporary scene of grief more clearly into view. Specifically, the texts I study here foreground a depressive response to the premature decline of the modern Civil Rights Movement and its attendant forms of faith and desire.

If the primary effort of this chapter is to provide a descriptive account of the body of presentist and near-historical writing that I am calling "the missing archive," then a secondary aim is to think through the relationship between the relative neglect of that archive, on the one hand,

and the critical prominence of the contemporary narrative of slavery, on the other hand. This line of inquiry affirms a core concern of prohibitive reading—that the form of the contemporary narrative of slavery may obscure or even foreclose other kinds of stories, particularly those that emphasize more proximate conditions of black political and psychic life. But where prohibitive reading identifies mistaken priorities that must be opposed, I want to forestall the gesture of judgment, to pose some agnostic questions about what it might mean for presentist, depressive narratives to materialize as the inassimilable remainder to historical narratives shaped by the structures of trauma or masochism.

## Racial Melancholia

In Freud's famous formulation, "melancholia" describes the grief of the ambivalent lover who wishes simultaneously to retain and repudiate her lost love object.[7] Fearing loss, the melancholic identifies with the love object as a means of preserving it. This unconscious identification "[substitutes] for the [earlier] erotic cathexis" and acts as a psychic defense against loss.[8] Resenting loss, the melancholic rages against the abandoning other who now lives, encrypted, under the guise of the self.[9] This self-beratement, which Freud identifies as the distinguishing symptom of melancholia, in turn reveals a psychic structure of split consciousness, "a cleavage between the critical activity of the ego and the ego as altered by identification."[10] Herein lies the crucial distinction between mourning and melancholia: Unlike mourning, which is Freud's term for the normative psychic response to loss, melancholia is a pathological process in which loss, or the perception of its imminence, provokes a complex, structural transformation of the ego. "Melancholia" thus describes a unique phenomenon in which grief powerfully restructures identity.[11]

For Freud, this hypothesis does not entail a cultural or historical context. He understands melancholia as alternatively arbitrary or an idiosyncrasy of personality—not as culturally conditioned or as a psychic response to systemic social or political forces. From his perspective, the "identity" melancholia restructures is identity in the psychoanalytic sense (i.e., the ego), not in the sense of the socio-politically interpellated self. It is Anne Anlin Cheng, eighty-five years after Freud, who returns to "Mourning and Melancholia" to produce a theory of the melancholic constitution of American *racial* identities. She contends that Freud's formulation of "a chain of loss, denial, and incorporation through which the ego is born" unwittingly elucidates the intricate and often nontransparent processes of racialization through which contemporary American identities are forged.[12]

Cheng describes the cultural phenomenon of racialization as one that entails two simultaneously operating forms of "racial melancholia." The first, "dominant racial melancholia," refers to how (white) American national identity is consolidated and "sustained by the exclusion-yet-retention of racialized others." Much as the Freudian melancholic hates and loves, reviles and needs, its lost object, Cheng posits that the American national imaginary is fueled by its constitutive "need" for "the very thing [it hates] or [fears]"—that is, racial minorities. Racial minorities thus function as the melancholic objects of hegemonic fantasies of national identity. "It is this imbricated but denied relationship" to them "that forms the basis of white racial melancholia."[13]

But even as racial minorities are made into the melancholic objects of American whiteness, they are simultaneously consolidating their own internal identifications as melancholic *subjects*. The second form of racial melancholia thus pertains to the internal negotiations of subjectivity performed by racialized others. This form of melancholia processes the experience of being interpellated through the contradictory hate and need of the dominant culture, and it consolidates legible identities through internalization of, and identification with, constitutive experiences of social loss. What are lost to the racialized other are social visibility and value, belonging, and the imaginative possibility of "self as legitimacy." What ensues is "the internalization of discipline and rejection" and "the installation of a scripted context of perception."[14]

In brief, racial melancholia is a two-pronged theory of identity formation that imagines subjectivity as at once socially and intra-psychically constructed. It posits that "racial grief" is an "invisible but tenacious" force at work in *all* modern American systems of identification, and it models the psychic "dynamic of retaining a denigrating but sustaining loss" through which de-/racialized identities are secured.[15] Unlike trauma-based theories of racial identification, which pivot on a crisis event and its ensuing, undesired repetition, racial melancholia foregrounds a logic of seduction—its engine is the libidinal excess that survives lost love. In this regard, melancholia and masochism may be said to serve a shared purpose of explaining the libidinal complexities that fuel internal and inter-personal negotiations of exclusion and loss. But whereas masochism takes shape as a relationship to power and punishment, melancholia describes a relationship to oneself, albeit as mediated by intrusive forces of sociality. As a drama of the self (as distinct from a drama of crisis event or a drama of punishment), melancholia is better suited than trauma or masochism to speak in the unexceptional and presentist register of the everyday.

Cheng's theory readily lends itself, for example, to a reading of Lee's protagonist as a melancholically racialized figure whose formative psychic dramas are mundane, presentist, and enmeshed with the sociocultural milieu of post-segregation America. The novella begins with a description of Sarah's conflicted love and denigration of a wealthy white stranger named Kate. When Sarah and her housemates (including the aforementioned, contemptible Henri) hear that Kate is being held hostage "by her present lover and an ex-boyfriend, who were collecting her allowance," Sarah takes pleasure in the "mock sorrow" of her companions but also, "sympathize[s] with [Kate]." "She seemed to be a kind of sister or alter ego, although she was white and I was black, and back in the States I'd undergone a rush of belated social fury at girls like Kate, whose complacent faces had surrounded me in prep school and college." The "identification" that Sarah claims with Kate is complexly wrought, merging feelings of affinity, "fury," and malice. For Sarah, "girls like Kate"—bearing the interchangeable faces of white feminine indifference—call to mind a history of social rejections that feel like loss and that sediment a re-configured and internally divided sense of self (3–4).

In a subsequent chapter, Lee elaborates upon this formulation when she tells us that, in high school, Sarah's misfit friend Gretchen "despised the school and often condemned it," but Sarah "had a secret": "I wanted to fit in, really fit in, and if Lissa Randolph or Kemp Massie, rulers of the Olympian band of suntanned, gold-bangled popular girls, shimmering in their Fair Isle sweaters, had so much crooked a finger at me, I would have left Gretchen and followed the way the apostles followed Christ. . . . At night I gloated over a vision of myself transformed by some magical agency into a Shetland-clad blonde with a cute blip of a nickname" (56). Like the racial melancholic, an adolescent Sarah incorporates the "gold-bangled popular girl" whose imagined attentions she has lost but whom she cannot grieve. "No one knew my secret—not my parents, who bragged with relief about my levelheaded adjustment; not my brother Matthew, who might have understood" (56). Quietly identifying with the inaccessible "Shetland-clad blonde" whom she both loves and resents, Sarah internalizes "a set of almost imperceptible closures and polite rejections" that "shut me off socially" (54). In Cheng's phrasing, "The social lesson of racial minoritization reinforces itself through the imaginative loss of a never-possible perfection, whose loss the little girl must come to identify as a rejection of herself."[16] Similarly, Sarah's ego is re-iteratively re-configured and abjected—as well as re-iteratively re-configured *as* abjected—by way of a complex and ambivalent relationship to an idealized whiteness. It is this under-acknowledged transformation of the self that accounts for Sarah's simultaneous "sympathy" and hostility toward Kate. Through her melancholic incorporation of Lissa and Kemp, she becomes both the agent of their racist discernment and the denigrated object they refuse to see.

As this cursory reading suggests, racial melancholia enhances our understanding of Lee's novella by exposing the "world of relations" that inhabit "the reductive notion of 'internalization.'"[17] This lens allows us to see a nuanced and generative social injury at the psychic core of Lee's often-unlikeable protagonist, and it pushes us to think through some of the invisibly pernicious effects of racism that may not garner our instinctive sympathies. But while Cheng's formulations help us to see how blacks and whites incorporate and rage against their respective racial others, they provide less guidance for our understanding of how structures of African American identification are cultivated through *intra-racial* negotiations of love, loss, and identification. Surely, Sarah's self-identification is forged not only in relation to Kemp and Lissa but also within the largely insular and racially homogenous domains of family and community. In this configuration, we may find a third form of racial melancholia—one that re-imagines the psychic genealogy of late modern African American subjectivity in relation to the intra-racially "lost" entity of the Civil Rights Movement's iconic, teleological faith.

I use the term "Civil Rights idealism" as a shorthand to describe this object of melancholic loss—an abstract "object" inhering in the powerful coalescence of a collectivizing self-story, a political affect, a personal ideal, and an itinerary for political action, peaking in the years between the Supreme Court ruling in *Brown v. Board of Education* (1954) and Martin Luther King, Jr.'s assassination in 1968.[18] King was not the singular or original author of Civil Rights idealism, but he is the iconic figure for this idea, par excellence. Conceptually, Civil Rights idealism made social and moral meaning of black suffering; to borrow language from Paul Gilroy, it upheld "the capacity of blacks to redeem and transform the modern world through the truth and clarity of perception that emerge from their pain."[19] More concretely, Civil Rights idealism attends a concentrated period of public protest, political action, and legal reform. It does not connote consensus or a singular voice of modern black progressivism; rather, it acknowledges a register of political *resonance* that reverberates through much of mid-century black discourse, consecrating widely shared ideals of progress, freedom, and moral truth.

Indeed, one striking measure of the reach of Civil Rights idealism may be found in the pained—if unrelentingly militant—eulogies that King's anti-integrationist, black radical critics wrote on the occasion of his death. The poet Nikki Giovanni, for example, declared, "the assassination of Martin Luther King, Jr. is an act of war";[20] Amiri Baraka, at the height of his anti-assimilationist ardor, expressed a devastating mixture of rage and despair when he asked why King "can/be killed by criminals";[21] and the nationalist psychiatrists William Grier and Price M. Cobbs interpreted the collective grief attending King's death as a portent of retaliatory violence. ("For a moment, be any black person, anywhere, and you will feel the waves of hopelessness that engulfed black men and women when Martin Luther King was murdered. All black people understood the tide of anarchy that followed his death.")[22] If such statements attest to the range of activist approaches that characterized mid-century black progressivism, then they also imply that even among dissidents, Civil Rights idealism figured as a "crucial collective [story]" by which African Americans lived.[23] Put another way, what Civil Rights idealism represents, at its core, is the affective and ideological potency of a set of ideals in relation to which modern African American political identity has been forged.[24]

Anchoring its plot in the loss of Civil Rights idealism, *Sarah Phillips* begins and ends with a symbolic familial death. In life, Sarah's father, James Phillips, was a prominent Civil Rights activist preacher whose ideology, legacy, and dexterous rhetorical style resemble (on a much smaller scale) those of Dr. Martin Luther King, Jr.[25] "When he wasn't preaching sermons, or visiting his parishioners from the New African Baptist Church, he seemed to spend his time in rooms full of men with dark suits—rooms in which the words 'civil rights,' constantly spoken, took on such gigantic significance that they seemed to be about to emerge from the clouds of cigarette smoke like the title of a Cecil B. DeMille movie" (48). James Phillips's passing inaugurates the novella and contextualizes Sarah's narrative project of recalling and reconstituting her identity alongside a scene of black congregational mourning in the early 1970s. It is in reaction to her sudden and devastating experience of father loss that Sarah flees to France, dreaming of "[casting] off kin and convention in a foreign tongue" (4). When, by the end of the first chapter, this escapist fantasy proves untenable, Sarah returns to her (personal, biographical) past by way of narrative memory, recounting a story of her life that culminates in the sorrowing event of her father's death and burial. Thus the vignettes of childhood, adolescence, and young adulthood that constitute the novella may be read as a circular eulogy, in which Sarah works through and finally apprehends the fact of loss.

Understood in this way, Lee's novella appears to accord with Freud's description of "profound mourning"—a condition whose presenting symptoms initially resemble those of melancholia but that slowly matriculates to a normative process of psychic detachment. Mourning, Freud tells us, entails a painstaking and "piecemeal" practice of "reality-testing": "Each single one of the memories and expectations in which the libido is bound to the object is brought up and hyper-cathected, and detachment of the libido is accomplished in respect of it." Similarly, in *Sarah Phillips*, the novella's chapters "bring up" Sarah's memories of her deceased father and re-contextualize those memories as artifacts of the past. Through this process, Sarah narratively solidifies (i.e., "reality-tests" and confirms) the fact of the Reverend's death. "The work of mourning" is thus "completed," and "the ego becomes free and uninhibited again,"[26] as we find Sarah, on the book's final page, preparing to "[move] in a direction away from anything [she] had ever known" (117).

What I am describing here is in many ways a familiar story of a daughter who struggles, but ultimately succeeds, in assimilating the fact of her father's death. This account of the novella is in some measure true, but it is also incomplete. For Sarah's grief attaches not only to her father as a private, familial figure, with whom she shared a relatively uncomplicated bond, but also to the Reverend as a public figure and avatar for the Civil Rights Movement. (His "entire soul," Lee tells us, was in the activist church [29].) Sarah's relationship to her father's public image and its attendant ideals is deeply ambivalent, and as Freud might predict, this ambivalence is re-activated, upon the occasion of loss, as the engine of melancholic processing. Much like the melancholic, who "knows *whom* he has lost but not *what* he has lost in him" (Freud's italics), Sarah mourns her father but proves profoundly unable to acknowledge, or "reality-test," the political and ideological losses that attend his death.[27] This abstraction, more precisely than the Reverend himself, becomes the once loved, now reviled entity whose loss resists apprehension and tacitly reshapes Sarah's identity when, "with a certain amazement at the ruthless ingenuity that replaced [her] grief, [she] left to study French literature in Lausanne, intending never to come back" (4).

On the night of the Reverend's funeral, Sarah is visited in her dreams by an apparition of the deceased, who appears to her as a "friendly" and familiar figure bearing an indecipherable message: "In the dream he had fallen overboard from a whaling ship—like the one in *Two Years before the Mast*—and had come up from the ocean still alive but encased in a piece of iceberg. Through the ice I could see his big hands gesturing in a friendly, instructive manner while he looked straight ahead at me and said something inaudible. It was the same word or syllable I had wanted to say to [his bereaved friend] Stuart Penn, and I couldn't figure out what it was" (114–5). The imagery of this scene resonates suggestively with that of Freudian melancholia: A lost object (the father fallen overboard) is unacknowledged as lost (he is "still alive"), but the fantasy of preservation requires a psychic technology of entombment and encryption (he is encased in ice and made "inaudible"). Significantly, what is rendered indecipherable to Sarah is not the person who is lost but the content of his message. As with melancholia, it is "the ideal that the person represents" that "appears to be unknowable."[28]

In this passage and the surrounding text, Lee indicates redundantly—though never in terms that suggest Sarah's own apprehension—that the word Sarah fails to discern is concerned with her father's progressive racial theo-politics. Sarah associates the dream with the Reverend's political ally, Stuart Penn, who, at the funeral, appealed to Sarah to carry on her father's legacy; she draws an unexamined stream-of-consciousness association between the dream and her memories of her father preparing sermons; and even the unexpected literary reference to Richard Henry Dana's nineteenth-century adventure novel obliquely alludes to the project of racial uplift, for Dana was a renowned abolitionist and co-founder of the anti-slavery Free Soil Party. Yet Sarah, a Harvard-trained literary critic, declines this easy interpretation, insisting that her father's message—which is "lost" to the ship along with his spontaneously entrapped body—is obscured, foreclosed from knowledge by a sedimented block of ice. Upon waking, Sarah registers some sense of failed connection, remembering that she wanted to say or hear something that she could not, but she fails to register that unarticulated "word" as something she has *lost*. Such is the opacity of melancholic loss. As Judith Butler explains, "Melancholia is precisely the effect of unavowable loss." "[The] object is not only lost, but that loss itself is lost, withdrawn and preserved in the suspended time of psychic life."[29]

I have suggested that upon the death of her father, Sarah loses not only the person but also his espoused ideals, even as she is unable to claim those ideals as loved or lost. But why should we imagine Civil Rights progressivism as the object of Sarah's ambivalent *love*—an entity whose desirability makes the idea of its loss a threat—in the first place? To date, the novella's critics have focused overwhelmingly on the protagonist's conspicuous disinterest in cultural history and racial politics or on her forceful rejection of an inherited tradition of "genuine gallantry in the struggle for civil rights" (4). But alongside this characterization, Lee repeatedly describes Sarah's mixed feelings toward her racial-cultural inheritance: "a mixture of pride and animosity" (18), "a mixture of hostility and grudging affection" (24). Furthermore, Lee casts Sarah's original disavowal of her father's theo-politics in a chronologically prior moment, which Sarah retrospectively apprehends as a scene of thwarted love. In the novella's shortest chapter, "Marching," a ten-year-old Sarah fantasizes an intense love for the "great" "symbol" of the 1963 March on Washington (51). This scene sets the stage for the future development of Sarah's conflicted and disavowed grief.

In "Marching," the protagonist nostalgically recalls a time when she was returning home to Philadelphia with her father, who had been attending meetings in Washington, D.C. Sarah overhears the Reverend and their cab driver discussing the upcoming march. Piecing together the words of her unwitting adult informants with her own, naïve fantasies of heroism, she envisions a glorious scene of human solidarity: "Something began to burn and flutter in my chest: it was as if I had swallowed a pair of fiery wings. . . . A tremendous picture appeared in my mind. . . . I saw a million men, their faces various shades of black, white, and brown, marching together between the blazing marble monuments. It was glory, the millennium, an approaching revelation of wonders that made blood relatives of people like my father and the cab driver" (49–50). In this scene, Civil Rights idealism appears (albeit in a naively reductive iteration) as the object of Sarah's own desire and as a register of political resonance through which she imagines herself as part of a racial community. It is a fantasy that stirs her, like "a pair of fiery wings," that summons her rapt attention and inspires an ardent love. Picturing herself among a magnificent community of "blood relatives," Sarah voices her love, declaring to her father, "I'll go to the march with you." But her love is thwarted (or perceived to be so), for her father responds with tepid excuses and the thinly veiled prohibition, "We'll ask your mother when she gets home" (50).

The march transpires as a historic and, by many measures, triumphant event, but Sarah's "tremendous picture" of her own, participatory engagement in "an approaching revelation of wonders" (49) is "lost [to her] as an object of love."[30] Barred from attending the march and "only grudgingly" allowed by her elderly caretaker to watch it on television, Sarah is made uncomfortably aware of her estrangement from the realization of her once-loved ideal. Viewing the event with her cynical teenage brother, from the dissonant space of "the creaky green glider that stood on the sun porch at home," Sarah's viscerally inspiriting fantasy of "glory, the millennium" is recast as a cryptic, foreign image of "a quiet gray crowd" and "on the screen, the face of Martin Luther King[, which] looked very round, with a somber, slightly Eastern air, like a Central Asian moon" (51).

Sarah's description of King by way of this conspicuously strained and irrelevant metaphor is perhaps most obviously a sign of her generational and class-based acculturation. According to Michael Awkward, the protagonist's "inability to recognize constitutive features of the racial past and present" is one feature of a deeper, "intractable [challenge]" of alienation that is nowhere more evident than in Sarah's inability to register "King's energizing speech" as a "unifying and transcendent occasion."[31] Awkward and others have compellingly prioritized the theme of African American class mobility and the resultant fracturing of collective black identification in readings of *Sarah Phillips*, and while these readings ring true, I wish to add to them another dimension of analysis. Sarah's baffling misreading of King is additionally significant because it signals her defensive encryption of a lost love object into an unknowable, foreign entity (a "Central Asian moon"). However naïve, Sarah's initial fantasy of the march evinces some measure of cultural literacy and collectivist political faith: Her vision is infused with shared, resonant feelings of hope and communal love, and its teleology conflates the registers of religion and politics in accordance with the most recognizable forms of Civil Rights activist rhetoric. Put another way, the interpellative force of Civil Rights idealism shapes Sarah's initial sense of identification, and it is only *after* her perceived slight that she acquires an exaggerated ineptitude for discerning the meaning of the march. Like the melancholic who must make both her love object and the fact of its loss opaque to herself, Sarah is suddenly convinced of the unknowable strangeness of the processional as it plays out before her. In a phrase that captures both her loss of an ideal and the obfuscation of that loss, Sarah recalls the embarrassment of discovering that, with regard to the march, "I wasn't sure what I really thought" (51).

Thus Sarah's early attachment to Civil Rights idealism progresses from love to disappointment to encryption and disavowal, producing a secret history of unresolved feelings that are later obscurely aggravated on the occasion of her father's death. In the Freudian drama, the stage for melancholic loss is set by a series of preceding but sublimated losses (or threatened losses) that persist in the unconscious as unresolved "memory-traces." These memory-traces harbor not only a relational history but also an unprocessed history of ambivalence that is re-activated when melancholia sets in. What the melancholic grieves, then, is more than the lost object itself. She also confronts anew a history of ambivalent attachment—of now ghostly, perceived "situations of being slighted, neglected or disappointed."[32] Similarly, Sarah's dream of her father encased in ice addresses not only his death but also an expansive, serialized embattlement with loss that we can trace back at least as far as the novella's prior textual scene of an illegible black, theo-political leader (King), captured and displayed in the impenetrable block of the family television. What Sarah loves, loses, interiorizes, and turns against, then, is not her father, as such, but her "lifelong" ambivalence toward the "outworn rituals of [her] parents" and their consecrated narrative of African American history as a progressive story of uplift—in Sarah's phrase, *"everything that made up my past"* (4, my italics). As melancholic rage emerges to conceal the unavowable facts of love and loss, Sarah reports that her grief transmogrifies into "a ruthless ingenuity," with which she constructs a new fantasy of her self, one predicated on the evasive desire to "cast off kin and convention in a foreign tongue" (4).

One might object that Sarah's felt exclusion makes her a problematic representative of the race, whose grief response to her father's death can hardly be read as a transparent allegory of post–Civil Rights black feeling. Indeed, her relationships to racial community and cultural tradition are most often described in terms of estrangement, alienation, and discomfort—feelings that point toward anything but a straightforward correspondence. And, in the days following her father's death, she describes the grief of fellow mourners not only as mysterious and unknowable but also as so many individuals' selfish attempts to "try to make my father's death into something all their own" (109). Nevertheless, I move to count Sarah as "representative" precisely insofar as her pronounced estrangement from feelings of racial unity registers widespread experiences of the post–Civil Rights period as, in Rolland Murray's phrase, "the time of breach."[33] Much as Sarah associates her father's death with the abrupt rupture of "the web of assumptions, memories, and old associations that make conversations within families as automatic as breathing" (106), popular historiographical accounts of the end of the Civil Rights Movement recount the loss of communal coherence and the exacerbation of once-latent ambivalence and animosity.[34] Foregrounding the loss of black theo-political leadership and a subsequent disorientation and melancholic grief response, *Sarah Phillips* points us toward an under-examined structure of identification and desire at work in the post–Civil Rights racial imaginary.

## Racial Depression

But perhaps we should push back against the psychoanalytic desire to confine identification to a consolidated, knowable structure— particularly, one that calcifies loss and injury in the psychic form of the racialized person. How else might we imagine the purview of racial grief's effects? Dilating on a keyword that at once evokes and turns away from the theoretical genealogy of melancholia, Ann Cvetkovich's recent monograph, *Depression*, draws on affect theory to reorient the discourse on racism and psychic life. Wary of psychoanalysis's capacity to distract us from direct and transparent ways in which political injustice produces psychic malaise, she encourages a retreat from the logic of internalization and the development of alternative, anti-pathologizing conceptualizations of psychic distress. Through a vocabulary that foregrounds neither symptoms nor identity types but *feelings*, she aims to tie systemic socio-political analyses directly to "everyday . . . feelings of despair and anxiety, sometimes extreme, sometimes throbbing along at a low level . . . feelings that get internalized and named, for better or for worse, as depression."[35]

Cvetkovich is one of several contemporary theorists who turn to affect theory to expand upon psychoanalytic understandings of depression by attending to feelings as important indices of social and psychic truth. The point is, not a disproof of psychoanalysis, but an inquiry into how feelings may amplify and texture a psychoanalytic portraiture of the self. As Eve Sedgwick asserts, where psychoanalysis meditates primarily on structures of desire and identification, affect theory gives us interpretive access to "an array of perceptual data . . . whose degree of organization hovers just below the level of shape or structure."[36] If this is so—if affect theory can illuminate our understanding of black psychic life by making the intensities of feeling that color loss available to discourse—then what does such a theoretical tool mean for our reading of post–Civil Rights racial melancholia?[37]

Let us return, briefly, to the scene with which I opened this chapter, a scene in which Sarah Phillips—a privileged constituent of the post–Civil Rights black bourgeoisie—appears to recognize herself in her boyfriend's wildly inaccurate, racist caricature of the American South. The versions of racial melancholia I have sketched in the preceding pages lend themselves to various logics for understanding this scene. We might, for example, claim that Sarah sees herself in this story because she has ambivalently internalized a racist gaze or because melancholia works by redirecting social rage into self-beratement. From this perspective, the narrative "event" is a scene of mis-recognition that brings into view a mappable, melancholic psychic structure. But just as surely, this is a scene that is *about* something other than event and structure. It is a scene that is at pains to describe an effusion of inconstant feeling that never matriculates to a psychoanalytically legible form: fury, shame, isolation, confusion, betrayal, resignation, and an intense and "nameless emotion" (12).

What if we imagined form as something short of the final word on meaning, heeding Sedgwick's warning that "to describe [affect] primarily in terms of structure is always a qualitative misrepresentation"? The alternative, she says, is to "enter a conceptual realm that is not shaped by lack nor by commonsensical dualities of subject versus object or of means versus ends."[38] Reading through this prism, we might argue that the protagonist's bafflement, rage, and felt impotence upon hearing Henri's story offer a self-sufficiently meaningful index of what racism *feels like*. We would shift critical attention from the question of whether or how Sarah incorporates or identifies with Henri's insult to the emotional impact and ephemeral reverberations of racism. Attention to affect as a primary axis for analyzing this scene would also yield an intricate view of how unwieldy, motile feelings are enmeshed with everyday processes of perception and communication that mediate experiences of identity and sociality. Our reading would remind us that the psychic life of racism consists not only in structures of identification coerced by social power but also in the production and dissemination of involuntary and unfair bad feelings.

Even more so than *Sarah Phillips*, James Alan McPherson's short story, "Elbow Room," offers a valuable occasion to zero in on what is at stake in elaborating a vocabulary of feelings to describe racial grief. Like *Sarah Phillips*, "Elbow Room" narrates the post–Civil Rights era in the moment of its emergence, yet it does not enshrine a central story of a phantom, lost object. Instead, it enlists an affect-driven conceptualization of depression, disarticulating the *feeling* of loss from the obsessive incorporation of loss. For McPherson, the post–Civil Rights era is a resoundingly depressing time of historical flux, most compellingly modeled by the proliferation of reverberating feelings that occasionally reference momentous events but more often spread diffusely, like an invisible contagion.

First published in 1977, "Elbow Room" is the periodically interrupted, first-person story of an unnamed black fiction writer seeking "new eyes, regeneration [and] fresh forms" amid an emergent zeitgeist of post-sixties political and existential despair (262). Through its prominent emplotment of a lost and searching writer, the story doubles as a fictional meta-commentary on the problem of post–Civil Rights black literary production: What directions will African American literature take in the uncharted future? Where will it find narrative forms commensurate to the needs of the beleaguered present? The story includes the symbolic fall of a character who personifies Civil Rights idealism, but the narrator's relationship to this character remains somewhat strained and superficial. His most earnest articulation of "the nature of the times" (277) consists in repetitious descriptions of the feelings that attend alienation. "There was a feeling of a great giving up" (278); "All around us, people looked abstracted, beaten, drained of feeling" (275); "Words seemed to have become detached from emotion and no longer flowed on the rhythm of passion" (260); "There were no new stories" (261). It is worth noting that, although "Elbow Room" does not announce the *end* of African American literature, its narrative project takes up Kenneth Warren's most enduring critical preoccupation: the practical, rhetorical and analytical inadequacies of "the racial commonsense of the twentieth century" to express the contents and serve the needs of our post–Civil Rights present.[39]

As a story about a search for stories, "Elbow Room"'s narrative path is somewhat difficult to grasp. Its framing conceit is a prolonged disagreement between the narrator/author and his white, male editor, represented in a progression of discontinuous, escalating debates. Ostensibly, these debates take as their object a story that the narrator is trying to tell, but in fact, they reveal little about that literary object and much more about the difficulties of cross-racial recognition and communication. With intensifying exacerbation, the editor repeatedly breaks into the unfolding, internal story with questions and critique. He finds the narrator cryptic and disturbingly rebellious, so he sets out to "discipline" the story, "to impose at least the illusion of order" (256).[40] In turn, the narrator feels frustrated and constrained by the editor's unimaginative, formal conservatism and reacts with cynicism, longing, and defiance. The narrator's feelings emerge in conversation with the editor, but they also frame, provoke, and seep into the story he is trying to tell.

In the internal story—the site of the battle for authorial control—the narrator follows an unlikely romance between two of his acquaintances: an African American woman named Virginia Valentine, and her white husband, Paul Frost. It is Virginia who first captivates the narrator and who figures as the story's closest approximation to an avatar for Civil Rights idealism. Egalitarian, aggressively utopian, and open to the diversity of the world, she represents a precious, vulnerable, and near-obsolete brand of political optimism. If Virginia is the "wounded" dream of Civil Rights idealism in the era of post-sixties, liberal declension, then Paul is a romanticized stand-in for the (white) American Dream.[41] An earnest, innocent, hardworking Midwesterner whom the narrator regards with unshakeable suspicion, he is the risky love object on whom Virginia settles. In a time of "grotesque sadness" (261), "vaguely haunted by lackluster ghosts" (282), this couple becomes a symbolic repository for the narrator's fragile, redemptive desire. Yet, even as he longs to enter and claim their story, Paul and Virginia's romance increasingly becomes an object of suspicion, derision, disinterest, and rage.

The narrator's initial pursuit of Virginia's stories represents his residual hope that Civil Rights idealism might be revived as the premise for the "new forms" he needs and craves, but he discovers that this is impossible because the stories he wants from her are lodged in the past and, as such, cannot speak to the anxious and amorphous time beyond loss. "More and more [her stories] fragmented into pieces of memory. There was no longer the sense of a personal epic" (278). Having begun the story as Virginia's ardent admirer and defender, the narrator ultimately declares, "I did not care about [Virginia and Paul] and their problems any more. I did not think they had a story worth telling. . . . I did not feel I owed them anything anymore" (281–282). The narrator's ultimate alienation from the couple becomes the story's most poignant illustration of its repeated assertion, that "old" articulations of politicized desire (Civil Rights idealism, the American Dream, a cross-racially unified "human family") have lost their currency.

As we did in *Sarah Phillips*, here again we find a sharp distinction between the depressive archive and the literature I have read under the rubrics of "trauma" and "masochism," for in his refusal to look to past forms to inspirit African American literature's future, McPherson's narrator eschews the constitutive move of the historical turn, which was beginning to take shape just as McPherson was writing "Elbow Room." It is not my assertion that McPherson's story overtly or deliberately critiques the historical turn; such a claim would be untenable given the simultaneity of "Elbow Room"'s emergence and the earliest wave of contemporary narratives of slavery. I am suggesting instead that "Elbow Room" marks a divergent mode of narrative response to the post–Civil Rights milieu that would later become subordinated to the historical turn, perhaps in part because of its internal disavowal of the past as a site of viable literary desire.

In a conspicuous departure from the narrative conventions of trauma and masochism-based fictions that unfold in relation to a temporally dissonant and intrusive racial past, "Elbow Room"'s racialized antagonists—most notably, the editor—filter an oppressive, uneven, and stubbornly presentist affective force. McPherson's meticulous sensory attention to *how people feel* de-centers the presumptive importance of origins (slavery) and telos (redemption) as the organizing parameters of African American self-story and brings a different set of narrative urgencies to the fore: Why does the narrator feel creatively stymied? Why is he unable to sustain interest in his narrative subjects? Why is his story unintelligible to his editor? These questions, which double as questions about how post–Civil Rights black literary practice will grapple with the mundane and isolating feelings that attend racial depression, lie at the heart of McPherson's story.

Here, the frame of racial depression allows us to apprehend something beyond the purview of racial melancholia, for where melancholia describes the unknowing enshrinement of loss through the formal reconstitution of the self, the narrator's sense that he has lost the sixties' "epic of idealism" disallows the repressive retention of that loved and lost object and gives way to a crisis in self-coherence (258). In lieu of melancholic form, racial depression here is apprehended through the narrator's meandering, itinerant loneliness, his poor instincts about his own interests, his intensifying skepticism and distrustfulness, and the anxious unraveling of stories that once gave shape to his identity and his being-in-community. "I began to feel cynical and beaten," the narrator reports. "Inside myself, . . . I heard only sobs and sighs and moans" (278). The story's own, unresolved suspension of narrative form produces an impression of dis-unification for the reader and, in so doing, redoubles the connection "Elbow Room" forges between the loss of Civil Rights idealism and the failure, the emptiness, or the inadequacy of extant narrative frames for understanding African American identification and desire.

All this is not to say that melancholia plays no role. If racial depression in "Elbow Room" involves feelings of self-fragmentation and cynicism that emerge from the loss of Civil Rights idealism and its attendant narrative and identitarian forms, then this cluster of feelings is compounded and framed by the persistence of (melancholic) societal racism, which mediates the narrator's identity by delimiting the terms of his social intelligibility. Recall that, for Cheng, the melancholia of the racialized subject in relation to white American hegemony is often experienced as invisibility: "Teetering between the known and the unknown, the seen and the deliberately unseen, the racial other constitutes an oversight that is consciously made unconscious."[42] In a similar fashion, the narrator's relationship to his editor and, later, his observations of Paul show how racial depression is amplified by the possibility—imminent and everywhere—of one's illegibility to others. Anticipating this motif, the story begins with the editor's aggressive and discrediting commentary that precedes the main text in an italicized and offset paragraph. Through this paragraph, the narrator is pre-empted by his own de-authorization, much as racialized individuals are preceded by an obfuscating and de-personalized racial discourse. Throughout the story, the editor interjects criticisms about what he does not understand in a succession of directive marginalia: "Analysis of this section is needed. It is too subtle and needs to be more clearly explained" (272); "Clarity is essential on this point. Please explain" (273); "Clarify the meaning of this comment. . . . Comment is unclear. Explain. Explain" (286). In short, as a concentric frame for the narrator's account of post–Civil Rights racial depression, the editor symbolizes and performs a distorting mis-translation through which the black speaking subject enters into the rhetorical field of sociality.

Like Cheng, José Esteban Muñoz theorizes racial depression—what he calls "feeling brown, feeling down"—as a phenomenon of misrecognition, but he departs from Cheng by asking how we might re-imagine the invisibility of the racialized subject with greater attention to affect. What interests Muñoz most is how racism asserts its psycho-affective power by simultaneously producing bad feelings in marginalized populations and obscuring from its lexicon the contexts of differential power and racial injury through which such feelings circulate.[43] This is precisely what happens when the editor goads, chastises, and criticizes the narrator in a relentless offensive, while his inability to fix or conquer the narrator's "meaning" aggravates his own, defensive myopia. "You are saying you want to be white?" he asks when the narrator expresses frustration over the literary constraints that racism imposes upon him. With mounting irritation, the editor persists: "You are ashamed then of being black? . . . Are you not too much obsessed here with integration?" (262).

Unable to see his interlocutor as a "mobile human personality" (271), the editor imagines himself in a "moral" struggle against the "unyielding material" (256) of African American psycho-affective domains.[44] Indeed, in a majority of the scenes that stage conversations between the narrator and the editor, the editor crowds out, obscures, or over-writes characterizations of the narrator's affective expressions, conveying to the (dubious) reader that the narrator is "paranoid," "shrill," oppositional, and in need of "discipline." Threatened by the editor's aggressive and mis-perceiving eye, the narrator responds more and more obliquely. The imagined struggle generates and intensifies feelings of terror and righteousness for both parties, which in turn foreclose communicative pathways and ironically seem to corroborate the editor's convictions about the narrator's fearsome foreignness. In this way, the relationship between the editor and the narrator models the curious phenomenon by which black psycho-affective illegibility is at once the stated basis and the veiled effect of an excessive, unclaimed white anxiety. By shifting his emphasis from identification to feeling in scenes such as these, McPherson redirects our gaze to the emotional frustration that ensues from experiences of being mis-seen and to socio-political forces that act on racialized subjects independent of our own psychic investments.

Like the editor, Paul's initial confrontation with blackness evades his existing frameworks for understanding social and psychic life, but unlike the editor, he is motivated by his love for Virginia to endure identitarian and epistemological crises to cultivate a revised racial consciousness. Paul's education in blackness is in part a historically and ideologically grounded introduction to the forms of racialized structural violence, but it also entails a difficult psychological and affective re-orientation. It unfolds as a kind of conversion experience that involves a restructuring of identification as well as Paul's subjection to feelings of anger, impotence, pensiveness, defensiveness, and sadness: the feelings of being made an object. Incrementally, we see:

> Paul began confronting the hidden dimensions of his history. . . . He read books hungrily for other points of view . . . what stuck in that private place in his mind made him pensive and silent, and a little sad. (275–276)

> In early February, while he was with Virginia in the parking lot of a supermarket, a carful of children called him nigger. . . . In late February, when he was walking with Virginia in the rain through the Sunset district, two younger children called him a nigger. "What's a nigger?" he asked me on the telephone. "I mean, what does it *really* mean to you?" (276, McPherson's italics)

> Something was also happening to Paul. In his mind, I think, he was trying desperately to unstructure and flesh out his undefined "I." But he seemed unable to locate the enemy and, a novice in thinking from the defensive point of view, had not yet learned the necessary tactics. Still, he seemed to sense that there were some secrets to survival that could be learned from books, conversations, experiences with people who lived very close to the realities of life. He cut himself off from the company of most white

males. . . . He denounced his father as a moral coward. He was self-righteous, struggling, and abysmally alone. . . . His large brown eyes still put the same question, though now desperately asked, "Who am I?" (279)

By depicting how confrontations with racism catalyze the unraveling of a subject who begins the story with (the white privilege of) his "soul intact" (264), the narrator pedagogically draws attention to experiential and affective dimensions of black life, whose apprehension by whites requires not only knowledge ("books, conversations . . .") but something like a *loss* as well—of whiteness, of naiveté, of "more than a million small assumptions" whose "totality guarded for him" an "ego that embraced the outlines, but only the outlines, of the entire world" (272–273).

For Paul, this loss compels a restructuring of identity—what Cheng might describe as a melancholic fall from "dominant racial melancholia." Corroborating such a reading, both Virginia and the narrator identify in Paul the gradual development of a defensive psychic posture that they associate with blackness, and Paul's father articulates a similar point from a different perspective when he "accused the son of beginning to think like a Negro" (268). But Paul's transformation also exceeds the contained and predictable terms of a shift in psychic structure. As important, Paul's loss of the self-oblivious fiction of white identity entails his experience of proliferating and at times unintelligible affects. He becomes "upset and determined" (268), "irritated" and confused (270), "pensive, and silent, and a little sad" (276). He grows "a long black beard" which "[merges] with his intense, unblinking eyes to give him the appearance of a suffering, pain-accepting Christ" (279). These descriptive details constitute an essential aspect of the story of Paul's transformation, even though they are never fully knowable to the narrator (or the reader) and never matriculate to something so cognitively accessible as an identitarian form. Demonstrating how black interior life consists not only in psychic structures that result from racism but also in idiosyncratic expressions of affective vitality that "[break] all the rules" (269), the narrator suggests that Paul's education in blackness hinges in large part on the intangible yet indispensable measure of his capacity to *feel* differently—to register at a visceral level the sting of the word "nigger" and to *sense* an answer to his own, unanswerable question, "What does it *really* mean to you?" (276, McPherson's italics).

As a point of clarification, the narrator does not posit that Paul becomes black by virtue of experiencing discrimination or that the feelings associated with being in an interracial relationship approximate the feelings of being personally marked as black. On the contrary, Paul's naïve question, "What's a nigger?" (276) is repeated throughout the remainder of the story as an index of the persistent limits of his efforts to understand or to "earn his own definitions" (284). In fact, although Paul's trajectory ostensibly offers an optimistic alternative to the editor and the surrounding social milieu, it does not ultimately bring him closer to the narrator or allow the two men to more fully see one another.

Refusing to emplot a direct and progressive development through which black feeling is finally and decisively transmitted to Paul, "Elbow Room" instead dilates on how Paul's new consciousness activates and stokes an array of contagious yet non-mimetic feelings among the story's diverse cast of characters. In this way, Paul's transformation provides McPherson with another tool for illustrating how racialized affects move through interior geographies and social space. Virginia recognizes in Paul "extraordinary spiritual forces" (264) that compel her love and protection; at the same time, "she could not understand why Paul became so upset" (276). Virginia's father is flummoxed by Paul and his daughter's bond and made to feel a curious and free-floating shame that evolves into uncomprehending but devoted acceptance. The narrator's capacity to "hear" and "feel" the "frequencies" of Paul's experience waxes and wanes in relation to his own, reactive emotions, which range from tender fellow feeling to unrelenting suspicion.[45] And the editor refuses or is unable to see the vast, affective complex that Paul's transformation produces. Discomfited and confused, he moves quickly to shut down this vaguely generative branch of the story, through the noise of his own, redundant complaint: "Unclear. Explain. . . . Clarity is essential on this point" (286).

To be sure, the premise of emotionally distressing racial misrecognition in a contemporary setting is neither unique to "Elbow Room" nor foreign to the contemporary narrative of slavery. Within the genre, such scenes often appear as the catalyst for a present-day protagonist's revelatory return to the slave past: Though painful in its own right, historicizing context becomes a corrective and a balm for contemporary social illegibility. But in the depressive archive, the scene of contemporary mis-recognition does not compel a pivot and displacement; instead, it demands uncomfortable dilation. Thus Henri's derisive joke floods Sarah with shame and impotent rage that she cannot escape. Rather than encountering her "true" past, she can only hide in a bathroom stall, feeling the impact of his insult. Similarly, the editor's persistent inability to understand the narrator does not compel him to explain their impasse through a story of historical origins. Instead, he redundantly describes the fatigue and frustration of missed connection.

Although "Elbow Room" is ostensibly a story about attempts to transcend alterity and know the other, with the possible exception of Paul and Virginia's love, it depicts connection among characters as categorically fleeting, embarrassing, partial, insincere, and unconvincing. A similar feeling of failed connection confronts the reader in her encounter with the text and militates against therapeutic reading as a hermeneutic approach to McPherson's story. For "Elbow Room" incapacitates readerly desires to access the text through immersive identification, romantic sympathy, or over-investment in a character's redemption. For one thing, the internal story is uneventful, predictable, and aggressively disrupted by the editor's critical interjections. By design, it is not a story in which one risks losing oneself. For another thing, its characters are stubbornly two-dimensional and even cliché, defensively concealing their "secret [selves]" from the narrator's—and the reader's—prying curiosity (263). Their secrets are not our own repressed truths, nor are they the narrator's; instead, they are symptoms of the story's depressive thematic. If the reader is drawn into the affective experience of the story, it is not through identification but through an opposite maneuver, in which the text's effect of emotionally shutting out its reader produces feelings akin to those that frustrate and impede the story's characters. Like the narrator and his acquaintances, the reader is brought into an affective world of confusion, irritation, stymied attempts to connect with others, distraction, and even boredom.

But if "Elbow Room" is saturated with missed connections and with descriptions of amorphous feeling that often substitute for plot, then McPherson nevertheless defines his narrator's central and enduring aim as the pursuit of form. The narrator wants not only new dimensions of feeling but also "new stories" (261), "fresh forms" (262), and "the insight to narrate [the] complexities [of a new story]" (286). The story's retreat from plot, in other words, does not represent a formal ideal unto itself but enacts a narrative tactic that allows the author to sit with perceived challenges and impasses for African American literature without the burden of teleological resolution hanging over him. Although the attainment of a suitably capacious and dexterous form remains beyond the frame of the story, the narrator holds out optimism that such forms will be the province of the future: He "wagers" that that it is neither he nor his discarded friends Paul and Virginia but the unforeseeable persona of their infant child who will evince a narrative "ambition" and "strength" that will eclipse his own, failed attempts to realize new expanses of narrative possibility (286).

## On Ambivalence

As a story that narrates the emergence of its own, unfamiliar present, "Elbow Room" opens but defers the question of what forms post–Civil Rights African American literature will take. Born of loss and its host of attendant feelings, the story carries its unfulfilled optimism in the unformed, forward-looking figure of the child. In the remainder of this chapter, I turn to Alice Randall's *Rebel Yell* (2009) to consider post–Civil Rights black fiction in hindsight. Set in the twenty-first century but punctuated with many protracted flashbacks, Randall's novel offers a fictional retrospective of the post–Civil Rights era through its depiction of the life and death of an anointed child of the Movement. As a novel in the form of a eulogy that foregrounds the perspective of the first post–Civil Rights generation, *Rebel Yell* may also be read as an inter-text and a rejoinder to *Sarah Phillips*, reviving and re-imagining the theme of loved and lost Civil Rights idealism from a twenty-five-year remove.[46] Whereas Lee brings Civil Rights idealism into view as a melancholic object for black literary consciousness and McPherson lends texture and dimensionality to a psychoanalytic portraiture of post–Civil Rights grief, Randall asks us to consider a more uncomfortable, antagonistic orientation toward the lost ideal.

Let us return to the problem of melancholic ambivalence by way of a question that remains unasked in my foregoing discussion of *Sarah Phillips*: If Civil Rights idealism is embodied in Sarah's father—a figure who invokes King—then what should we make of the fact that it is her father who thwarts her desire to participate in the movement's scenes and sentiments of racial collectivity? To re-articulate this question in terms of its metaphorical significance, what would it mean to locate an agency of aggression or dis-unification *within* a beloved trope of black political optimism? Recent scholarship on literary representations of the Civil Rights Movement has shown how fantasies of segregation-era racial unity often belie pervasive socio-cultural fractures, particularly along demographic lines of class, generation, gender, and sexuality difference.[47] And indeed, each of this chapter's primary texts may be said to engage in a deconstruction of the familiar bourgeois, patriarchal leader of Civil Rights iconography. Prompted by Randall, I want to consider an additional manifestation of ambivalence toward Civil Rights idealism, keying in on a "hatred" that consists less in an alternative opinion voiced by dissidents than in the underside of a love attachment itself. Put plainly, my point not simply that some people objected to Civil Rights idealism all along while others loved it but also that the very tenets of fraternity, pacifism, and hope in the face of unrelenting racist brutality were shadowed by feelings of resentment, terror, and hatred. This internal tension lurks within *Sarah Phillips*, surfacing, for example, when Sarah's mother alleges that "[the Reverend's] work killed him" (108). But it is Lee's contemporary, Randall, who most emphatically brings this dimension of ambivalence to the fore.

Like *Sarah Phillips*, *Rebel Yell* stages the figural death of the promise of the Civil Rights Movement, but this time, the deceased is not a King-like figure but a member of the next generation. The only son of a prominent Civil Rights lawyer, Abel Jones III rose through the ranks of academic and professional success but "[betrayed] his special birthright in the black community," growing up to become a neo-conservative CIA agent and government lawyer complicit in the defense of the second Bush White House's war crimes.[48] Posthumously recounted through the grief of his survivors, Abel's life allegorizes a historical narrative in which political hope gives way to liberal declension.

Born on the precipice of social change, when "black was just about to bust out beautiful," Abel is hailed by African American civic and political leaders as a "a new prince" (15) and "a citizen for whom [one] can prepare a future" (16). Randall cultivates his symbolic significance with good-natured heavy-handedness. "Related by blood or marriage to both

W. E. B. Du Bois and Booker T. Washington" (14), Abel, who shares a name with his distinguished patrilineage and the biblical first martyr, grows up to marry a woman called Hope before "a predominantly black but integrated congregation" (147). To have danced at their wedding, it is said, was to be "convinced that Lyndon Johnson was the greatest president who had ever lived—that his dream of a Great Society had become a reality" (148). Their marriage is brief and gives way to divorce, but "for a moment they were side by side in the same place and the future outstretched before them was alluring and obtainable" (169).

With his energizing love of hope and his successful matriculation through Harvard and Duke to the highest levels of government office, Abel embodies the extraordinary optimism and unprecedented possibilities for racial advancement brought about by the Civil Rights Movement. But, if Abel's attachment to his inheritance of Civil Rights idealism may be characterized in terms of love and optimism, then it is also an attachment formed in terror, rage, and resentment. As a toddler, Abel loses his babysitter to the 1963 Birmingham church bombing, whereupon Carole Robertson's grieving mother implores him to remember, "These men, these black men . . . used you children to fight this war" (10).[49] He absorbs her injury and promises, "I hate them too" (11). Abel's childhood is described as "a time and place of terror, a place of bombings and shootings, a place of funerals and wakes, a place of police dogs and fire hoses turned toward children, a land red with the blood of the recently slaughtered" (52); he remembers the sixties as "his Civil War" (132).

Indeed, although the novel frequently indulges a nostalgic sensibility—toward the leisure culture of the black bourgeoisie in the mid-to-late twentieth-century, toward the folk history of Hope's native West Virginia, and even toward certain unlikely inter-racial romances staged in the antebellum South—Randall staunchly disallows for a sanitized memory of the "trenches" of Civil Rights activism. Complicating popular memories of the Movement as a site of political unity and affective purity, she portrays a profoundly ambivalent cultural scene and a tragedy of lost innocence. Both the beginning and the end of the novel scandalize with rhetorical questions about whether God will forgive King, who knew "just how precious" the Movement's child martyrs were (11).

Randall's metaphoric references to "Abel's Civil War" invoke both the extraordinary violence of the sixties ("the bombings, the murders, the funerals" [182]) and Abel's corresponding interior drama of a bitterly divided self, ever negotiating a volatile conflict between hope and fear, love and hate. Much of the drama of Abel's ambivalence toward the principles and material effects of Civil Rights idealism is told through the story of his consummated but dismantled marriage to Hope. To this end, one way of reading the book is as a grief-driven re-counting of the promise of the Civil Rights Movement with and after hope; another way is to read it as the story of hope's resilience, since Hope is the character who twice survives her loss of the "prince" of Civil Rights idealism, first in divorce and later in death. But despite the novel's foregrounded commitment to the genre of romance, its central conflict—which is also its melancholic core and the site of its teleological revelation—lies not in marital discord but in a primal scene of father-son conflict. Alluded to and repeated in variations over the course of the novel, this scene operates as a site of narrative origins (i.e., the sub-plot to which all other sub-plots can be traced) that inspires a range of competing interpretations.

Those closest to Abel are privy to the knowledge that his thirteenth birthday is the occasion for a personal trauma that profoundly alters him. On this day, his party is disrupted when celebrants become aware of a seven-foot cross burning in the front yard. Terrified, Abel wets himself. Then, with shame, he watches his father, who is unable to put out the fire or speak back to the "rednecks" who call to ask "how [he likes his] boy's birthday present" (298). When a couple of white policemen arrive, Abel "[mistakes] their disinterest for courage" and runs "to stand in the sheltering space he [imagines] between their two bodies" (297). After the fire is put out, his father summons him to "get a strap and wait [in his] room" (299). In early accounts of these events, Abel implies that his father proceeds to physically and sexually abuse him, although he persistently withholds a specific accounting from his loved ones and even from himself.

In the novel's penultimate scene, as he lies in an ambulance foreseeing his imminent death, Abel remembers what happened between him and his father with new and painful clarity. This time, it is a story that begins with paternal mercy. When he enters the room, Abel's father "[reaches] to reassure" his crying son. But, for Abel, this mercy is maddening and oppressive. "The father takes you in his arms and tries to stop your shakes. . . . His hands are nowhere near your neck, near any part of you he shouldn't touch, but it feels like he is strangling you and violating you and you shake harder to shake him off." Abel announces that he is ashamed of his father, and this abject interpellation ensnares them both. "This new connection, a shared and profound cocreated humiliation, is immediate and volatile" (361).

Let me first sketch some ways in which different formulations of racial melancholia can help us to interpret the scene of the hate crime and the subsequent father-son confrontation. In Cheng's sense of the term, we may note that what Abel recounts is a scene of identitarian reconstitution mediated by loss: Abel's "internalization . . . of rejection" ensues from his loss of safety and from his "imaginative loss of a never possible perfection."[50] Coveting the fantasy of absolute power the white policemen represent, he disavows his blackness, though he can never fully relinquish it. For in spite of his disavowal, the burning cross represents a rite of humiliation that casts him out of whiteness. Waiting for his father to beat him, reflecting on his powerlessness and his unanswered desire for recognition, Abel says to himself, "*I am wrong.* He repeated the same sentence over and over again" (302, Randall's italics). Much as Cheng describes the melancholia of the racialized other, Abel realizes himself as "both a melancholic object and a melancholic subject, both the one lost and the one losing."[51]

We may also read the scene as one in which Abel's "mature" identity is reconstituted through the melancholic incorporation of his father as a powerful Civil Rights leader. Such an interpretation returns us to the burning cross, which now appears as a site of thwarted love. The adolescent Abel is focused not on the fire but on the prolonged and shocking enactment of his father's impotence. His father hits a white child in frustration; he "[struggles] with the spigot on the [slashed] outdoor waterhose" but achieves only "a half trickle out the nozzle"; he cries out in desperation, "*Get me some fucking tape . . . no, get the hose from next door . . . no, don't fucking call the police*" (296, Randall's italics). This spectacle discredits the idealized object of Abel's father love by exposing the father as one who "wasn't powerful" (298). True to Freud's maxim that no one ever willingly abandons an attachment,[52] Abel resists relinquishing his beloved image of the powerful father, saying to himself,

*"Can I not know tomorrow what I know now? . . . Big Abel can't protect me. Can I not know tomorrow what I know now?"* (ibid., Randall's italics).

In melancholia, impossible love cannot be registered by the conscious mind, so it takes cover in identification. Likewise, Abel disguises his lost ideal of the powerful father through a fantasy of paternal brutality with which he comes to identify. (His consequent incorporation of masculinist, brute power materializes most perversely in his future as a white-collar perpetrator of extraordinary military violence.) Though factually untrue, the beating fantasy keeps faith with the affective history of Abel's ambivalent, fearsome attachment to the powers his father symbolically consolidated, both as a familial disciplinarian and as a civic warrior through whom Abel came to apprehend the violent dangers facing the black South. Throughout his childhood, Abel's personal relationship to his father *and* his relationship to the patriarchal leadership of the Civil Rights Movement more generally are marked by admiration and fear, emulation and resentment, love and hate. Thus, his loss of the idealized patriarch is inassimilable because it is an unwilling loss that nevertheless enacts a wish fulfillment; the beating fantasy appeals because it sublimates a mutually implicated trifecta of aggression, love, and loss. Read allegorically, this plot progression may imply a broader cultural ambivalence about the stature and authority that accrued to male leaders of the black bourgeoisie as self-designated representatives for an illusory black unity.

But if Abel's fantasy of his father's brutality suggests one history of post–Civil Rights racial melancholia, then his memory of his father's *mercy* uncovers another. Here we arrive at an interpretation of the melancholic, father-son confrontation that turns on the love and loss of the forgiving father, who imbues suffering with dignity and love, but whose "shivering hug . . . can not matter enough" (362). In Abel's near-death memory, his father repeatedly moves to embrace him, while Abel repeats, in variations, the word "shame." The scene is saturated with the language of reflection, porousness, and contagion, so that the enactment of father love becomes inextricable from the experience of humiliation. Shifting to second-person narration, Randall writes, "Your eyes are mirrors." "Your shakes are contagious." There is a "new connection, a shared and profound cocreated humiliation" (361). What humiliates is love itself—both the individual love of the father and love as the father's political and identitarian ideal. It is 1972, the year of the last major legislative gain of the Civil Rights Movement and the year of Nixon's re-election. The ethos of Civil Rights idealism appears at once superior and inadequate to the counter-presences of vigilante violence and the impassive state (the burning cross, the indifferent policemen).

From a psychoanalytic perspective, humiliation exposes the values we hold closest to the ideal self, and the ideal self is the one thing we can never mourn. "Tell me what makes you . . . feel truly diminished," Adam Phillips writes, "and I will tell you what you believe or what you want to believe about yourself. What, that is, you imagine you need to protect to sustain your love of life."[53] By this logic, humiliation reveals Abel's love *of love*, for it is love's inadequacy that he cannot abide, that he feels as a violation. "The father takes you in his arms and tries to get you not to shake but it feels like he is strangling you and you shake harder." Love is the precious, self-exposing thing he rages against when he later "translate[s] an utter and tender, complete and mutual defeat into the oldest and most powerful male story [he knows]." When, in the novel's final pages, Abel returns his memory to what we might call its original language, he arrives at an unexpected conclusion: "Ultimately it is not strange and dramatic occurrences that shatter: it is a shivering hug that can not matter enough" (362).

Because the drama of Abel's thirteenth birthday prompts the identitarian re-constitution that governs all subsequent stories about him, we may infer, at least in the context of this novel, that the loss of Civil Rights idealism re-forms the very conditions of narrative possibility. But how shall we understand the concept of "translation," through which Randall links the range of interpretations rehearsed above, and, more concretely, two ostensibly dissimilar quantities—"strange and dramatic occurrences that shatter," and "a shivering hug that can not matter enough"? Melancholia lends itself to one compelling logic of "translation," since, as a symptomatic mode of expression, melancholic speech encodes a clue about the thing it cannot say; it wears a "disguise" to "[make] desire accessible by making it tolerable."[54] Put another way, melancholic speech, like translation, describes a substitutive economy, in which one entity stands in for another. It is susceptible (psychoanalysts hope) to an interpretive key that will enable a drama of revelation, a return to the event in its "original language." If the rape story is a lie, then it is also a melancholic translation: a disavowal that substitutes for the impossibility of mourning the ideal self, and an encryption of love and loss through which the self is remade.

Affect theory lends itself to another interpretive approach, whereby the narrative telos of "corrected" memory need not be read as the event's full and final meaning. By bracketing melancholia's mechanical description and its fundamental commitment to the logic of repression, attention to affect may illuminate another understanding of "translation" that operates through the density and distribution of feeling. If melancholic translation consists in something like a practice of decoding, then affective translation might entail something more like an art of approximation, whose success is measured through resonance with, or felt closeness to, an original expression.

To explain how affective force travels and transforms through speech, Sedgwick presents an analogy to the act of wandering through adjoining neighborhoods. In this analogy, performative utterances—such as Abel's interpellation of his father through shame—constitute the "prestigious centers" of real estate zones; they are sites of power from which influence reverberates, albeit "unevenly, [and] even unpredictably."[55] Using the term "periperformatives" to describe utterances that cluster around performative speech acts, she notes, "If the periperformative is the neighborhood of a performative, there might well be another performative neighborhood not so very far off to the north or northwest of this one; as I amble farther from the mother lode of my own neighborhood, my compass needle may also tremble with the added magnetism of another numinous center to which I am thereby nearer."[56]

As described here, affect's movement is at once mysterious and mappable. The model for associative connection is not "truth" and "disguise" but geographical sprawl, through which feeling "rarefies or concentrates in unpredictable clusters [and] outcrops," becoming vulnerable to "powerful energies that often warp, transform, and displace, if they do not overthrow, the supposed authorizing centrality of [the original, or central] performative."[57] Similarly, we might imagine that a propulsive force in the form of a compelling, if idiosyncratic, resonance clears the pathway that begins with Abel's declaration of shame and leads toward his allegation of sexual abuse. It is worth noting that, when Abel finally recalls his "untranslated" memory, the scene is not a single, stable revelation but three consecutively repeated memories of the same moment, "ambling" in the direction of his original declaration of shame.

In Abel's recollection, shame feels like confinement, violence, and the loss of bodily self-control. "Your thought is narrow, compressed, flattening." "[The father's] touch constricts." "Your nose continues to bleed. . . . You taste your own blood and cry harder" (361). Shame reverberates through the room, attaching to everything—Abel, his father, Abel's soiled clothes, his father's belt. It feels like contagion *and* isolation.[58] "Your eyes are mirrors. . . . You see him and he sees how you see him." "You come undone and he comes with you" (361). "You push him away." "The breach is a reciprocal bond" (362).

But shame is not only the scene's affective milieu; it is also the transformative speech act at the heart of the novel. More than a confession, it is the core of a repetitious, performative declaration that coheres and transmits the feeling it identifies. "'You. Ashamed of You, Daddy,' you say." "'Shame,' you say like it's his name" (361). Randall's pervasive use of the second person throughout her description of Abel's deathbed memory further amplifies this effect, since the appellation "you" contains volatile capacities for intimacy and accusation. "You are ashamed of him," she writes. "The breach is a reciprocal bond" (362). In the stifling confines of Abel's bedroom, unbearable love is felt like the most intimate injury. Love and injury are made congruent through a standard of affective fidelity. Like a translation, the apprehension of love as injury bespeaks both consistency and conversion.

I want to emphasize that this affect theory–based concept of "translation" insists upon a measure of credibility for the "cover story" of abuse, not in keeping with any juridical standard, of course, but still pertinent to a rich understanding of the psychic dynamics that accrue to the novel's central scene. We know that the rape story is invoked to obscure or disguise Abel's feelings toward vulnerability and love. But we can say this even as we hold on to an ostensibly opposite claim, that the "strange and dramatic" story of Abel's sexual trauma is meant to capture something authentic about how mercy felt like violence and likely also about Abel's adolescent feelings toward patriarchal power and disciplinary violence.[59] If melancholia helps us to understand how and why Abel obscures from consciousness the meaning and trajectory of grief, then affect theory supplements this logic with a description of how "translation" keeps faith with an original feeling (here, shame) by way of a traceable path of resonant feeling.

Since Abel goes on to become a neo-conservative war criminal (in the fashion of his good friend, Secretary of State Aria Reese!), it is easy to read his biography as a cautionary tale, warning that the refusal to mourn the most tender and personal losses of the Civil Rights era will corrupt black political subjectivity's authentic trajectories of feeling, desire, and identification. But might we also read the story of "translation" as a parable about Randall's milieu of contemporary black literature and its criticism—a discursive domain in which "strange and dramatic" historical plots may be seen as covering or displacing or "translating" more proximate and familiar narratives of loss? Put plainly, might we interpret the novel's epiphany as a reflection on the contemporary narrative of slavery, whose spectacular scenes of violence and trauma themselves emerge as symptoms of racial melancholia? (Ursa, the protagonist of Gayl Jones's *Corregidora*, seems to surmise something like this when she laments that her mother could bear witness to her enslaved foremothers' traumas but could not disclose "what she had lived." Ursa concludes, "[The ancestral slaver and rapist] Corregidora was easier than what she wouldn't tell me.")[60] Much as melancholia operates as a mode of censorship, in which the thing that cannot be declared comes to govern speech through its pre-emptive power, the loss of Civil Rights idealism haunts the contemporary narrative of slavery, which compulsively disavows or downplays the near past as a primary site of love or loss.

Commonly heralded as the first contemporary narrative of slavery, Margaret Walker's *Jubilee* was published a year after Malcolm X's assassination and two years before King's. In the decades that followed, running parallel to an escalating panic about a post-King vacuum of black leadership, the contemporary narrative of slavery became the most celebrated and widely circulating form of mid- to high-brow African American literature. Yet, even as these novels publicly articulate racial grief in the immediate and extended aftermath of the Civil Rights Movement's premature end, the great majority of them do not represent substantive scenes of contemporary political loss at all. Instead, and in keeping with melancholic grief, they refuse to mourn the lost faith of the near past, forestalling the apprehension of loss through self-punitive returns to the past. To be sure, my point is not that slavery has been sufficiently grieved or that trauma offers an inappropriate lens for the study of contemporary black literature. Nor is it that we can have no credible feelings about the distant past. Rather, I am suggesting that historical plots of slavery and the rhetorical device of traumatic time may *simultaneously* offer an earnest, resonant representation of grief that attaches to the past and work to forestall or encrypt other forms of unspeakable love and loss.

Perhaps unexpectedly, the melancholic psychic trajectory I articulate carries a certain indebtedness to formulations that emerge from prohibitive reading—most notably, from Warren, who begins *What Was African American Literature?* with the hypothesis that the field's historical turn bespeaks a wounded attachment to the apprehension of the Civil Rights Movement as loss. He writes, "Recent claims that either distinctly African traditions or the experiences of slavery and the Middle Passage constitute the center of African American imaginative and expressive practice should be seen as symptoms of the breakdown of a former coherence."[61] Rephrased to highlight our shared conviction, Warren suggests that the backward gaze of black literary discourse bears a coded expression—a "symptom"—of something unspeakable in the present.

Here is where we part ways. Prohibitive reading surmises that the contemporary narrative of slavery is at best self-delusional and at worst a liar's discourse. It treats African American literature's historical turn as a diversion, whose content has no bearing for the comparatively undertheorized social and political demands of the post–Civil Rights era. By contrast, I want to sever the idea that the historical turn is not fully self-transparent from the conclusion that it has no useful or "true" content. Which is to say, I move to re-think the relevance of the lie as a category *for literature* and to turn a curious eye toward the figure of translation. What might we discover by "translating" the contemporary narrative of slavery's "strange and dramatic" account of loss and longing if, indeed, it carries within it, and in its narrative traces, the very stories it eschews?

# 4

## Reading African American Literature Now

I am bored with the topic of Atlantic slavery. I have come to
be bored because so many boring people have talked about
it. So many artists and writers and thinkers, mediocre and
genius, have used it because it is a big, easy target. They appropriate it, adding no new insight or profound understanding, instead degrading it with their nothingness. They take
the stink of the slave hold and make it a pungent cliché, take
the blood-soaked chains of bondage and pervert them into
Afrocentric bling. . . . What's even more infuriating is that,
despite this stupidity, this repetitious sophistry, the topic of
chattel slavery is still unavoidable for its American descendants. It is the great story, the big one, the connector that
gives the reason for our nation's prosperity and for our very
existence within it. . . . Turns out though that my thorough
and exhaustive scholarship into the slave narratives of the
African Diaspora in no way prepared me to actually become
a fucking slave.
—Mat Johnson, *Pym*, 2011

Midway through Mat Johnson's exhilarating, novelistic response to
Edgar Allan Poe's faux travelogue, *The Narrative of Arthur Gordon Pym
of Nantucket*, Johnson's protagonist, a professor of African American literature, pauses to remark upon his fatigue with black studies' prolific
discourse on the slave past. This passage is remarkable not only because
its irreverence scandalizes historical trauma but, moreover, because it
assumes a degree of familiarity with the protagonist's complaint: The
reader must comprehend slavery's ubiquity in black writing in order to
be in on the joke. Johnson, of course, is ironizing his own position as
an author grappling with slavery and the African American past within
a saturated, twenty-first-century literary marketplace. Our hero, Pro-

fessor Chris Jaynes, bespeaks a desire to be released from the past and what he perceives to be its hackneyed, inadequate re-vivifications. Yet this desire is belied by his enduring attachment to the history of slavery, where he envisions "the great story, the big one" whose causal reverberations produce the content and meaning of the American present. Chris, as a literary historian and expert on the genre of the slave narrative, is consumed with the "fossil record . . . of modern racial thought," and his research is directed by his belief that combating racism in the present requires an excavation of the literary past.[1]

Though he is an African Americanist by training, Chris's recent teaching and research focus singularly on "the intellectual source of racial whiteness"[2] that he argues—after Toni Morrison in *Playing in the Dark*—is concentrated in Poe's writing.[3] Early in the novel, Chris is denied tenure, but he forestalls despair when he happens upon the papers of Dirk Peters, the thought-to-be fictional, "half-breed Indian" companion of Poe's titular Arthur Gordon Pym.[4] Chris discovers that, in fact, Peters was African American and real. This discovery initiates the protagonist's post-academic life as an independent researcher-cum-adventurer retracing the routes of Pym and Peters. Undertaken as Chris's destiny and desire, the voyage to Antarctica and its environs that occupies the remainder of the text conflates the geographically exotic expedition with the professor's conquest of the very literary and cultural archetypes that purportedly bore him: the fantasy of a "great undiscovered African Diasporan homeland . . . uncorrupted by Whiteness";[5] the fantasy of historical revision, redemption, or repair; the terrorizing idea of contemporary black subjects enslaved to monstrous forces of whiteness; and the specifically literary will to speak back to an inherited corpus of racist writing.

Thus *Pym* reveals the potent endurance of its hero's historical desire in spite of a competing will to be done with the past. Yet it declines to endorse that inextinguishable desire as useful or inherently valuable. When Chris is forcibly made the property of a band of brutish "snow honk[ies]," his epiphany is this: "Turns out . . . that my thorough and exhaustive scholarship into the slave narratives of the African Diaspora in no way prepared me to actually become a fucking slave."[6]

Put differently, Chris's absurdist descent into slavery—which begins with a literary encounter with Peters's "Negro servant's memoir"—leads him to detect his previous hermeneutical error. He had been reading with the expectation of liberation or redemption, hoping to cure racism, or to "redeem" Peters by returning his skeleton (which Chris acquires) to a fantastical "island of blackness," or to rediscover himself in the context of a blackness untouched by "the Diasporan dialogue." "There was a group of our people," Chris deduces through his reading of Peters's papers, "who did achieve victory over slavery in all its forms, escaping completely from the progression of Westernization and colonization to form a society outside of time and history."[7] But each of these fantasies of meaning's confirmation remains beyond the frame of the novel, inaccessible to its questing, internal reader. Instead of deliverance, *Pym* gives us proliferating, successive scenes of Chris's imperilment, each the effect of mis-interpretation on his part. Might this crisis in interpretation, which manifests as reading that gets us stuck (in various enemies' traps), circle back to the protagonist's complaint of boredom and impasse in the contemporary discourse on slavery? And, if this is so—if certain habits of reading black historical fiction have calcified into restrictive habit— then how might we re-fresh and re-imagine our readerly task?

For many critics, *Beloved* is the exemplar of black fiction's historical turn: It is the book that taught us how to read as we read now. Its lesson is construed variously, as the necessary or dangerous command, or the inscription of the impossible wish, that literary encounters with the slave past will compel a reparative catharsis for the contemporary reader. More fundamentally, *Beloved* is regarded as *the* unparalleled cultural text that confirms the register of trauma and the topic of slavery as the foremost concerns of black literary study. Taking *Pym* as cue and cautionary tale, I want to ask, What if we displace *Beloved* as the central or singular prism through which to understand the agency of post–Civil Rights African American literature and the demands of historical desire? How, and with what effects, might we re-imagine the contours of our critical enterprise—say, through an iconoclastic alternative to Morrisonian poetics like Charles Johnson's *Oxherding Tale* (1982) or through Morrison's own rejoinder to *Beloved* in the form of her 1997 novel, *Paradise*?

In lieu of a conclusion, the present chapter performs an open-ended experiment in reading African American literature differently. Rather than argue that we must be done with the past or that we must vigilantly preserve its place in contemporary consciousness, I seek out alternative literary-critical genealogies to de-familiarize the investments and allegiances that dominate our field today. My intention is not to prescribe a new methodological hegemony (though, like any critic, I carry my biases) but to unsettle received ideas about what black literary studies *should* want and do. If, thus far, my book has made its claims in the negative—how not to read, what we miss when we read through certain habits of thought—my intention, now, is to re-imagine such critique in terms of the positive.

## *Oxherding Tale* and the Problem of History

First printed by a university press where Johnson claims to have found "the only editor in America . . . able to understand and willing to publish [it],"[8] *Oxherding Tale* is an unusual take on the contemporary narrative of slavery. Its wry humor, literary historical commentary, and epic adventure position it as a noteworthy precursor to *Pym*, but unlike *Beloved*, which so often serves as the basis for generalizing pronouncements about black historical fiction, Johnson's novel is neither representative of a major literary trend, nor is it especially remarkable for its commercial or pedagogical popularity. In fact, Johnson has somewhat fastidiously fashioned himself as the anti-Morrison of contemporary black letters: irreverent, anti-identitarian, and complexly misogynistic, he dismisses *Beloved* as "an interesting middle-brow book" that falls short of measurable "intellectual achievement."[9] Emplotting a "literary vision of slavery as ludic as Toni Morrison's is tragic," *Oxherding Tale* sits in irreducible tension with the literary tradition of which it is part.[10] It is decidedly atypical in style, tone, and its embedded philosophy of race; it is densely meta-fictional and deliberately, unapologetically comedic; and its playful use of a traumatic strain of racial history (i.e., slavery and fugitive escape) is by all accounts unusual and, by many accounts, offensive.[11] But despite its distinctive, comedic façade, *Oxherding Tale* also unfolds a deeply serious and self-consciously ambivalent meditation on history, literature, identity, and desire—those thematic concerns at the generic heart of the contemporary narrative of slavery. Precisely because of its status as a brother-outsider text to the genre, I turn to this novel to illuminate the normative boundaries of generic and hermeneutical practice. How do we read now—through what desires, attachments, and disavowals—and how might we read otherwise?

Originally drafted under the working title "The Last Liberation," *Oxherding Tale* follows and flouts the formal conventions of the antebellum slave narrative—a genre the text internally describes as those "authentic narratives written by bondsmen who decided one afternoon to haul hips for the Mason Dixon line."[12] The novel's narrative action spans the twenty-three-year period between 1838 and 1861, during which time its mixed-race protagonist, Andrew Hawkins, is born a slave, suffers through various ordeals of bondage, becomes a fugitive—aided by literacy and book learning, as well as his ability to pass for white—and finally escapes the pursuit of a villainous slave catcher. But bursting from the seams of this predictable narrative progression is a far more unusual plot, full of hijinks, philosophizing detours, and intricate and outrageous twists.

The novel begins in 1838, nine months before Andrew Hawkins's birth, when Jonathan Polkinghorne, owner of the Cripplegate Plantation, orchestrates an absurd and calamitous prank. "Literally inebriated with power,"[13] Jonathan demands to trade places for the night with his favorite slave, George Hawkins. Andrew is the product of a mutually non-consensual sex act between George and Jonathan's wife, Anna. His conception signals the downfall of each of his parents, for the following day, George is remanded to the fields and Anna descends into a long period of shame and isolation. Andrew's own relation to race, status, and family are ambiguous from the start. He is raised, he tells us, "caught" in the "crossfire" of two families—one black, one white (8). Although the law designates him as Jonathan's property, he is spared hard labor and afforded unusual benefits, including the procurement of a brilliant, reclusive tutor. Thus, Andrew gains a comprehensive understanding of Western and Eastern philosophy (both of which will underwrite the novel's culminating visions of freedom) before the tutor dies of heartbreak in 1853.

In 1858, Andrew falls in love with a fellow slave from a neighboring plantation, Minty McKay. Moved by love and its extension into a romantic vision of collective, liberationist politics, he approaches Jonathan to express his desire to buy his freedom, as well as Minty's, George's, and his stepmother Mattie's. In a sinister twist, Jonathan agrees but requires that Andrew earn his wages in the service of Flo Hatfield—an "opium-taking, candy-munching,"[14] hyper-sexual proto-feminist, whose hunger for power is emblazoned in the name of her plantation, Leviathan. There Andrew spends an ambivalent year as Flo's male concubine. His indignity is mitigated by comfort and sensual reward but made suddenly intolerable by the news of an unsuccessful slave revolt at Cripplegate. Fearing the scattering loss of family and loved ones, Andrew approaches Flo for back payment, and their discussion escalates to violence. After Andrew punches Flo in the face, she sentences him, along with Leviathan's coffin maker, Reb, to hard labor in the mines.

Here, the story of fugitive escape begins. Assuming the role of Reb's white owner, Andrew re-invents himself as an unlucky heir to a family that made, then lost, their fortune in American shipping. (He calls this personality William Harris.) Under this guise, the two enslaved men flee the mines of Abbeville, though their journey north is forestalled by Andrew/William's unmanageable heroin withdrawal. Forced to stop, for his medical care, in Spartanburg, South Carolina, the dangers of fugitivity are indefinitely prolonged. They are also exacerbated by the appearance of a notorious slave catcher, Horace Bannon (alias: the Soulcatcher). A monstrous antagonist astride "a great war-horse with padded hooves" (66), Bannon represents the immediate and embodied threat of capture, though his terrorizing physicality is complicated by the curious, psychologizing rule that governs his trade: He will enact his capture only when the fugitive himself admits an internal surrender, desiring his own predation. Thus, the Soulcatcher maintains a shadowy, suspenseful perch, as Andrew/William's life continues. The protagonist is returned to health by the local doctor, he assumes a role as a schoolteacher in order to pay the doctor's bill, and he courts and finally marries the doctor's daughter, Peggy Undercliff.

In 1860, realizing that Andrew will never chaperone him north, Reb flees Spartanburg for Chicago, pursued by Bannon. Bannon is unable to capture and kill Reb, but he procures the coffin maker's ring, which he sends to Andrew as false testament to his victory. Grieving the loss of his former companion, Andrew finally begins to despair, though he knows that despair will be his demise—the first stage of the death wish that is the Soulcatcher's cue. He goes out in search of Bannon but instead comes upon a slave auction, where the last person to be sold is his childhood sweetheart, Minty, now grotesquely ill. Professing a sense of duty, Andrew purchases Minty, and he and Peggy tend to her in her final days.

Then the Soulcatcher returns. Upon Minty's death, Bannon appears in Andrew's doorway, and, in a state of resignation, Andrew submits himself to his tormentor. The Soulcatcher, however, meets him with surprising news. Because Reb has bested him, he has been compelled to resign. So, through Reb's heroism, Andrew's life is spared, delivering him from fugitivity to freedom. Andrew's apprehension of freedom is accompanied by a vision of life as intensely and dynamically interconnected, and in 1861, as the novel's culminating event, Andrew and Peggy have a daughter. "This," the protagonist-narrator tells us, "is my tale" (176).

How does such a fantastical story position the contemporary reader in relation to the slave past, and what structures of feeling is it meant to produce or disrupt? Let us find our first clue in Johnson's self-announcing "essayist interlude" (119), whose condensed, meta-fictional commentary appears approximately two-thirds of the way through the novel, under the title, "On the Nature of Slave Narratives." Here, an unidentified narrator—ostensibly, someone other than our usual first-person protagonist, Andrew—interrupts the story to describe to the reader the genealogy of antebellum slave narratives. Spanning just over a page, what begins as an annotative digression on the "archival tomb of literary history" (118) turns into a description and endorsement of literary historical *retrieval*. Put another way, what begins as an explanation of the antebellum slave narrative becomes a theory of the contemporary narrative of slavery.

Starting from the premise that the antebellum slave narrative is "related, as distant cousins are related," to earlier literary forms, including the Puritan conversion narrative and *The Confessions* of Saint Augustine, the narrator hypothesizes that "no form . . . *loses* its ancestry; rather, these meanings accumulate in layers of tissue as the form evolves." But in a curious turn, the narrator goes on to describe contemporary writing, not as an ongoing accretive enterprise (the accumulation of more layers of history), but as the work of dis-interment (an excavation of history). He proposes: "It is perhaps safe to conjecture that the Slave Narrative proper whistles and hums with this history . . . and all a modern writer need do is dig, dig, dig—call it spadework—until the form surrenders its diverse secrets" (119, Johnson's italics).

At once confessional and brazenly academic, this narrative "intermission" purports to contextualize the novel, identifying its constitutive, generic ambition. "The modern writer," we are told, sets out to perform a kind of de-repressive labor, not simply imitating but unearthing and bringing to consciousness a past that is buried but not lost, with a host of "diverse" and promising "secrets." History, in this view, is invisible but imperishably present and enduringly useful. It is retrievable for modern life, if we will only "dig, dig, dig"—though we are cautioned that the "hole is very deep, the archaeological work slow" (119). Read in isolation, this explication of (late) modern writing would seem to corroborate the hypothesis that under-girds therapeutic and prohibitive reading: that contemporary narratives of slavery work, through performative claims to historical revelation, to effect a meaningful psychic experience. Their achievement is the revelation of secrets, the apprehension of "the wheels as they whir beneath the stage" (118). The implied will of the text, to borrow language from Angelyn Mitchell, is to "emancipate [its] readers from the cultural and historical amnesia that has surrounded the issue of slavery in the United States."[15]

But, for Johnson, there is a catch. This position, presented in the moment of its articulation as an earnest, intellectual hypothesis and meta-fictional self-disclosure, has already been ironized by the novel's preceding 117 pages. For the past that *Oxherding Tale* recounts consists not in a set of historical facts retrieved and laid bare, like the spoils of an archeological dig, but in a flamboyant fantasy of the slave past that, from the start, renounces its referential duty to any governing ideal of the historical real. With zany plot twists, internal confessions of a history that is "ruin now, mere parable" (3), and conspicuous, comical anachronisms that mock the conceit of historical authenticity, the novel mercilessly, peremptorily contradicts its later, textual instruction to "dig, dig, dig" for a past that will eventually, inevitably, disclose itself (119). So, although Johnson offers a historical plot, rendered roughly according to a familiar literary historical form, it is impossible to believe that, in reading the novel, one is directly encountering the past. We are not, per Morrison's narrative standard, "thrown ruthlessly into an alien environment as the first step into a shared experience with the book's population,"[16] for in

*Oxherding Tale*, the temptation to forget oneself in the text is summarily, if pleasurably, foreclosed.

Through his twinned representation of historical irretrievability and the contradictory desire to exhume and reconnect with the past, Johnson at once endorses and renders absurd the fictional gesture of historical return. The "archaeological" desire of the contemporary narrative of slavery does not matriculate to fulfillment but, rather, generates a stubborn tension around the subject of history, as the impossibility of historical return is held uncomfortably alongside the persistence of historical desire. How shall we make sense of this internal contradiction whereby *Oxherding Tale* espouses and mocks, fantasizes and forecloses, the desire for a reparative, historical return?

On this matter, the critical tendency has been to privilege one of the novel's orientations toward history over the other, to regard one as (triumphant) thesis and the other as (defeated) antithesis. By this rule, either *Oxherding Tale* succeeds as a contemporary narrative of slavery, by bringing the past to bear on contemporary psychic and political life, or it fails as a contemporary narrative of slavery because it thwarts the post-traumatic imperative to remember. Keith Byerman, a spokesperson for the former view, writes, "At a time when the president himself [Ronald Reagan] was declaring that racism no longer existed as anything other than an individual aberration, Johnson constructed narratives that described the holocaustlike experience of slavery and that implicated current social practices in that history."[17] Arlene R. Keizer, representing the opposite view, foregrounds the novel's anti-historical bent to assert that its anachronistic lexicon works to evacuate rather than instill historical consciousness. She warns, "*Oxherding Tale* runs the risk of allowing the reader to forget the real conditions of slavery, and to view the condition of bondage as primarily an existential problem."[18] Though these perspectives diverge in their respective estimations of Johnson's literary accomplishment, they share a common governing standard whereby literary explorations of racial memory *should* speak with moral clarity and therapeutic efficaciousness; black historical fiction is deemed supremely valuable when it works collectively and "constantly . . . against . . . the desire to forget," showing its readers that "the possibility for change is in memory."[19]

But as I show now, *Oxherding Tale* imagines its task otherwise, as evidenced by its overt and protracted use of allegory to *expose and displace* the very structures of feeling the contemporary narrative of slavery is expected to provoke. If, as proponents of therapeutic and prohibitive reading maintain, black historical fiction is meant to act with immediacy, through a transparent psychic technology of reader identification, then allegory—derived from the Latin *allos* (other) and *agoreuein* ("open, declarative speech")—defies the most basic requirement for such immersive storytelling, "that our words 'mean what they say.'"[20]

To be sure, allegorical meaning is not the negation of a story's ostensible content; the "otherness" of its speech is not self-canceling, but self-abstracting. Although *Oxherding Tale's* use of allegory conforms to the agenda of prohibitive reading insofar as it interrupts the possibility for readerly transference and over-identification, it does so, not by renouncing that desire, but by turning the ideal of transcendent therapeutic reading into a "double signpost."[21] Under Johnson's hand, the complexly wrought human pathos of the fantasy of reparative return is both asserted *and* abstracted beyond itself; the literary articulation of therapeutic reading redoubles as a story about the desire for therapeutic reading. Through this maneuver, *Oxherding Tale* elicits a hermeneutical approach that invokes and exceeds the critical horizon of therapeutic/prohibitive reading. The foundational question it puts in the mouth of its implied reader is not, "How will the literary representation of the slave past facilitate or renounce the task of the reader's psychic betterment?" but "What objects and economies of desire propel African American literature's historical turn, and what is the role of literature as such in mediating that desire?"

Of course, as the preceding chapters demonstrate, it is not unusual for contemporary narratives of slavery to make use of allegory as a narrative strategy, nor is allegorical reading uncommon within the extant criticism. My own analyses have repeatedly turned to allegory to discern a meta-literary and meta-historical discourse implicit to black historical fiction, and indeed, allegory is one of the most common devices through which writers and critics have encouraged us to draw meaningful connections between historical and contemporary conditions of racial subjectivity, sociality, and unfreedom. Nor is *Oxherding Tale* anomalous for its refusal to fulfill its internal fantasies of historical desire. On the contrary, a central argument of the present study has been that therapeutic and prohibitive reading too often obscure the contemporary narrative of slavery's generic skepticism toward the possibility of the catharsis it desires.

What is remarkable about *Oxherding Tale* is how it enlists allegory and humor as its primary and unrelieved narrative strategies to enact its foreclosure of historical desire. The novel calls up familiar and sincere forms of longing—for historical redemption and repair, for contemporary heroism in the face of unrelieved historical suffering, for assuagement of the losses of the Civil Rights era—but it allows us to see these desires always and only through the prism of exaggerated and self-conscious narrative artifice. The novel's inclination to pathos is itself inhabited by an inclination to abstraction, such that profoundly vulnerable articulations of love and desire strain against a milieu of merciless humor. Theresa M. Kelley has argued that "because it is wayward, provisional, and openly factitious, modern allegory can assist a line of reasoning that breaks open self-enclosed symbols or systems and thus break out of the 'habitus' of culture, whose patterns of received knowledge would otherwise close off inquiry."[22] In what follows, I make a similar case for *Oxherding Tale*'s capacity to unsettle the presumptive meanings and functions of black historical fiction's familiar network of symbols, systems, and feelings.

## Four Allegories

*Oxherding Tale* describes the contemporary narrative of slavery's relationship to the past through its protagonist's encounters with four allegorical figures, each standing in for a distinct aspect of African American literature's historical desire. These figures are Andrew's first love, Minty; an eccentric novelist named Evelyn Pomeroy; Andrew's father, George; and the bounty hunter, Horace Bannon. They represent, respectively, the desire for lost origins, the novel's own ambivalence toward modern black writing, post–Civil Rights racial melancholia, and the contemporary narrative of slavery's psychic attachment to historical injury. Roughly translated to the idioms that organize this volume, they represent trauma, depression, and masochism.

## Andrew's First Love

Although she is absent from the great majority of the novel's narrative action, Minty's presence frames the text at the levels of plot and signification. At the beginning of the novel, Andrew's love for her catalyzes his pursuit of freedom. At the end, the demands of her suffering and the fact of her premature death compel his moral self-reckoning. Before she dies, her suffering affords Andrew an opportunity for heroism.

Presumably, the protagonist's relationship with Minty is intended to fulfill the reader's desire and expectation: to extend recognition to an abject past, to alleviate historical suffering, and to mourn the unmourned dead. In each of these respects, Minty bodies forth the promise that we may counteract the oppressive weight of our impotence, in the present, to redress the wounds of history. Yet, with acerbic self-consciousness, Johnson represents Minty in outrageous caricature, ridiculing the imagined and predictable desire for a character like her in the very act of fulfilling that desire.

A couple of years after he leaves her behind at the Cripplegate Plantation, Andrew accidentally stumbles upon Minty at a covert Spartanburg slave auction. This woman, who once "ensorcelled" him with her "flawed, haunting beauty" (15), has become, by age twenty-two, "unlovely, drudgelike, sexless, the farm tool squeezed . . . for every ounce of surplus value, then put on sale for whatever price she could bring" (155). Andrew purchases her at an outrageous markup, securing his heroism when he offers the reassurance, "I've purchased you not to put you to work but, as I promised years before, to buy your freedom" (157). Minty responds with hyperbolic gratitude that undermines the scene's already tenuous claims to tragedy. Per Andrew's report, "There is a place where southern women retire when their nervous systems short-circuit, a pleasant region much like a sanatorium, or a Writer's Colony, and I have often heard it referred to as a *swoon*; I can describe it no further, having never been there: Men pass out, a few faint, others are knocked out, but men do not *swoon*, and I thought it improper to trouble Minty about the details of the Ladies' Psychic Powder Room after she checked back in" (157–158, Johnson's italics).

Upon recovering from her "swoon," Minty is taken to Andrew's home, where she makes herself useful. She cleans, cooks, and instructs

Andrew's new wife, Peggy, on how best to care for him. But in time, illness incapacitates her, and she is confined to bed. In a gesture of love, Andrew attempts to comfort her by inventing an alternative future to her unsalvageable past. He extemporizes a sentimental fantasy of Minty "[standing as] a freewoman" on "eastern beaches [whose] blues and browns . . . contrast the warm hues of her skin," and it is against the backdrop of this image of redemption that Andrew's muse dies before him (167).

If Minty stands for the irredeemable suffering of the slave past and Andrew for the redemptive desire of the contemporary, African American literary imagination, then the depiction of her belated rescue suggestively approximates a presentist fantasy that is harbored within therapeutic reading. In this fantasy, the contemporary narrative of slavery becomes the saving grace of historical trauma, extending a holding hand, a soothing voice, a loving eye. It is hardly unorthodox that the desire for trans-historical healing announces itself within the text, nor is it unusual for such a wish to come up against its tragic foreclosure; a similar narrative of reparative desire and its incompletion unfolds in nearly every other historical novel that appears in this study. But Johnson goes further to turn this fantasy on its head. He presents our desire to redeem the past as a desire to make the past swoon. He accentuates our inclination to romanticization and possessiveness, and he confesses, by way of Minty's domestic generosity, the under-articulated wish that, in return for our remembrance, history will work for us, ordering and repairing the fabric of our daily lives. (Let us not forget, as Keizer rightly notes, that as a matter of law, Minty has become Andrew's slave.)[23] When Minty finally dies, Johnson represents the scene in crude, corporeal detail, refusing his readers both Andrew's redemptive fantasy and the release of righteous sympathy: "A gush of black vomit bubbled from her mouth onto my hand. The Devil came and sat on Minty, his weight pressing open the valve to her bladder and bowels" (167). To the end, Johnson's articulation of the forceful, contemporary longing for reparative return is interrupted and undermined by the impossibility of un-self-critically inhabiting that desire.

In order to achieve its intended effect, Johnson's allegory requires that Minty's interior life remains inaccessible to Andrew because Minty stands for history, and the point of her character is precisely the impossibility of history's appearance as a self-articulating *presence*. Thus, like the bard who sees in his lover the reflection of his own desire, Andrew is unable to parse Minty's true essence from his projective longing. He admits: "How much of her beauty lay in Minty, and how much in my head, was a mystery to me" (15). But Minty must also and nevertheless stand for a more substantive conception of the historical real, for however irretrievable the immediacy of its experience may be, the history of slavery is a certain fact, the painful reality that propels historical desire in the first place. Thus, Minty bears the burden of representing both the abstracted, imprecise, reparative desire of the present and the still-potent, graphic wound of the slave past. To this end, she alternately appears as an un-harnessable fantasy object ("voluptuously sleepy, distant, as though she had been lifted long ago from a melancholy African landscape" [15]) and, as stunningly, even grotesquely, corporeal (with "work-scorched stretches of skin and a latticework of whipmarks," a "belly pushed forward [from] the cholesterol-high, nutritionless diet of the quarters," and the accelerating dis-figurement of untreated pellagra [154–155]).

In light of such characterization, what might the reader *feel* for Minty? What is the tenor of our sadness when she reappears at the end of the novel, brutalized and dying, or when her body is literally consumed by disease at age twenty-two? Made witnesses to a tragedy that is repeatedly interrupted by the asynchrony and irreverence of Johnson's narrative voice—a tragedy, in other words, that can never fully come into view—we are unable to inhabit her suffering or to internalize it as our own. Rather than feeling Minty's pain, we find ourselves in a position akin to Andrew, the narcissistic lover who looks to Minty for confirmation of his heroic loyalty, who frantically, quixotically imagines her redemption, and who struggles to relinquish the history he could not save. "I raved, all my eloquence empty, refusing to release her hand," Andrew tells us, upon Minty's death. "In my chest there commingled feelings of guilt I could not coax into cognition" (167).

For the feminist reader (or even her most lukewarm sympathizer), the question of reader response encounters additional complications, most of all because we cannot escape the conspicuous and profoundly unnerving fact that Johnson's suggestive discourse on historical desire uses, as its allegorical prop, a black woman's brutalized body, whose self-consciousness is overwritten by that of her passing male purchaser. In the case of Minty, the cost of Johnson's representational choice—and, some have argued, of Andrew's own freedom—is revealed to be the extreme disparagement of black, female embodiment. (Is this one source of the "guilt" that Andrew cannot or will not know?) For me, as for other feminist critics who have engaged with *Oxherding Tale*, this representational economy produces an alienation from the text that exceeds the intended effects of curtailed identification and ironic distance.[24]

There is more to be said about the feminist recoil Minty inspires, and I return to this topic shortly. Yet I also want to note a complication within this critique. For even if, as Jennifer Hayward suggests, the sadism that befalls Minty is a symptom of Johnson's own "conflicted attitude toward women," this interpretation does not exhaust the meaning of Minty's intersectional subjection to textual disparagement.[25] Not as a negation but as an addendum to this view, her fate may be read as a satirical critique of (often gendered) literary displays of suffering, insofar as the gratuitous spectacle of her death aligns with the appropriative righteousness of certain fictions of slavery. Put another way, one may find, in the excess of Minty's suffering and the emptiness of her character, both a troubling negation of black feminine subjectivity (to which I will return) and a provocative interrogation of literature's long-standing investment in the spectacular pain and pathos of enslaved women. In the latter respect, Minty's characterization anticipates Saidiya Hartman's famous disapprobation of "the ways we [readers] are called upon to participate" in literature's fixation and relentless "display of the slave's ravaged body."[26] For Johnson, too, the spectacle of suffering anchors the idea—the false promise—that we can exchange the psychic discomfort of witnessing terror for our own catharsis, therapeutic self-epiphany, or moral inoculation. But where Hartman's response is to look away from the spectacle, replacing its visual and rhetorical centrality with analyses of "mundane" forms of suffering that are too often overlooked,[27] Johnson's response is to explode the spectacle, to break it apart through intense, satirical magnification.

### An Eccentric Novelist

If *Oxherding Tale* is a comedy whose currency is cynical excess, then does its mercilessness become the limit of its critique? Is *Oxherding Tale* reducible to a "clever, sneering lampoon" of the fictions of slavery, reveling in the "faults" of its satirical object? (143). I borrow these cited phrases from the novel's internal description of an unfinished book by a peripheral character named Evelyn Pomeroy. A number of critics have read Evelyn, an aging schoolteacher and a novelist within the novel, as a humble portrait of Johnson himself.[28] I encounter her from another angle, not (quite) as a figure for Johnson's authorial self-indictment, but as an intratextual confession of ambivalence—and *love*—that tempers and textures *Oxherding Tale*'s aggressive animus toward the constitutive fantasies of the fictions of slavery.

Evelyn's narrative arc is short and, for the most part, insignificant to the broad strokes of the plot. Her allegorical significance is concentrated in a secondhand anecdote that Peggy shares with Andrew about Evelyn's struggle against the anxiety of influence. Suggestively, this anecdote pivots on the most famous, and most controversial, novel about American slavery ever written: Harriet Beecher Stowe's *Uncle Tom's Cabin*. It was Stowe, Peggy tells Andrew, who inspired Evelyn to become a writer. Evelyn "read her novel and loved it—and loved her—and thought, 'I *have* to do that.'" Peggy continues:

> "Evelyn is not, as you know, a crusader. . . . Nothing she has written will equal the influence of Stowe. When she *saw* that, after writing a hundred pages of a protest novel, she also discovered that she hated Stowe's book. She found faults, first with her novel, then turned on the Novel itself. She dismissed it as dead. She wrote a parody of *Uncle Tom's Cabin*, a clever, sneering lampoon that was, after the first few laughs, *ugly*—ugly and spiteful because it burlesqued something it couldn't be, and all because Evelyn *did* love Harriet Beecher Stowe. . . . Can you," Peggy asked herself, not me, "still love and believe in something when . . . you *know* you can't have it? (143, Johnson's italics)

Rather explicitly, Peggy's description of Evelyn's literary genealogy points to Johnson's own, meta-fictional self-reckoning. Like Evelyn, he is a novelist who was first moved to write by the example of politicized art and the moral cause of black history. As he recounts elsewhere, it was Amiri Baraka, in place of Stowe, whose charismatic performance at a public reading left Johnson "in a daze." "I wondered: What if I directed my drawing and everything I knew about comic art [at the time, Johnson was a cartoonist] to exploring the history and culture of black America?"[29] Yet, again recalling Evelyn, Johnson's early literary efforts were subsequently cast "into the bottom drawer of my filing cabinet," as the author developed a piercing critique of the forms and figures that originally inspired him.[30]

But *Oxherding Tale* is not Evelyn's "ugly" "lampoon," precisely because it is painfully, irresolvably aware of its mixed feelings for the overlapping forms of the novel of slavery and the protest novel. Although it parodies these forms with "clever" glee that occasionally sours into meanness, Johnson's novel persistently declines to "dismiss as dead" those objects of its original, impossible love: the fantasy of reparative return, and the fantasy of literature's direct and transparent transformative power. Instead, love is resurrected again and again, though it is also demeaned and though it is revealed to be an inconvenience, an embarrassment, and an impracticable wish. Minty, for example, is made ugly and undesirable to absurdist proportions, but she is also kept alive until the very end. The novel overwrites its love object with gallows humor and grotesquerie, but this act of disparagement may well be a melancholic rejection—a rejection that is not one—powered not by organic derision but by defensive projections of the lover's own failure, resentment, and foreclosed love.

Holding in tension romantic desire and cynical critique, Johnson offers a critical, yet non-annihilative rejoinder to the familiar wish that we, as subjects of the present, are charged with the task of de-repressing and psychically reconciling with the slave past. His counter-claim— which stealthily undermines his own fantasy of a secret-baring literary archaeology—is not that we must abandon historical desire altogether but that perhaps we have fundamentally mistaken the nature and object of repression. Might it be that the repressed of contemporary black fiction is not slavery itself, or even the un-mourned slave, but the difficult knowledge that the desire to redeem the slave past is simultaneously inoperative and inextinguishable? On this view, Peggy's question gives language to the novel's most elemental pathos and uncovers, in a new light, the heart of the contemporary narrative of slavery: "Can you . . . still love and believe in something when . . . you *know* you can't have it?" (143, Johnson's italics).

### Andrew's Father

Minty—and with her, the idea of the slave past tendering itself for its or our redemption—is one of *Oxherding Tale*'s impossible love objects. She represents not only the enduring potency of the slave past in the cultural imagination but also a structure of grief and desire through which contemporary literary consciousness approaches the slave past. Ever elusive and unknowable, (dis-)appearing as a missed encounter, Minty bears the characteristic marks of traumatic memory. In Andrew's father, George Hawkins, Johnson presents a second impossible love object and an attendant origin story for the contemporary narrative of slavery. This story locates the conception of the modern slave narrator (Andrew) in what George comes to call "the Fall" (7), a scene of disappointed love and foreclosed idealism whose allegorical counterpart is the crucible of post–Civil Rights grief. If the register of feeling that characterizes Minty's representation is dramatic, romantic, and catastrophic, then George's depiction retreats from this scale. Where Minty is ethereal and distant, George is commonplace, tangible, "a practical, God-fearing man" (3). And rather than bearing the traumatic sign of belatedness, George is marked by ambivalence and disavowal, the signature of melancholia and its constitutive repression.

At the outset of the novel, George is his master's favorite slave, but when Jonathan's drunken prank backfires, George is cast out of the house, losing "in one evening . . . a lifetime of building a good name for himself, winning his master's confidence, and disproving the grim Negro wisdom that no effort served to alter history and nature" (101–102). Like an ungenerous cliché about the Civil Rights–Black Power era, George moves from naïve hope in gradual, assimilationist progress to an aggressively separatist politics of grievance and recrimination. But before his conversion is complete, he experiences a period of profound, unmasked grief.

Put simply, when George is expelled from the master's house, he falls into a depression. "His head was lowered . . . [and] his voice was lower, too, softer, more unsure" (101). "I feel like a daid man gettin' hup ever' mawnin," he tells a friend. "There ain't nothin' to hope for, work toward. How kin you go on, knowin' that?" (105). What George describes is not only disappointment at his reduced circumstances but, more important, disappointment of belief as well—a radical disruption to his long-standing optimism, which held that patience, loyalty, and the assumption of good faith would eventually bring the promise of freedom. "Didn't those years of service count for something? In all this, George decided, he'd been duped" (102).

Denied his belief in the righteousness of history and the eventuality of freedom, George is consoled and saved from catastrophic despair by a lazy, womanizing narcissist who convinces him that his Fall may in fact have been an awakening, "a period of purification of all things European." (This friend, who is also Minty's father, is *Oxherding Tale's* most cutting "clever, sneering lampoon" of black cultural nationalism.) The friend's perspective initially provides George with an adaptive strategy in the face of certain nihilism, but it quickly deteriorates into a "spell of hatred" that interminably forestalls his full apprehension of loss and grief (142). If melancholia is, by definition, a remaking of the self through the foreswearal of an impossible love, then it is surely the psychic model for George's post-lapsarian reconstitution. The love and loss of something resembling Civil Rights idealism give way to George's politicized rebirth as a proto-black cultural nationalist.

Furthermore, this love and loss pre-figure the formation of another new identity, as Andrew's birth into slavery metaphorizes the invention of the contemporary narrative of slavery. Born of post–Civil Rights melancholia and bearing an impossible love for Minty, the unsalvageable slave, Andrew's biography takes shape as a thinly veiled genesis story of African American literature's historical turn. In this story, the melancholic devastation of George's optimistic worldview produces the (re-)birth of a slave, figured as a modern son who will carry an impossible (melancholic) attachment to trauma.

Complicating Johnson's narrative, Andrew is not a static and transparent representation of George's proto–post–Civil Rights melancholia but an ambivalent heir to that psycho-affective disposition. Like all children, he identifies with and against his parent; like an ambivalent child, the parody of the contemporary narrative of slavery identifies with and against its original form. Indeed, much as Evelyn begins to write a protest novel only to discover its impossibility and to rage against her forsworn love, Andrew enacts a similar pattern in the name of the contemporary narrative of slavery, initiating an emancipatory labor he cannot fulfill and later converting his impossible desire into a "burlesque" of the love that "couldn't be" (143). Reflecting the wish that the contemporary novel might redeem the reverberating injuries of the near and distant past, *Oxherding Tale* begins with Andrew's vow that "[Minty] and I, George and Mattie—all the bondsmen in Cripplegate's quarters and abroad—would grow old in the skins of free man" (15). Yet, by the novel's end, Minty is made grotesque, while George becomes simple, cowardly, and ridiculous.

And yet. "Can you . . . still love and believe in something when . . . you *know* you can't have it?" (143, Johnson's italics). Although George is the novel's most mercilessly ridiculed character, he is also, persistently, its most beloved. So many of Andrew's cruelest utterances against his father dovetail with professions of love—a disenchanted love, but one that will not be relinquished. "He would reject me, claiming that I had rejected him, and this was partially true," Andrew concedes. "But I loved my father. What would I not have given for him to be . . . proud of me?" (142). Denying Andrew both the catharsis of reparative return, on the one hand, and the relief of self-emancipation from historical feeling, on the other, Johnson instead introduces a dynamic and anti-teleological model for conceptualizing the interplay of impossible attachments and warring desires. If Minty, Evelyn, and George collectively produce Johnson's commentary on African American literature's historical desire, then a fourth allegorical figure, the Soulcatcher, reorients the reader to this discourse by representing a critical alternative to the hermeneutics of therapeutic/prohibitive reading.

### The Bounty Hunter

The Soulcatcher—or Horace Bannon, as he is otherwise known—is a villain who is a caricature of a villain. "The slave catcher of all slave catchers,"[31] he is an uncouth, sadistic, cloaked "tormentor" with "weapons up the yin-yang, [who] seemed able to sniff out slaves anywhere" (53, 77). Yet the ostensible one-dimensionality of Bannon's "villainy" is in fact a façade. Bursting from the seams of stereotype in unusual and often alarming ways, he bodies forth an unpredictable threat within a seemingly formulaic and known plot. The most minimally seasoned reader expects Bannon's appearance to signal for Andrew one of two familiar fates—entrapment or escape—but Bannon surprises both the protagonist's and the reader's expectation. We assumed we knew the economy of the book's fictional reality, we anticipated its movement from slavery to fugitivity to freedom or recapture. Instead, the Soulcatcher discloses that the terms of the hunt are not what they appeared to be, and we find ourselves, with Andrew, "in a different, new . . . relationship with everything [we hold] dear" (148).

More than any other character in *Oxherding Tale*, Bannon acts directly on the reader, not through his manipulation of sympathetic identification or vicarious traumatization, but by unsettling the reader's relationship to a known plot, in ways that produce uneasiness, defamiliarization, and terrorized suspense. Blurring the line between the familiar and the unfamiliar to act on the reader's "moods" and "expectations," the Soulcatcher brings to mind Freud's theory of the uncanny—a "species of the frightening" whose mechanism of terror consists precisely in the eerie, self-contradictory co-habitation of familiarity (*das Heimliche*) and unfamiliarity (*das Unheimliche*).[32]

Bannon channels the uncanny not only in his manipulations of the slave narrative as literary form but also in his role as our protagonist's foil and unnerving double. Freud illustrates the uncanny through the figure of a double that contains the parts of our ego from which we estrange ourselves through repression. This double holds not only "what is objectionable to self-criticism" but also "all the possibilities which, had they been realized, might have shaped our destiny, and to which our imagination still clings, all the strivings of the ego that were frustrated by adverse circumstances, all the suppressed acts of volition that fostered the illusion of free will." Bearing the ghostly psychic burden of unfulfilled histories and inoperative desires, "the double [becomes] an object of terror, just as [gods] become demons after the collapse of their cult."[33]

Consider Bannon in this way: Recalling the image of his would-be victim, the Soulcatcher bears a startlingly hybrid phenotype and dons "clothes [that] were a cross between house . . . and fields" (68), evoking the potent, though unverifiable, suspicion that he is a fugitive in disguise. Moreover, he consolidates Andrew's most shameful values and traits with a catalog of lost possibilities and unfulfilled desires. He is ruthless, amoral, and anti-heroic, and, as we will see, his mystical body houses the history of Andrew's lost attachments. Andrew runs from this unwelcome mirror but indicates his covert identification with Bannon when he confesses, near the end of the book, that "only the Soulcatcher knew the secrets of my history and heart. . . . I was . . . bound to him, had produced him from myself" (169–170).

In the constitutive tension that binds and divides Andrew and Bannon, Johnson locates an intra-psychic conflict at the heart of the contemporary African American literary imagination. The Soulcatcher, Andrew's dogged pursuer, is what the contemporary narrative of slavery represses: its "wounded attachments" to the traumatic past, its vulnerability to seduction by nihilistic despair. These are the shadow impulses Andrew runs from and aspires to out-maneuver, though he feels, persistently, the force of their encroachment. Andrew's fugitive escape enacts the contemporary narrative of slavery's avowed impulse toward freedom, but—recalling the Freudian maxim that what is repressed is not banished but continuously strains toward consciousness[34]—the specter of the Soulcatcher looms over the latter half of the novel, where Andrew lives under the escalating pressure of the warning, "he'll kill you if you slip" (116).

Again recalling the uncanny, the method of Bannon's "delicate, difficult hunt" involves the performative duplication of his prey. "It ain't so much overpowerin' him physically, when you huntin' a Negro, as it is mentally," he explains. "Yo mind has to soak hup his mind. His heart. . . . You *become* a Negro by lettin' yoself see what he sees, feel what he feels, want what he wants" (114–115, Johnson's italics). Over the course of his pursuit, the Soulcatcher gradually absorbs the history of his antagonist's visions, feelings, and desires. This "[explains] Bannon's Negroid speech, his black idiosyncrasies, tics absorbed from the countless bondsmen he'd assassinated." In turn, the fugitive becomes a grotesquely literalized split subject, inhabited by the bounty hunter's destructive desire (which, Bannon hopes, was the fugitive's secret desire all along). When the duplication is complete—when the Soulcatcher's mimetic study locates the fugitive's countervailing wish for unfreedom—only then does the bounty hunter capture and kill: "His capture happens like a wish, somethin' he wants, a destiny that come from inside him, not outside" (115). Will Andrew come to *desire* slavery and thus ensure his demise, or will he remain steadfast in his pursuit of freedom? Can the contemporary narrative of slavery as a literary form out-maneuver the destructive desire that swells within it? Like those novels that take masochism as their organizing trope, these are the questions that push *Oxherding Tale*'s plot forward.

Yet they are also questions that Johnson provocatively evades. For Andrew does "slip" when he despairs at Minty's death and the attendant loss of his fantasy of romantic heroism. In this moment, as his tormentor foretold, he sees in Bannon "the familiar quirks of my friend" (169) and "[realizes] the futility of resistance" (170). But in the same moment, Andrew becomes the beneficiary of Reb's fortitude, and because the Soulcatcher's retirement precedes Andrew's onset of nihilism, the plot matriculates neither to Andrew's victory nor to his defeat. Departing from the plot structure that it ostensibly adopts, *Oxherding Tale* declines to become a book about Andrew wresting freedom from Bannon or Bannon quashing this desire. The novel's constitutive tension is not resolved but de-escalated and supplanted by a new model of historical feeling and relationality.

When Andrew learns of his unexpected freedom, he feels a pang of remorse for his father, who died years ago at Bannon's hands. He asks after George—his question a mixture of mockery, shame, and genuine sorrow—"and then the Soulcatcher did a strange thing." Unbuttoning his shirt to reveal his upper body, he exposes to Andrew

> an impossible flesh tapestry of a thousand individualities no longer static, mere drawings, but if you looked at them long enough, bodies moving like Lilliputians over the surface of his skin. Not tattooes at all, I saw but forms sardined in his contour, creatures Bannon had killed since childhood. . . . The commonwealth of the dead shape-shifted on his chest, his full belly, his fat shoulders and yet all were conserved in this process of doubling, nothing was lost in the masquerade. . . . Behind every different mask at the party . . . the selfsame face was uncovered at midnight, and this was my father, appearing briefly in the dead boy Moon as he gave Flo Hatfield a goodly stroke and, at the instant of convulsive orgasm, opened

his mouth as wide as that of the dying steer Bannon slew in his teens. . . .
The profound mystery of the One and the Many gave me back my father
again and again . . . and, in the final face I saw in the Soulcatcher, which
shook tears from me—my own face, for he had duplicated portions of me
during the early days of the hunt. (175–176)

In this bizarre and fantastical mirror scene, Johnson re-invents the arc
of the freedom quest itself by rejecting the possibility of an un-burdened,
autonomous hero. When he first determines to free himself, Andrew
makes a vow that prohibitive reading would welcome: that, "whatever
my origin, I would be wholly responsible for the shape I gave myself in
the future" (17). But the "freeman" Johnson delivers at the novel's end is,
not such a self-determining, monadic subject, but a speaking self per-
petually ghosted by that which it necessarily—but never completely—
discards. If Andrew's hopeful premonition was that he would "escape
destruction" by eschewing his father and the "strategies that poisoned
[him]" (117), then surely he is surprised at the moment when freedom
arrives, to be "[given] back [his] father again and again." Yet neither is
patrilineal reconciliation tangible or complete, as proponents of therapeutic reading might wish. Contradiction, bad feeling, lost and embarrassing love objects, impossible desire: These are neither available
to retroactive change nor what Andrew must give up in the name of
self-possession; they are the inextinguishable conditions of life, which
the hero finally confronts in the self-reflecting image of Bannon's "flesh
tapestry" (176).

Making reference to a Zen parable in which enlightenment looks like
the transcendence of identity, the novel's title invites a reading in which
the epiphanic revelation of the Soulcatcher's "tattoo" releases Andrew
from his figurative enslavement to the concomitant notions of the liberal
subject and the racial self. By abandoning Western taxonomies of identity,
the argument goes, Andrew evades the false choice between traumatic
enmeshment with, or total detachment from, history and community.
Reading thusly, Jonathan Little describes "Andrew's sea change of consciousness, in which he moves from a primarily ego-centered Western
perspective to a Buddhist and Hindu conception of the benefits of the
loss of the self." Similarly, Rudolph P. Byrd finds that, by "achieving moksha [the Buddhist term for enlightenment]," Andrew comes to "[stand]

within as well as on the outside of the conventional constructions of race and consciousness. . . . By virtue of this complex positioning, he literally and figuratively bodies forth an alternative mode of being in the world 'that constitutes an affirmation beyond opposites of all kinds.'"[35]

To the degree that readings of this culminating scene suggest a triumphalist view of Andrew's maturation, I am inclined to push back. For one thing, we would be wise to remember that Bannon's revelation is not the fruit of Andrew's spiritual achievement; it's Reb's.[36] As our protagonist clarifies, Reb's "Way" is one of "strength and spiritual heroism," but "it was not *my* Way" (77). Indeed, Hayward, Keizer, and Ahsraf Rushdy have ably shown that, to the novel's end, Andrew remains flawed and un-self-aware in persistently "Western" and profoundly consequential ways: most of all in his "resolute denial of [the] social forces" that prop up his life of white, "bourgeois contentment."[37] But suppose the Soulcatcher's "body mosaic" (175) appears not to signal Andrew's matriculation to the status of post-racial hero but to occasion, for Andrew, the ephemeral wonder of the reader who discovers, in the "text" of Bannon's body, a new way of seeing the known world. Suppose, in other words, that the triumphalism of the novel's final pages pertains not to *identity* but to *hermeneutics*.[38]

Like a text, the Soulcatcher's body bears the inscription of the slave past, mimetically copied in the forms and psychic structures of the dead. "Yo mind has to soak hup his mind. His heart," Bannon candidly explains, when in an early encounter he instructs Andrew to read him as a faithful record of the un-redeemed, ever threatening to overtake the soul of the present (114–115). In this way, Bannon initially appears as one of the novel's several descriptions of history's manifestations in the present, alongside "the archival tomb of literary history" (118) and the romantic fantasy of Minty's rescue. But when the villain retires, he presents his body to Andrew as a different kind of text, revealing, in his "flesh tapestry" (175), a revision and critical alternative to previously articulated visions of how history may appear in and for literature. Now the history transcribed on the Soulcatcher's body is a history outside of time. Its disorderly contents are a trove of lost affects and objects, old and new, inherited and acquired. They are not frozen in place, in the strict order and form of their happening, but mobilized in fantastical, irreverent, internally inconstant ways.

Having abandoned the hunt, Bannon is no longer a familiar threat or villain, coercing our hero's righteous purpose and direction. Discarding the ideals of historical fidelity and redemptive witnessing, he comes into view as a vibrant but aimless repository—a proliferating, "shape-shifting," ungovernable psychic record of what we still miss, love, or otherwise feel. Through this culminating image of infinite "doubling" and "masquerade," the Soulcatcher directs the reader toward an alternative hermeneutical expectation: that the act of reading need not deliver us from impossible desire, and that the agency of literature may consist simply in the creative, propulsive recycling of desire. What Bannon offers Andrew in the name of freedom is thus a figure for what African American literature's historical turn holds out to the contemporary reader: the endless re-presentation of desire as revelation and disguise, the realization of desire's capacity for unpredictable transformation, and steadfast resistance to the will to be done with desire.

## Subjects of Historical Desire

I want to hold on to what strikes me as the useful core of *Oxherding Tale*'s alternative approach to African American literature, premised on the free-form, re-combinatory circulation of historical desire. But it is also essential to confront the limit of Johnson's proposed hermeneutic, which we find symbolically condensed in the fact that women are literally *unreadable* in the text of Bannon's body. Though the scene of Bannon's revelation is brief and the sample of his constituents is accordingly small, it is remarkable that neither of the novel's black women—be it the tragic Minty or the benevolent stepmother Mattie—surfaces in the culminating image of infinite flexibility in our psycho-affective attachments to the past. Indeed, only one woman qualifies for Andrew's descriptive inventory of the Soulcatcher's magical display: She is the white slaveholder Flo Hatfield, whose femininity is mitigated by both her infiltration of a masculine economy and the protagonist's obscuring declaration that "she was the creature of men; she was me" (72). (Even so, Flo's appearance within "the profound mystery of the One and the Many" reproduces her exclusively as the passive object of male sexuality; 176.)

This limitation is not accidental, nor is it anomalous to the spirit of the book. In fact, throughout the novel, Andrew remains stubborn and explicit in his insistence that women are "remote and strange" to the world of men (16). Following the example of his childhood tutor, he learns to harness his lust and fear by equating women "with Nature (and with terror)," regarding them as "passive objects of fecundity [and] deliberate agents of doom."[39] Thus cloaked in the protagonist's dread and desire, *Oxherding Tale*'s women—most of all, its black women—inhabit the book like "a strangely absent presence,"[40] imbued with literary meaning but evacuated of character. Which is to say, not only does the novel tend to represent women stereotypically or not at all, it relies on women's mis- and non-representation in order to produce its system of literary meaning. We may recall, pessimistically, the problem of Minty's representational abjection, and her enduring subordination to Andrew's metaphorical needs.

To be sure, this literary stage on which women are ever "illusory like moonlight on pond water" more accurately describes Andrew's mindset than Johnson's (16). I would be remiss if I did not mention that the author often seems to be winking at the reader, mocking Andrew's interpretations by depicting them in comedic hyperbole. Indeed, this is one of the great pleasures of *Oxherding Tale* for the feminist reader: its teasing caricature of a self-indulgent and objectifying male gaze. Here, for instance, is how Andrew describes Minty in the early stages of his infatuation:

> I was stung sorely, riveted to the spot, relieved, Lord knows, of my reason. . . . I saw her eyes—eyes green as icy mountain meltwater, with a hint of blue shadow and a drowse of sensuality that made her seem voluptuously sleepy, distant, as though she had been lifted long ago from a melancholy African landscape overrich with the colors and warm smells of autumn—a sad, out-of-season beauty suddenly precious to me. . . . Her name, now that I think on it, might have been Zeudi—Ethiopian, ancient, as remote and strange, now that something in me had awoken, as Inca ruins or shards of pottery from the long-buried cities of Mu. (15–16)

Even in this abbreviated form, the extraordinary excess of such a soliloquy (to say nothing of its anachronistic ribbing at the masculinist language of racial romanticism) undermines its content. It invites the reader, through laughter, to take the self-serious Andrew down a notch.

In this peculiar way, and particularly in earlier portions of the book, *Oxherding Tale* embeds its own feminist critique of itself in its plainly revealed textual self-consciousness.

What disappoints, then, is not that Johnson is blind to his protagonist's misogynistic worldview but that he offers no viable alternative through which women can enter into representation. We know that Andrew's narration is not entirely to be trusted, but this knowledge does not allow the novel's female characters—their losses, their grievances, their loves, their desires—to come more fully into view. Moreover, this knowledge does not unmake the text's strategic, symbolic use of women as the primary, often abusively "embodied [sites]" for the novel's "highly abstract and metaphysical speculations."[41] Without discarding the ambitious promise of *Oxherding Tale*'s final revelation, what might it look like to more fully realize the gendered dimensions of our thinking about historical desire, particularly from the vantage point of complexly developed women subjects?

For several reasons, this question directs me to Morrison's *Paradise* (1997), a novel whose central dramas revolve around the masculinist narration of history, the interior lives of women, and intra-racial embattlements over the task of interpretation. Despite obvious differences in register, style, and plot, *Oxherding Tale* and *Paradise* share a strikingly similar narrative project. Both are "serious [works] of fiction which also [function] as [parables]"—and, "effectively and ironically, [as works] of literary criticism";[42] both are concerned with what forms racial remembrance will take in the post–Civil Rights era; both are attentive to the seductions of traumatic and melancholic memory yet critical of nostalgia and wounded attachments to a history of racial injury; both envision history as a palimpsest, at once ineradicable and irretrievable; and both culminate in utopian images of self-consciously—indeed, joyously—impure access to history's psycho-affective residuum. But to this catalog of shared and fascinating attributes, *Paradise* adds a direct feminist rejoinder to the feminine absence in books like *Oxherding Tale*, reproducing for critique a range of assumptions, correlations, and gendered norms and stereotypes that consolidate a dangerous and flawed sense of history as "a male concept of time."[43] Moreover, *Paradise* issues this critique from a deftly imagined, poly-vocal space of feminine interiority—symbolically concretized as a makeshift refuge for transient, homeless women, at the outskirts of a town "deafened by the roar of its own history."[44]

Thus I submit that a reading of *Paradise* will complicate and extend Johnson's hermeneutical ideal while also demonstrating its profound applicability and force. In addition, because it is the third and final installment of Morrison's "love trilogy"—the sequence of novels beginning with *Beloved*, whose narrative arc spans from the antebellum period to the post–Civil Rights era—*Paradise* will enable the present study's circuitous return, through Johnson's rogue take on the contemporary narrative of slavery to a refreshed encounter with the genre's ur-text. Here I read *Paradise* as neither a correction nor a straightforward continuation of *Beloved* and *Jazz* but as a diffuse relation that becomes a prism for encountering *Beloved*'s field-changing exploration of the slave past differently.

*Paradise* is set in the all-black town of Ruby, Oklahoma, whose dwindling population descends from an insular band of post-Reconstruction homesteaders. Driven out of the Deep South by racist vigilantism and unwelcome in the settlements of their light-complexioned, more affluent brethren, fifteen founding families establish a town called Haven (later relocated and renamed Ruby). Their traumatic origin story becomes sacred communal lore, repeated and reenacted with fidelity so it comes to stand like "some fortress you . . . built up and have to keep everybody locked in or out" (213). Set primarily in the years between 1968 and 1976, the novel follows two conflicts over how to read the past, one internal to Ruby and the other at Ruby's border with the outside world.

The former conflict grows out of a generational divide. The town patriarchs wish to preserve and transmit the past through mimetic, unadulterated repetition. "As though past heroism was enough of a future to live by. As though, rather than children, they wanted duplicates" (161). The sons question the relevance of Ruby's traumatic history for their present, marked by communal fracturing and "the desolation that rose after King's murder, a desolation that climbed like a tidal wave in slow motion" (160). They wish to abandon or transform it, "to kill it [or to] change it into something they made up" (86).

The second conflict pits Ruby against a motley collective of unattached women living at the town's margins. Rumored to be witches, abortionists, and lesbians, the women defy Ruby's terms of conservative sociality and historical legibility. Their home, commonly known as the Convent, stands in dramatic contrast to Ruby's ideal of a restored, insular, and continuous racial genealogy. Whereas Ruby invests in a social fiction of historical constancy, the Convent (which is not really a convent) bears the traces of its re-purposing over time: It has been an embezzler's mansion, a Catholic school for indigenous girls, and now a sanctuary for women fleeing misfortune. On occasion, women, misfits, and even town elders wander from Ruby toward the Convent, but such action is discreet, proscribed, and generally disavowed.

Here are the plot's most rudimentary touchstones: Between 1968 and 1973, the Convent acquires four new residents, following disparate, accidental routes from different personal histories and corners of the country. Each woman flees from dangerous or despairing personal circumstances: abusive and unfaithful husbands and lovers, child loss, mother loss, political violence, rape. Stopping at the Convent, "the one place they were free to leave," they join Consolata, a blind and aging healer who bears witness to their personal histories of unrelieved suffering (262). Consolata is the Convent's oldest tenant, having arrived nearly fifty years prior, in the care of a nun who rescued or abducted her from an exploited childhood in the streets of Brazil.

When the Ruby patriarchs panic about the families' diminishing numbers and the next generation's apathy, the women at the Convent become convenient scapegoats, common enemies to bridge the town's generational divide. An inter-generational gang of Ruby men plans and executes a raid on the Convent. The raid comes on the heels of a euphoric communal cleansing ritual, in which the Convent women matriculate, to borrow a phrase from Carola Hilfrich, to an "anarchically embodied enunciative position [as] historical and narrative subjects."[45] In a crime of convenience and displaced aggression, the Ruby gang shoots them, but they vanish into the grass.

*Paradise* is decidedly unsubtle in its depiction and critique of history as a masculinist discourse. Because Ruby's self-story is secured through a ritual of devotion that requires the replication of the present in the image of the past, its persistence in its being is contingent upon a carefully controlled, insular system of "unadulterated and unadultried" reproduction (217). The continuous narrative of Ruby's history, in other words, depends upon patriarchal policing of communal boundaries, particularly at the site of women's sexuality and reproductive potential. As the town historian discovers, "everything that worries [the ruling patriarchs] must come from women" (217).

Moreover, the debate over how to represent and transmit historical legacy is staged as an exclusive dispute between the patriarchs and their would-be successors. Ruby's public forums are dominated by men, while women's speech is alternately cast as interior, peripheral, relegated to the private sphere, or otherwise informal. Although the younger men defy their father's vision of historical legacy, they have no quarrel with masculine power as such. Thus the town's most prominent public debate takes as its topic the prerogative of the younger men to re-interpret historical decree in their own image, and a hotly contested youthful rebellion consists in a young man's exogamous sexual pursuit of a forbidden Convent woman. (One recalls Andrew Hawkins's individuation from George, wrested in declarations of rejection and sexual congress with white women). These sites of conflict and others like them reveal a contested historical discourse that nevertheless consolidates a selective account of what happened—the stories of "Great Men"—and perpetuates an exclusive apparatus of gendered power.

The novel's critique of patriarchal (or fraternal) historiography finds concise and explicit critique in the mouth of Patricia Best, the town genealogist. Initially reminiscent of the historian-hero of David Bradley's *Chaneysville Incident*, Pat begins to record town history through a method that prioritizes the meticulously fact-checked, bare-bones documentation of patrilineal descent: "a collection of family trees; the genealogies of each of the fifteen families. Upside-down trees, the trunks sticking in the air, the branches sloping down" (187). In infrastructure and content, this "history project" reifies Ruby's "official story" as it is passed down and recited by the patriarchs (187, 188).

But Pat quickly finds herself dissatisfied with the absence of "footnotes, crevices, or questions," so she begins to "supplement the branches of who begat whom" with increasingly detailed, digressive, and subjective annotations (188, 187). If the family trees recapitulate the authorized public history of Ruby, then Pat's notes turn to conventionally feminine discursive domains—family Bibles, gossip, and "her students' autobiographical compositions" (187)—to assemble a more substantive but suppressed account of the past that "starts with the local, the immediate, and the personal."[46] As her notes proliferate, Pat "[gives] up all pretense to objective comment" and discovers that "she didn't want or need any further research" (187). The family trees remain at the center of her notebooks and continue to exert force over the general direction of events, but the ever-amassing annotations apply a counter-force against the story of patriarchal descent, reframing the focus of familial history within an unruly web of relations.[47]

To be sure, Pat's redirected interest does not anticipate her overthrow of Ruby's patriarchy. On the contrary, she remains subject to the law and logic of Ruby—she is even a ruthless enforcer of the town's disciplinary judgment—and she ultimately determines that her notebooks are "unfit for any eyes except her own" (187). Still, the content of Pat's study highlights women's central role in perpetuating or foreclosing the insular continuity of patriarchal society, alerting Pat to women's potential to be subversive historical actors. And the form of her study, with its sprawling narrative overgrowth, exposes the official history as selective and partial and foreshadows the Convent women's radical, anti-genealogical challenge to Ruby's accepted modes of historical engagement and representation.

If Ruby is a social and narrative space in which women's counter-memories must be contained or occluded, then from the vantage point of the town's official history, the Convent women are literal excess. They are "detritus: throwaway people" (4), not only exotic to the numbered bloodlines that make up the town's population, but unmoored as well from the very formations that would confer social legibility, such as family, genealogy, or a claim to place. Like Haven's founders, the women are driven to a "backward noplace" (308) by rejection and disappointment, but in almost every way, their micro-society inverts the traits and values of the town. The town is a hermetic space of genetic continuity while the Convent is populated by "drifters"; the town is controlling while the Convent is permissive; the town is consumed with a singular, original trauma while the Convent accumulates discrepant voices like a palimpsest; the town is ordered by patriarchal governance while the Convent is "permeated with a blessed malelessness, like a protected domain, free of hunters but exciting too" (177).

Thus, when the Ruby men descend upon the Convent, what they see is history's "outside": what is not only foreign to existing knowledge but fragmentary, meaningless, unable to cohere. Measuring the Convent's assorted contents against the recognizable structure of the town's historical self-story, they find nothing legible and nothing worthy of interpretation. Yet, much like Pat's sparse family trees that cannot hold back the uncontainable proliferation of meaningful detail, the oppositional logic that divides Ruby from the Convent repeatedly breaks down. As Patricia Storace enumerates, "Two Ruby men have affairs with Convent women; another, an alcoholic, experiences a wild detoxification there, unable to admit his addiction within the Ruby city limits. Arnette Fleetwood, who is pregnant by the scion of a prominent Ruby family, a condition all Ruby suspects but will not acknowledge, goes to the Convent with the equally unacknowledged purpose of aborting the child." Rather than a foreign and unknowable "out there," the Convent "inadvertently becomes the vault for all of Ruby's secrets. . . . [Its] dangerous witchiness is as much Ruby's as its own."[48]

Mimicking but exceeding the images of the corrupted distance between town and Convent, and Patricia's once-orderly but now irrevocably unruly notebooks, *Paradise* itself crowds out the tidy, redundant narrative of Ruby's founding through a sheer abundance of women's voices that de-center and overwhelm it. Morrison allocates an eponymous chapter to each of the Convent women, in which she introduces them through intimate portraits of personal traumas they endure prior to arriving at the Convent. The women are historically situated, and some of their complaints are heavy with historical meaning, but the narration consistently denies the register of historical epic in favor of rich, local detail. In turn, the effusion of detail strains against the contained, linear narrative that the simple chapter titles might lead us to expect. Though the women's stories are irreducible to one another, they are also porous, meandering, and uncontained by the designated boundaries of the chapters.

Many critics have commented on the difficulty of reading *Paradise* in light of its unwieldy construction. Louis Menand, for example, makes note of "the energy we have to spend puzzling out the various pieces and getting them into some kind of satisfactory narrative shape." For Menand, this "obscurity" is classically Morrisonian: "Morrison," he reminds us, "has always been careful to make her writing elliptical."[49] Without disputing this stylistic point, I would add that the nature and function of *Paradise*'s narrative complexity is markedly different from that of, say, *Beloved*. *Beloved* is challenging and elliptical because its task is to represent the elusive violence of psychic trauma, which is so often experienced as a kind of interruptive recursivity. But traumatic time is not *Paradise*'s narrative mode (except in some of its internal recounting of Ruby's history). Rather, the latter text's difficulty results from a feminist effort to explode the "upside down tree" (*Paradise*, 187) as the presumptive shape of historical narration. In spatial terms, *Beloved* destabilizes its chronology by sprawling backward in time; *Paradise* destabilizes its narrative coherence by sprawling outward in an ever-expanding web of sociality.

The point is not that women are anti-historical or outside of history or beyond historical comprehension—or, as Andrew Hawkins's tutor posits, that historical thought stands in irreducible opposition to women's "rhythms of birth and destruction, the Way of absorption, passivity, cycle and epicycle" (*Oxherding Tale*, 31). Rather, *Paradise* challenges us to re-imagine or re-invent history's narrative form, with attention to how gender, a social form, structures our most entrenched understandings of the legible world. What constitutes an event? What kinds of relationships or attachments merit representation? What forces—psychic and material—bind the self to the community? Through what kinds of formations do we recognize historical continuity or discontinuity? What do we long for, and what do we long to expunge when we look to the past? If the consuming question facing contemporary black literary studies has been how to conceptualize the meaning and relevance of the racial past, then *Paradise* seeks to understand how this inquiry is pre-figured by the gendered politics of who and what get to count as historical in the first place.

Symbolizing both what Ruby represses and a fantasy space that defies extant norms of historical intelligibility and organization, the Convent is the edifice through which Morrison most expansively imagines alternative and foreclosed approaches to historical representation, interpretation, and desire. Significantly, its built environment invites us to imagine, not an Edenic history without patriarchy, but a *post*-patriarchal domain of possibility, where the articulation of "every true thing is okay" (38). Morrison actively avows our inheritance of a violently masculinist record of American history in the Convent's architecture and interior design. "This masculinist mansion of iniquity, turned Convent"[50] bears the traces of history's obfuscating desire, fear, and reverence for women in its bizarre and unfocused assortment of objects and signs: The embezzler's lewd and opulent décor peeks through the nuns' austere and pious remodeling. What is novel about the Convent, then, is neither its content nor its infrastructure but the manner in which it is inhabited and repurposed when it becomes, in Erica R. Edwards's words, "a sanctuary for women and a queer space that allows for the doing of different things."[51] Carrying their own psychic baggage and material effects, the drifting women overwrite their dwelling like a palimpsest, allowing the Convent to come into view as a site of arbitrary and intentional human interaction antedated by past events that unevenly intrude upon the conditions of the present. As a lens on to the past, *Paradise*'s post-patriarchal Convent is capacious, accommodating, and dis-interested, as well as mystical, female, and multi-ethnic. This is why it is precisely what the Ruby patriarchs must excise to reify their own, immobilized and over-determined account of a teleological, self-authorizing past.

How and what do the women write on the palimpsestic text of history? In the novel's climactic scene, Morrison depicts this act as a healing ritual and an exorcism, which begins in the mansion's cellar and matriculates to its garden. Consolata—familiar yet deified, the women's "ideal parent, friend [and] companion" (262)—officiates a ceremony that begins with a series of acts resembling "a ritual practice of the Afro-Brazilian religion, Candomblé."[52] First, the women undress and lie naked on the floor, bearing witness to Consolata's personal testimony of love and loss, as she paints outlines of their bodies in each woman's chosen posture. "How should we lie? However you feel" (263). Literally etching the "sensualized externality of [each woman's] inward [life]"[53] onto the subterranean chamber—the unconscious—of the house of historical accretion, Consolata's "templates" allow the women to convert their shapeless histories of suffering into a collaborative and open-ended search for "what [they] are hungry for" (262). Rising from their templates, they join in a collective act of testimony: "That is how the loud dreaming began. How the stories rose in that place. Half-tales and the never-dreamed escaped from their lips to soar high above guttering candles. . . . And it was never important to know who said the dream or whether it had meaning. In spite of or because their bodies ache, they step easily into the dreamer's tale. . . . In loud dreaming, monologue is no different from a shriek; accusations directed to the dead and long gone are undone by murmurs of love" (264).

The women's speech acts are accompanied by embellishments to their sketched bodies. They fill the outlines with figurative and abstract symbols—"careful etchings of body parts and memorabilia." "They spoke to each other about what had been dreamed and what had been drawn," urging the conversation forward "but gently, without joking or scorn" (265). Eventually, after their arduous labor of coming into representation, they emerge from the Convent, free to express without encumbrance "the rapture of holy women dancing in hot sweet rain" (283).

As a unique form of expressing the past, "loud dreaming" defies the most basic requirements for coherent, historical representation. It is uninvested in narrative wholeness, it demands no proof or attribution, it is poly-vocal and not homogenizing, and it accommodates abstract, non-narrative expression. Perhaps most surprisingly, it subordinates the reification of meaning to the experience of speaking and witnessing. This is why it never matriculates to a fixed and repeatable story, even as it compels engagement and leaves a lasting mark.

Morrison stresses that, although the women succeed in wresting narrative form from the "cellar" of their repressed possibility, their stories remain largely incomprehensible to the uninitiated. "A customer stopping by would have noticed little change" (265). More consequentially, when the Ruby men raid the mansion, they find nothing more than a succession of disorderly and indecipherable scenes—pornography, they surmise, and "Satan's scrawl" (303). Thus the achievement of self-representation is rendered distinct from the guarantee of reception, and the act of the women's triumphant testimony does not mitigate their vulnerability to attack. (If anything, it does the opposite.)

And yet, the ritual of "loud dreaming" *does* appear to usher the women into a space of magical existence, ambiguously kin to immortality and figuratively reminiscent of the indefinite afterlives of literature itself. Shortly after the raid, all of the women are presumed dead—four of them shot down as they ran "like panicked does" through the grass behind the mansion, and one shot and killed in plain sight (18). But when the undertaker arrives to retrieve the bodies, all of them have mysteriously vanished. The reader learns none of the details that might explain this magical disappearance, nor is she privy to how or why, in the book's final pages, the women flicker back into view, in a series of brief, de-contextualized fantasies of each woman's narrative resolution. If, as Storace cleverly proposes, the Ruby men "treat Ruby like authors who want to stop the life of their work at the moment of writing, [unable to] endure . . . the myriad readings and misreadings it will encounter beyond the author's conception of it,"[54] then Morrison's implausible re-introduction of the women at the novel's end would seem to express an opposite wish, inviting the reader to engage in the imaginative, promiscuous re-circulation of the Convent women's stories.

Presenting an imaginary space in which traces and symbols of the past circulate in indefinite, recombinatory relation, the Convent ritual and its aftereffects bring to mind the lively necropolis of the Soulcatcher's tattoo. Both retain the un-fixed residue of trauma, loss, love, and desire. They value and invite memory as a psychoanalyst might: as "the past, ghost-written as desire, [and] driving us into the future."[55] But Morrison also offers an important variation on Johnson's vision of such an ideal. As we have seen, Andrew's description of the Soulcatcher's "flesh tapestry" tacitly reifies the domain of the historical in conventionally masculine depictions of hero and event—hunting, sexual conquest, and father-son reconciliation dominate the scene, and indeed, the author's awesome vision of creative infinitude is tellingly contained in the hyper-masculine body of a violent man. Bursting through the apparatus of narrative containment, Morrison gives us the figure of magical, vanishing women, and radically reimagines what counts as worthy of narration, delving into the mundane and dramatic depths of women's lives.

Here, we must note that the Convent holds more than the specific history of this fictional frontier town. It is also inter-textually penetrated by other ghostly formations that produce a dreamy, intangible exchange between the women's twentieth-century memories and feelings and a broader range of historical event and affect. This is how *Paradise* asserts its place within the series that begins with *Beloved*: not through genetic connection, in the way that *Jazz* introduces us to Beloved's probable son, but through the kind of compulsive figural, thematic, and imagistic repetition Freud associates with serial dreams that "[form] part of the same whole, . . . giving expression to the same impulses in different material."[56] Infusing *Paradise* with the uncanny sensibility of a serial dream,

Morrison redescribes a house of women haunted by ghost children and saturated with mother and daughter loss; the mysterious arrival of a ravenous daughter who emerges from a watery trauma and introduces herself by spelling her name; a spiritual mother figure who guides a collective in reclaiming and loving their pained bodies; the merging of women in a ritual of grief closed off from the outside world; the exorcism of ghosts; and the magical vanishing of women in the grass behind the haunted house.

What, we might wonder, does *Beloved* mean in and for *Paradise*? Taking my cue from Morrison's un-catchable women, I want to resist the impulse to a fixed, teleological interpretation. One could argue, of course, that *Beloved* is *Paradise*'s true origin, so that the latter text's meaning is ultimately traceable to the former text's discussion of slavery's traumatic persistence in memory. Or, following Freud's belief that repression is often loosened through repetitious speech, one could read *Paradise* as a later version of *Beloved* that brings to the surface some of the earlier novel's latent content. But I submit that the repetition of cryptic images moves, not toward resolution, but toward a thicker description of Morrison's historical impulse as it appears in "different materials." Its priority is not the discernment of cause (which historical locus is origin, and which is effect?) but a more intimate apprehension of historical desire's multi-directional pathways.

On this view, we may accept the tautology that historical trauma intensifies the grief of contemporary loss, while contemporary loss triggers, and perhaps hides itself in, a catalog of earlier, linked losses. Reading the love trilogy in this way, as part of an irreducible, non-teleological composite, displaces *Beloved*'s widely conferred status as primary or original and recasts the novel's singularity of focus on the slave past as part of a broadly constellated literary discourse on post–Civil Rights, African American historical desire. To the degree that *Beloved*, *Jazz*, and *Paradise* work together as a trilogy, they do so by co-producing an open circuit of proliferating re-description and interpretive possibility, leading the reader away from the expectation of certain, "sermonizable" meaning (*Paradise*, 297), toward "the threshold of mystery."[57] Evocative and un-containable, the recurring figure of the woman who escapes or disappears or "erupts into her separate parts" (*Beloved*, 323) bears the trilogy's hermeneutical key: an ideal of interpretive non-closure.

# Postscript

From its inception, African American formal writing has troubled conventions and norms of how to read. The slave narrative and, later, the protest novel, with their purposeful, often sentimental appeals and their urgent calls to action, plainly asked to be read for their literal truths, their moral and emotional claims, and their repudiation of (in Henry Louis Gates, Jr.'s unforgettable phrase) "the Western fiction of the 'text of blackness.'"[1] This is not to say that early African American literature is without beauty or attention to form but, more pointedly, that in its utmost urgency it belonged to the province of political speech. Above all else, its representational aims were activist, pedagogical, and documentary; its premise was that the act of reading would inspirit social change.

The conditions for today's black literary production do not demand literature's political agency above all else, and yet, from the perspective of the present, it remains un-realistic to imagine an African American literature that wholly supersedes or divests from *the political*. For if the political is the public realm in which individuals and collectives negotiate the terms of their aggregated representation, then "blackness" itself, however problematically, is a constitutively political sign. As Elizabeth Alexander argues in her extraordinary book, *Black Interiors*, African American racial representation is always, "regardless of the artist's intent," staged "against a history of deformation and annihilation of the black body and [thus] challenged with resisting or redirecting the current (though ancient) vogue for a stereotypical black realism."[2]

Of course, to say that a literature cannot shake its ties to the political is not to say that it must look or act according to a certain, fixed prescription. Nor is it to say that black writing is categorically or ideally instructive, transparent, or confined to "the face of the social self."[3] Indeed, Toni Morrison argues just the opposite when, in "The Site of Memory," she posits that her unique capacity and duty as a black writer in late modernity is to restore an "unwritten interior life" to our historical conceptions of African American subjectivity. In other words, her response to the stubborn publicity of the Gatesian text (and counter-text) of blackness is to illumine what it obscures: the human complexity that is denied by racism, on the one hand, or excised in the name of political expediency, on the other.[4]

Morrison's call to interiority may be interpreted as the mantra of the contemporary narrative of slavery more generally—that voluminous and proliferating archive of post–Civil Rights fiction which regards the traumatic past as its painful inheritance and the object of its reparative desire. Tacitly or explicitly, this genre presumes that if the "text of blackness" is an economic, political, and materialist formation (as surely it is), then it is also a historical discourse, a record of personal and collective psychic injury and resilience, and an axis of identification and desire. It depicts dramas of black interiority that exceed the frameworks of "resistance" or political action while nevertheless insisting on psychic life as a space of political potentiality.[5] This tradition of writing represents one origin of the present study, which similarly aims to dispel the esoteric reputation too often associated with the investigation of the inner life.

Contemporary narratives of slavery are by no means the first or only books to foreground intricacies of black psychic life, but I am drawn to them as objects of study because of their collective longevity and impact, because of the poly-vocal force with which they identify a cathected site in the contemporary racial imaginary (i.e., the slave past), and because they have inspired such impassioned critical debate about how they should be read and what happens when we read them. Critics have wondered: When we read the fictionally restored interior lives of enslaved African Americans, does the act of reading assume the status or function of political agency? Is our reading directed by our desire to, or our belief that we can, "claim the lives and efforts of history's defeated as ours either to redeem or to redress?"[6] Alternatively, does the reading of contemporary narratives of slavery embolden us to confront past and present in a way that is false, dangerous, or maladaptive? One assertion of the present volume has been that the question of how contemporary narratives of slavery enshrine hermeneutical approaches to depictions of black interiority is a central question for black literary studies today.

Against the grain of the questions listed above, this volume uses a critically re-imagined, somewhat idiosyncratic iteration of psychoanaly-

sis as a hermeneutic to interrupt received habits of reading black fiction and to access a unique store of conceptual and linguistic resources
for thinking about interior life. As a tool for reading African American
literature, psychoanalysis' shortcomings are various; some of them are
enumerated in the preceding pages. What attracts me to psychoanalysis in spite of its flaws is its complication of specific modes of reading
that residually attach to African American literature—modes of reading
that encounter black textuality as (always, only) literal, performative,
and heroically "resistant." Psychoanalysis can help us to uncover veiled,
disavowed, and inconsistent feelings and desires, as well as the ways in
which "oppression . . . both [compromises and conditions] the very possibility of subjecthood."[7] Access to this kind of nuance and contradiction
is, I believe, essential to the serious recognition of the human mind. It is
also crucially important to the present study because the major archive
under consideration is one that defies the transparent rationality of the
political directive. Claiming the distant past as the psychic property of
the present and investing, however ambivalently, in a moral logic of redemptive suffering, the contemporary narrative of slavery *requires* an
interpretive rubric that is accountable to the indirect routes and complex
mechanisms of psychic life.

By way of psychoanalysis, I have told a story about the forms of unfinished and un-acknowledged mourning—not just over the un-resolved
trauma of the slave past but also over the political, civic, and psychic dismantling of the modern Civil Rights Movement—that inhabit and drive
today's black literary discourse. I have argued, more specifically, that the
psychic logics of trauma, masochism, and depression can help us to decipher how the grief and desire imbuing the contemporary moment attain clarity (or find disguise) in narratives of historical return. The point
is not to cure, or even to mobilize, but to invite a more supple and comprehensive reading of blackness, one that necessarily engages but also
strains against "the politics of representation," with its "determination
to see blackness only through a social public lens."[8] The ability to read
individuality and human complexity within blackness seems to me an
irreducibly important pre-condition for politics—and a pre-condition
that literature is uniquely equipped to address.

Far be it from me to prescribe or prohibit any reader's experience of
textual encounter, whether by insisting on the "appropriate" psychic im-

pact of a text or by diminishing the reader's experience of being moved and transformed by literature. On the contrary, my intention has been to release the contemporary narrative of slavery from such interpretive strangleholds. I separate the question of how representations of psychic life work in literary fiction (which is my primary interest) from the question of how literary fiction works on actual readers (which is not). Although I have gravitated toward psychoanalysis and made a case for its hermeneutical legitimacy, I do not mean to suggest that psychoanalysis is the only—or even the singular best—way to interpret black interiority. I hope that the titular "how to" will be read, not as a self-righteous command, but as a deliberative and inconclusive invocation of the question *how?* that animates my approach to contemporary literary depictions of black interiority. Taking inspiration from Andrew Hawkins and the magical Convent women in their respective moments of hermeneutical revelation, I have endeavored to approach reading as a practice of wonder that agnostically recuperates the density of inner life.

# NOTES

## INTRODUCTION

1 Morrison, "Site of Memory," 77.

2 Arlene Keizer coins the much-used taxonomical term "contemporary narratives of slavery" in her 2004 monograph, *Black Subjects*. I find this term particularly useful (as opposed to variously named sub-categories of the contemporary narrative of slavery) because it is deliberately capacious, accommodating "a wide variety of works," including "the historical novel of slavery . . . , works set in the present which explicitly connect African American/Afro-Caribbean life in the present with U.S./Caribbean slavery . . . , and hybrid works in which scenes from the past are juxtaposed with scenes from the present" (*Black Subjects*, 2).

3 By most accounts, African American fiction's renewed interest in the slave past begins with Margaret Walker's *Jubilee* (1966), a novel based on an oral history of the author's grandmother and published as the Civil Rights Movement was giving way to more militant strains of black nationalism. Combining revisionist historiography with the imaginative un-encumbrance of fiction, *Jubilee* anticipated, and perhaps even catalyzed, what Deborah E. McDowell calls "a post-sixties phenomenon" of "novels about slavery [appearing] at an unstoppable rate" ("Negotiating between Tenses," 144).

4 Best, "On Failing," 453.

5 In this vein, Keith Byerman writes that black historical fiction is "potentially therapeutic in that it insists on revealing the fullness of the past" (*Remembering the Past*, 9); Arlene Keizer opines that "these texts [contemporary narratives of slavery] seem to be saying that we need to imagine [enslaved] ancestors as psychically free if we are to imagine ourselves as psychically free" (*Black Subjects*, 17); Angelyn Mitchell offers that the "objective" of a subset of contemporary narratives of slavery is to "engender a liberatory effect on the reader" (*Freedom to Remember*, 6); Ashraf H. A. Rushdy asserts that a prominent subset of black historical novels "make[s] the point that the past influences a present that can be modified and made better only by returning to and understanding [the] past, [specifically,] that personal and national family secret of slavery" (*Remembering Generations*, 7); and Lisa Woolfork contends that a proliferating set of "books, films, exhibitions [and] reenactments . . . use the contemporary body as an invitation for the reader, viewer, or patron to locate themselves in the past; readers, viewers, and visitors are prompted to ask themselves, 'What would I do?' in the context of Ameri-

can slavery" (*Embodying American Slavery*, 1). To be sure, one may adopt the hermeneutic of therapeutic reading as a critical premise without making it one's sole or primary object of study. In identifying this common feature that pervades much recent scholarship on black historical fiction, my aim is not to reduce that scholarship to a singular, shared "meaning" but to gesture toward the critical reach of the hermeneutic of therapeutic reading, which informs a capacious and multi-faceted body of research.

6 Variations on this figure appear in novels such as Toni Cade Bambara's *Salt Eaters*, David Bradley's *Chaneysville Incident*, Octavia Butler's *Kindred*, Paule Marshall's *Praisesong for the Widow*, Gloria Naylor's *Mama Day*, and Phyllis Alesia Perry's *Stigmata*, as well as in a number of acclaimed films, including Julie Dash's *Daughters of the Dust* and Haile Gerima's *Sankofa*.

7 Marshall, *Praisesong for the Widow*, 245.

8 Throughout this book, I invoke the figure of the "contemporary reader" to describe an abstracted consumer of post–Civil Rights black fiction. One approach to thinking through such a figure might emphasize literary history and the sociology of reading, giving attention to data on who reads and how, as well as political and generational differences among post–Civil Rights writers and critics. Such a project, however, is beyond the scope of the present work. My primary interest attaches, instead, to the implied reader—the projected addressee of literary discourse. Rather than speaking for the tastes or desires of a particular demography, this imaginary figure consolidates a sense of how particular texts and genres imagine their readers and curate the reading experience. This "contemporary reader" is historically specific insofar as post–Civil Rights authors necessarily speak to an audience positioned at a significant distance from the slave past. Yet, as an index of narrative construction, this reader cannot be accountable to the particularities of experience, perspective, and idiosyncrasy that mark actual readers and their textual encounters.

9 Perry, *Stigmata*, 24, 17.

10 Ibid., 7, 47.

11 Ibid., 88.

12 Perry, "Confronting the Specters of the Past," 637.

13 Warner, "Uncritical Reading," 37n. Warner's catalog of hermeneutical norms is meant to expose the tacit bias through which scholarly practices of "critical reading" work to de-legitimize texts and reading strategies that operate outside of its hegemony. In this respect, Warner could easily be describing the critical marginalization of so many earlier forms of African American literature—most notably, the slave narrative and the protest novel, with their purposeful, sentimental appeals and their urgent calls to action. Since black print culture has, from its inception, been charged with particular modes of representation—activist, pedagogical, documentary—it is not a stretch to say that African American literature's availability to Warner's enumerated interpretive conventions has been powerfully

and persistently interrupted. On the long history of how African American literature has been framed for consumption and evaluation, see Gates, *Figures in Black*.

14 Mitchell, *The Freedom to Remember*, 6; Byerman, *Remembering the Past*, 9.

15 Michaels, *Shape of the Signifier*, 137.

16 Hartman, *Lose Your Mother*, 6.

17 Tate, *Psychoanalysis and Black Novels*, 16.

18 Adam Phillips, *Promises, Promises*, xv.

19 As Shoshana Felman puts it, psychoanalytic literary theory replaces the question
"*What* does the story mean?" with the question "'*How* does the story mean?' How
does the meaning of the story, whatever it may be, rhetorically take place through
permanent displacement, textually take shape and take effect: take flight" ("Turning the Screw," 119).

20 As an inquiry into how psychic forms travel in and through black historical fiction, the infrastructure of this book takes a cue from Caroline Levine's
unorthodox re-imagining of formalist analysis. Levine invokes a broad definition of form as any recognizable "ordering principle" to demonstrate how forms
travel in and through ostensibly disparate cultural territories such as literature,
politics, popular culture, and so forth. Mobile and adaptable, forms are available
to repurposing but indivisible from their constitutive properties. To repeat one of
Levine's examples, the form of the whole may alternatively describe a unified text,
a "nation-state," or a "seminar room"—three indisputably non-identical entities—
but in each iteration, the whole retains certain unaltered capacities—the capacities to contain, enclose, exclude, bring together. A formalist analysis after Levine
begins with a curious eye toward *what forms can do*—an index of potentiality that
she terms "affordances." Thinking about form in terms of affordances invites an
orientation toward meaning that is dynamic, non-reductive, trans-disciplinary,
and open to surprise but also finite and generalizable (*Forms*, 3, 48, 6).

  In a similar way, I would like to think of psychoanalysis as a collection of
psychic forms whose meaning concentrates, not in diagnostic power, but in
the capacities of those forms to express and conceal attachments, desires, and
other interior processes. What are the affordances of the psychic forms that
prominently and repeatedly appear in post–Civil Rights African American
literature—trauma, masochism, and depression? Posing the question in this
way allows me to shift the interpretive endeavor from taxonomy to exploration.
To continue with my example, instead of asking, *Are contemporary narratives
of slavery masochistic?* I set out to understand what masochism can *do* for contemporary African American literature. What kinds of narratives about power
and desire does the form of masochism enable, and what kinds of narratives
does it foreclose? Why might this be an appealing form (or not) for conceptualizing the longue durée of black disenfranchisement and political longing?

21 Adam Phillips, *On Flirtation*, 24.

22 Spillers, "All the Things," 379.

23 Madhu Dubey offers a particularly astute analysis of this phenomenon, keyed to its implications for contemporary black literary and cultural studies. See *Signs and Cities*.

24 Brand, *Map to the Door*, 50.

25 Spillers, "All the Things," 381.

26 Friedman, *Joyce*, 25.

27 "Freud also breaks down the autonomy of the dream-text by reading dreams in relation to other dreams, decoding a series of dreams as a composite text. 'A whole series of dreams,' he writes, 'continuing over a period of weeks or months, is often based upon common ground and must accordingly be interpreted in connection with one another'" (ibid., 25).

28 The voluminous critical literature on contemporary narratives of slavery includes illuminating research on many of these recurring tropes. To scratch the surface, see Byerman, *Remembering the Past*; Keizer, *Black Subjects*; Rody, *The Daughter's Return*; Rushdy, *Remembering Generations*; Tillet, *Sites of Slavery*; and Woolfork, *Embodying American Slavery*. Through their selective and sustained emphases, these studies and others implicitly corroborate the foundational claim that I am moving to establish: that contemporary black fiction may be read for and through thematic and figural resonances among texts, to illuminate an archive that comprises something like a "composite text."

29 Lee, *Sarah Phillips*, 14.

30 In a closely related argument, Michael Awkward offers an expansive consideration of the novella's split allegiances to black literary and cultural traditions, on the one hand, and to the radical abandonment of these traditions, on the other. He highlights in particular the "notable disparities between the narrator-protagonist's myopic observations about race and Lee's informed allusions to black-authored texts" (*Philadelphia Freedoms*, 126).

31 Brown, *Edgework*, 100. Here, Brown is speaking about the decline of feminism in late modernity.

32 McBride, *Song Yet Sung*, 286–287.

33 Manning Marable offers one representative iteration of this cultural narrative when he outlines an inter-generationally continuous trajectory of "yearning for freedom" that takes root on "America's plantations and slave society" and persists as a unifying, collective racial self-story through the late 1960s. Again resonating with McBride's novel, Marable identifies Martin Luther King, Jr., as the final prophet of a "cultural tradition of salvation and liberation" (*Beyond Black and White*, 18–19).

34 McBride, *Song Yet Sung*, 254.

35 Ibid.

36 Adam Phillips, *On Flirtation*, 34.

37 Ibid., 24.

38 Best, "On Failing," 459, 455.

39 Kenan, *Visitation of Spirits*, 188.

## CHAPTER 1. AGAINST PROHIBITIVE READING (ON TRAUMA)

1 Warren, *What Was*, 1.

2 Nielsen, "Wasness" (Neilsen's italics).

3 Warren, *What Was*, 82.

4 Best, "On Failing," 454.

5 Morrison, *Beloved*, 248. The space gap appears in the original, near the beginning of a nine-page break from conventional prose. Further citations to this work are given in the text.

6 Leys, *From Guilt to Shame*, 167. To be clear, Leys makes only a fleeting reference to African American literature, and she is not directly engaged in the disciplinarily specific conversation that I address in this chapter. The immediate focus of her book is the evolution of shame theory in relation to post-Holocaust Jewish studies. I reference her in passing because, despite this substantive difference, her notion of "radical expropriation" (167) crystallizes a central concern she shares with critics like Warren: that contemporary uses of trauma theory calcify victimization as a social identity and falsely position "those of us who were never there" at the center of historical meaning (180).

7 Michaels, *Shape of the Signifier*, 137.

8 Douglas Jones, "Fruit of Abolition," 43.

9 I borrow this economical phrase (somewhat out of context) from the philosopher Alasdair MacIntyre, who proposes that both historiography and virtue depend upon the possibility of imagining human life as a unity. See MacIntyre, "The Virtues."

10 "The event is not assimilated or experienced fully at the time, but only belatedly, in its repeated *possession* of the one who experiences it." See Caruth, "Introduction," 4.

11 Luckhurst, *Trauma Question*, 88, 89.

12 For an excellent study of this literary trope, see Rody, *Daughter's Return*.

13 Morrison, *Beloved*, xviii.

14 Caruth, "Introduction," 4 (Caruth's italics).

15 Snitow, review of *Beloved*, 26n.

16 Felman, "Betrayal of the Witness," 167.

17 Christian, "Fixing Methodologies," 6–7.

18 On this tradition, see Gilman, *Difference and Pathology*.

19 Daryl Michael Scott, *Contempt and Pity*, xix.

20 Awkward, *Philadelphia Freedoms*, 6.

21 Some noteworthy exceptions to this pattern of exclusion are Eyerman, *Cultural Trauma*; Felman, *Juridical Unconscious*; Hirsch, "Maternity and Rememory."

22 Marriott, *Haunted Life*, xxi.

23 Best, "On Failing," 459.

24 Michaels, *Shape of the Signifier*, 136. By contrast, Michaels regards modern socio-economic disparity as the dominant and reliable "real" of American life.

As he writes in *The Trouble with Diversity*, identitarian racial discourse is "at best a distraction, and at worst an essentially reactionary position" in relation to the class-based justice projects that he deems the work of "equality" (16).

25 Michaels, *Shape of the Signifier*, 136.

26 Morrison, *Beloved*, 44.

27 Hirsch, "Generation of Postmemory," 107.

28 La Capra, *History in Transit*, 108.

29 Hirsch, "Surviving Images," 10 (my italics).

30 In the introduction to *Renewing Black Intellectual History*, Reed and Warren write, "Much black studies scholarship remains unreflectively moored to notions such as race leadership, unitary racial interest, as well as an intellectually and politically naïve rhetoric of racial authenticity on which those notions rest. Yet these notions—all of which emerged within the patterns of elite discourse that evolved between the second half of the nineteenth century and the middle of the twentieth—have become increasingly problematic as frames for interpreting black American experience" (*Renewing Black Intellectual History*, viii).

31 Joan Dayan's critique of Paul Gilroy's *Black Atlantic* epitomizes this argument: "Gilroy announces that it's time to reconstruct 'the primal history of modernity' from the 'slaves' point of view,'" she writes. "But . . . . Where, oh where do we find the slaves' point of view?" Still more pointedly, she concludes with the claim that, by "taking writing anchored in a specific time and place out of its *roots* and into abstraction, Gilroy turns poverty and racial stigma into an obscurantist, if rhythmic aesthetics of pain" ("Paul Gilroy's Slaves," 8, 13; Dayan's italics).

32 Brown, "Wounded Attachments," 72, 74.

33 Consider the crescendo of Reid-Pharr's case for prohibitive reading, which simultaneously magnifies the allure of power and the mechanism of censorship that drive prohibitive reading. In this excerpt, Reid-Pharr casts himself in the third person as the hero of contemporary black intellectualism:

> He refuses to privilege the rhetorics of return and nostalgia that so burden much contemporary criticism of Black American literature and culture. . . . He does not mourn fallen martyrs, nor does he tremble in the face of forgetfulness, alienation, isolation, peculiarity, funniness, or estrangement. . . . Instead he has suggested that the notion that the Black American must forever despise what he holds in his hands in favor of what is already lost is, in fact, part of the very defeatist nonsense that would not only disallow any true form of Black American intellectualism but that would also disqualify Black Americans as self-conscious agents of history. (*Once You Go Black*, 172)

34 In her fascinating study of anti-victim rhetoric, Alyson Cole argues that a key strategy of anti-victim discourse has been to discredit "therapeutic culture" as disinterested in the truth. Imitating the discourse through which her antagonists devalue victims' claims, she writes, "Truthfulness is not a therapeutic concern. Any claim of injury or need is prima facie valid and merits compensation" (*Cult of True Victimhood*, 33).

35 Warren, *What Was*, 84.

36 I borrow this phrase from Wendy Brown's chapter of the same name, "Wounded Attachments."

37 Bradley, *Chaneysville Incident*, 197. Further citations to the work are given in text.

38 Caruth, "Introduction," 5.

39 Morrison, *Beloved*, 44.

40 Elsewhere, Bradley elaborates on this desire for historiographical mastery. He writes: "[Most] of us have learned to accept the idea that we will never know everything, so long as we labor here below. But we also believe in Historians' Heaven: a firmly fixed chamber far removed from the subjective uncertainties of this mortal coil, where there is a gallery of pictures of [the past] taken constantly from every angle, and motion pictures, and cross-sections. And we believe that if we have been good little historians, just before they do whatever it is they finally do with us, they'll take us in there and show us what was *really* going on. It's not that we want so much to know we were right. We *know* we're not right (although it would be nice to see exactly how close we came). It's just that we want to, really, truly, utterly, absolutely, completely, finally, *know*" (*Chaneysville Incident*, 264; Bradley's italics).

41 La Capra, *Writing History*, 35.

42 Warren, *What Was*, 102.

43 Bradley, "Business of Writing," 26.

44 Best, "On Failing," 461.

45 Warren, *What Was*, 103, 105 (my italics).

46 Morrison, *Jazz*, 229. Further citations to the work are given in text.

47 Adam Phillips, *Becoming Freud*, 17.

48 Morrison, "Site of Memory," 70, 69.

49 Ibid., 71.

50 Morrison, *Playing in the Dark*, 5.

51 See ibid.

52 Reid-Pharr, *Once You Go Black*, 172.

53 Michaels, *Shape of the Signifier*, 137.

54 Reid-Pharr, *Once You Go Black*, 33.

55 Muñoz, *Cruising Utopia*, 32.

56 Freeman, *Time Binds*, 3.

57 Muñoz, *Cruising Utopia*, 27, 26.

58 Cvetkovich, *Archive of Feelings*, 20, 22.

59 Juxtaposing curt, narrative descriptions of so many micro-aggressions with poetic accounts of anti-black surveillance, brutality, and murder, Claudia Rankine's *Citizen*, which culminates in a magnified detail from J. M. W. Turner's painting "The Slave Ship," is organized by just such a tension.

60 In fact, as Thadious Davis points out, *A Visitation of Spirits*'s temporal dexterity is even greater than it seems, for the novel is haunted by Kenan's historiographical short story, "Let the Dead Bury Their Dead," which elaborates a *Chaneysville-*

like reclamation of the main family's history in slavery and marronage. "'Let the Dead Bury Their Dead,'" Davis writes, "began as a section of [Kenan's] 1989 novel *A Visitation of Spirits*," but it became uncontainable within the novel's frame. In separating the story from the novel, the author was able to develop a multi-textual, palimpsestic take on historical desire (Davis, *Southscapes*, 315). The focus of the present chapter, however, will limit itself to *A Visitation of Spirits*. Further citations to the work are given in text.

61  Set awkwardly alongside each other, the play and the historical vision are os-tensibly opposite renditions of a shared referent—the one is jovial, celebratory, and apologist, while the other is harrowing, sorrowful, and demanding. The play purports to look back on history, while the vision presents itself as his-tory's own summoning, unappeased voice. The play is endorsed by corporate money and local governmental organizations, while the vision is of a kind with oral counter-history. Wildly divergent in content and register, these clashing representations of slavery model the inconsistent and inaccessible contexts in which Horace apprehends a sense of his past and the resultant terms of his interpellation.

62  Judith Butler, *Undoing Gender*, 29.

## CHAPTER 2. FOR CONTRADICTION (ON MASOCHISM)

1  Byerman, *Remembering the Past*, 10.

2  Evelyn Brooks Higginbotham is the original theorist of this concept, which is now widely (if somewhat inconsistently) used. See Higginbotham, *Righteous Discon-tent*. For Higginbotham's recent response to misconceptions about respectability in contemporary political and activist discourses, see Higginbotham, "Wrestling with Respectability."

3  For a sampling of this scholarship, see Abdur-Rahman, *Against the Closet*; Hol-land, *Erotic Life of Racism*; Keizer, "Obsidian Mine"; Morris, *Close Kin*; Musser, *Sensational Flesh*; Jennifer Nash, *Black Body*; Darieck Scott, *Extravagant Abjection*; and Sharpe, *Monstrous Intimacies*.

4  Sharpe, *Monstrous Intimacies*, 148.

5  Cole argues that in contemporary American culture, the credibility afforded to victims "has less to do with the veracity of petitions or the facts of injury than with the sufferer's personal qualities." Each of the four qualities she describes—propriety, responsibility, individuality, and innocence—sits at odds with popular understandings of the masochistic posture:

> *Propriety*: The True Victim is a noble victim. He endures his suffering with dignity, refraining from complaining or other public displays of weakness. *Responsibility*: The True Victim commands his fate; he does not exploit his injury to excuse his failures. He assumes victimhood reluctantly or, even better, rejects the status altogether. *Individuality*: Victimhood is an individual status even when a group is injured collectively. A True Victim is not a vic-tim by affiliation or by engaging in "victim politics"; victimization must be

immediate and concrete. *Innocence*: This is the most important virtue of True Victimhood. Anti-victimists apply the category of innocence in two distinct ways. First, with respect to his victimization, the victim's innocence must be complete and incontrovertible. True victims have not contributed to their injury in any way. Second, the victim is morally upright; he must be pure. This totalizing conception of innocence encompasses every facet of the True Victim's character. (*Cult of True Victimhood*, 5; Cole's italics)

6 In her anthropological study of BDSM (bondage, dominance and submission, and sadomasochism) in California's Bay Area, Margot Weiss describes an additional, pragmatic disincentive for African American engagement with masochistic desire or s/m practices. Weiss reveals that BDSM communities tend toward demographic homogeneity (white, upper middle class) and that black participation is often limited to "race play that mimics social power" in un-self-conscious ways. Although most practitioners envision their fantasies and performances as politically benign, Weiss observes that "scenes require enough of the real to work— black bodies or German commands and uniforms." "Indeed, effective scenes find and push hot buttons, buttons that access the power that coheres with national imaginaries that structure citizenship, belonging, and subjectivity through affective relations." In such a milieu, masochism requires African Americans to inhabit and claim a particular kind of victimhood: a victimhood of "choice" that is shielded from political critique by its appeal to the "private" domain of the sexual (*Techniques of Pleasure*, 199, 207, 214).

7 Dubey, *Black Women Novelists*, 25.

8 Delany, *The Game of Time and Pain*, 57, 34.

9 Keizer, "Obsidian Mine."

10 Kara Walker, quoted in English, "New Context," 87.

11 Sharpe, *Monstrous Intimacies*, 25.

12 Richard von Krafft-Ebing, quoted in Lenzer, "On Masochism," 277.

13 Lenzer, "On Masochism," 280.

14 Freud, "A Child Is Being Beaten," 189.

15 Brown, *Politics out of History*, 53, 59.

16 Ibid., 52, 55.

17 Octavia Butler, *Kindred*, 28. Further citations to this work are given in text.

18 Intermittently throughout the novel, contemporary repudiations of Dana and Kevin's marriage are echoed in the historical tense. For example, when Dana first tells Rufus that Kevin is her husband, his spontaneous reaction is, "Niggers can't marry white people!" Later, the taboo against interracial marriage is more explicitly tied to traditions of non-recognition for *all* African American romantic unions. "No slave marriage was legally binding," Dana learns (ibid., 60, 133).

19 Baker, *Blues, Ideology*, 48. Baker elaborates: "What Douglass's certificate of marriage . . . signifies is that the black man has *repossessed* himself in a manner that enables him to enter the kind of relationship disrupted, or foreclosed, by the economics of slavery" (ibid.).

20 Litwack writes, "If [legacies of freedom and opportunity] are the grounds for commemorating the anniversary of the Constitution, they reveal a perverse and limited reading of the American past. [To celebrate uncritically] is to read American history without the presence of black men and women, to define them out of American identity, to exclude a people who enjoyed neither liberty, impartial government, nor the equal protection of the law ("Trouble in Mind," 317).

21 To be sure, Brown herself acknowledges this limitation and does not purport to "psychologize political life directly [or] to reflect on the ways that sexual life bears on political life, but rather to allegorize a historical-political problem through the story of desire and punishment that Freud constructs" (*Politics out of History*, 47). My critique should not be read as an allegation of Brown's shortcomings but, rather, as an attempt to put pressure on what the idea of political masochism can do for contemporary black fiction's explorations of the slave past.

22 Cvetkovich, *Archive of Feelings*, 87.

23 Freeman, *Time Binds*, 142, 143.

24 Ibid., 138.

25 Ibid., 144.

26 Octavia Butler, "Persistence" (Butler's italics).

27 Octavia Butler, "Interview" by Rowell, 51.

28 Octavia Butler, "Persistence."

29 Octavia Butler, "Interview" by Snider, 214 (Butler's italics).

30 Morrison, *Beloved*, xix.

31 Freeman, *Time Binds*, 95, 99, 101.

32 Ibid., 191n.

33 Butler underscores the idea of the excessive inarticulacy of historical pain in her extraordinary overuse of two impactful yet imprecise words: "pain" and "hurt." In the course of the mid-length novel's 264 pages, Butler deploys the word "pain" 62 times, and the word "hurt" a stunning 114 times. As I see it, her strained reliance on language that is at once necessary and inadequate gestures toward the affective excesses of contemporary African Americans' legible and "appropriate" relationship to an abusive racial history. Furthermore, Butler's deliberate and redundant verbal vagueness operates as an indictment of historiographical standards of distance and objectivity, gesturing toward a wealth of experience that cannot be apprehended on these terms.

34 Cvetkovich uses this language to describe the "safe space" of a feminist mosh pit, where sexual trauma is performatively re-enacted (*Archive of Feelings*, 87).

35 Freeman, *Time Binds*, 141, 139.

36 Mitchell, "Not Enough of the Past," 52–53.

37 Gayl Jones, *Corregidora*, 184. Further citations to this work are given in text.

38 For an expansive discussion of the trope of the family secret in temporally split contemporary narratives of slavery (including *Corregidora*), see Rushdy, *Remembering Generations*.

39 Brown, *Politics out of History*, 53.

40 Sharpe makes a similar point when she writes, "*Corregidora* allows us to explore how the family's demands on the subject to keep visible (but also keep repressed) horrific experiences of violence in slavery—in this case, the demands of the formerly enslaved on their descendants—become congruent with the law of the (slave) master" (Sharpe, *Monstrous Intimacies*, 32).

41 Brown, *Politics out of History*, 56.

42 Rushdy, "Relate Sexual to Historical," 277.

43 Freeman, *Time Binds*, 191n.

44 Dubey, *Black Women Novelists*, 83.

45 Freeman, *Time Binds*, 144.

46 Ibid., 141, 144.

47 In the vein of queer theorists like Leo Bersani and Lee Edelman, Freeman imagines the mystical power of s/m as wrapped up with "sado-masochism's temporary destruction of the subject." She diverges from Bersani and Edelman, however, in her refusal to regard this destruction as evidence of sex's fundamental ahistoricity or apoliticism. For a more detailed description of how Freeman positions herself in relation to both Bersani's critical tradition and "white lesbian-feminist" strains of queer theory, see *Time Binds*, 142–144.

48 Brown, *Politics out of History*, 55.

49 Dubey, *Black Women Novelists*, 81.

50 Gayl Jones, *Corregidora*, 185. Surely this contrast is at least in part a matter of genre. Dana's access to the fantastical possibility of time travel allows her to confront a history that Ursa can only find spectrally, projected onto her similarly wounded, African American lover.

51 Halberstam, *Queer Art of Failure*, 129.

52 Ibid., 139.

53 Darieck Scott, *Extravagant Abjection*, 23.

54 Ibid., 9–12, 258–259.

55 Ibid., 49 (Scott's italics).

56 In fact, Scott makes a point to disarticulate his preferred term, "abjection," from the more broadly familiar concept of masochism, although he avows a family resemblance between these terms and includes within his book, sustained considerations of s/m fantasy, desire, and play. In the introduction to his book, Scott writes that "such familiar (if nevertheless endlessly fascinating and near limitless) terms [like] *masochism* and *castration* overlay, overlap, and even partly describe the relation between blackness and abjection, and the powers that inhere in that relation, [but they] do not fully encompass that relation and those powers, adequately name them, or exhaust them." In my own engagement with Scott, I have treated his "abjection" and my "masochism" as comparable and even interchangeable terms, but I have taken care to do so only in ways that preserve the arc and content of his argument (ibid., 28–29; Scott's italics).

57 Ibid., 270, 264.

58 Ibid., 265.

59 Ibid., 263, 265.

60 Lotman, *Structure of the Artistic Text*, 213, 212. Elsewhere, Madhu Dubey elegantly ties the non-ending of *Corregidora* in particular to the blues form when she writes:

> In a narrative structured by the cut, it becomes irrelevant to ask the bildungsroman question of whether, at the end of the novel, Ursa succeeds in articulating a radically new identity that ruptures her ancestral heritage. The movement of her plot is, rather, an accumulation and variation on her foremothers' stories. Any notion of the present as a new and decisive break from the past . . . is simply incongruent with the novel's structure and temporal vision. The device of the cut achieves a sense of structural and temporal continuity, and allows a formal containment of the potentially discontinuous terms, past and present. This formal containment must be distinguished from the problem-solving impetus of classic linear plots; the blues structure of *Corregidora* . . . formally accommodates rather than erases the text's thematic contradiction between past and present. (Dubey, *Black Women Novelists*, 83)

## CHAPTER 3. THE MISSING ARCHIVE (ON DEPRESSION)

1 Lee, *Sarah Phillips*, 10–11. Further citations to this work are given in text.

2 The capacious language of "feelings" that I employ throughout the chapter—in addition to, and at times as a critique of, the particular language of psychoanalysis—is indebted to Cvetkovich's recent writing on the topic. In *Depression*, Cvetkovich explains her effort to generate a critical vocabulary that "encompasses affect, emotion, and feeling, and that includes impulses, desires, and feelings that get historically constructed in a range of ways (whether as distinct specific emotions or as a generic category often contrasted with reason)." She elaborates:

> I also like to use *feeling* as a generic term that does some of the same work: naming the undifferentiated 'stuff' of feeling; spanning the distinctions between emotion and affect central to some theories; acknowledging the somatic or sensory nature of feelings as experiences that aren't just cognitive concepts or constructions. I favor *feeling* in part because it is intentionally imprecise, retaining the ambiguity between feelings as embodied sensations and feelings as psychic or cognitive experiences. It also has a vernacular quality that lends itself to exploring feelings as something we come to know though experience and popular usage and that indicates, perhaps only intuitively but nonetheless significantly, a conception of mind and body as integrated. (*Depression*, 4)

> I follow the example of Cvetkovich's tensile vocabulary of affect and feeling, although my own work preserves more of an inclination toward psychoanalysis than does hers.

3 Smith, "Foreword," x.

4 Washington, "Young, Gifted and Black," 3.

5 To date, two critical emphases have dominated discussion of *Sarah Phillips*: The first alternatively condemns or defends Sarah's relationship to progressive racial politics, while the second elucidates the novel's emplotment of unprecedented African American social and class mobility in post–Civil Rights America. For examples of the former, see Hogue, "The Limits of Modernity"; McCormick, "Is This Resistance?"; Smith, "Foreword"; and Washington, "Young, Gifted and Black." For examples of the latter, see Awkward, *Philadelphia Freedoms*; and Murray, "The Time of Breach."

6 McPherson, "Elbow Room," 260–261. Further citations to this work are given in text.

7 "The loss of a love-object," Freud writes, "is an excellent opportunity for the ambivalence in love-relationships to make itself effective and come into the open" ("Mourning and Melancholia," 250–251).

8 Ibid., 249. A subsequent phrasing of this defense is especially poetic. Freud writes, "So by taking flight into the ego love escapes extinction" (257).

9 Ibid., 249.

10 Ibid.

11 Nevertheless, Freud unwittingly enables future appropriations of his theory for thinking through the forms of *social* identity, for his theory of melancholia becomes the basis for his understanding of universal, non-pathological processes of subject formation. As Judith Butler explains, the very notions of interiority, and of the ego as a "psychic object," require the technology of melancholia in order to come into being, as the fiction of the self is produced through serialized negotiations of loss (*Psychic Life of Power*, 168). See also Laplanche and Pontalis, *Language of Psycho-analysis*, 230.

12 Cheng, *Melancholy of Race*, 8.

13 Ibid., 10, 12.

14 Ibid., 20, 17.

15 Ibid., 4, 10.

16 Ibid., 17. Cheng's analysis here refers to the character Claudia in Toni Morrison's *The Bluest Eye*, though it is offered in the service of a generalizable argument.

17 Cheng, *Melancholy of Race*, 20.

18 The chronology I employ here is similar to that which the historian Jacquelyn Dowd Hall identifies and critiques as the "dominant narrative" of the "short civil rights movement." By her account, this narrative

> chronicles a short civil rights movement that begins with the 1954 *Brown v. Board of Education* decision, proceeds through public protests, and culminates with the passage of the Civil Rights Act of 1964 and the Voting Rights Act of 1965. Then comes the decline. After a season of moral clarity, the country is beset by the Vietnam War, urban riots, and reaction against the excess of the late 1960s and 1970s, understood variously as student rebellion, black militancy, feminism, busing, affirmative action, or an overweening of the welfare state. A so-called white backlash sets the stage for the conserva-

tive interregnum that, for good or ill, depending on one's ideological persuasion, marks the beginning of another story, the story that surrounds us now. Martin Luther King, Jr. is this narrative's defining figure.

Hall goes on to make a very persuasive case for imagining instead a "'long civil rights movement' that took root in the liberal and radical milieu of the late 1930s," but this argument is, for the time being, beyond the scope of my study. I bracket the narrative of progressive continuity not because I believe it is untrue but because I am interested in the "dominant narrative" precisely as an index of how historical events and effects have been publicly registered and represented (Hall, "Long Civil Rights Movement," 1234–1235).

19  Gilroy, *Black Atlantic*, 216.

20  Giovanni, "Reflections on April 4, 1968," 54.

21  Baraka, "Afrikan Revolution," 244.

22  This passage reads in full: "For a moment be any black person, anywhere, and you will feel the waves of hopelessness that engulfed black men and women when Martin Luther King was murdered. All black people understood the tide of anarchy that followed his death. It is the transformation of *this* quantum of grief into aggression of which we now speak. As a sapling bent low stores energy for a violent back-swing, blacks bent double by oppression have stored energy which will be released in the form of rage—black rage, apocalyptic and final" (Grier and Cobbs, *Black Rage*, 210).

23  In this summative statement, I adapt language and a conceptual gesture from Wendy Brown's description of modern liberalism, which she describes as an amalgam of "certain crucial collective stories . . . by which we live." Brown's study proceeds as an inquiry into what happens when "fundamental premises of an order begin to erode, or simply begin to be exposed as fundamental premises" (*Politics out of History*, 3).

24  The idea that the denouement of the modern Civil Rights Movement has been accompanied by feelings of collective loss is by now fairly common within African American literary and cultural criticism, although affective and analytical responses to this narrative of loss vary widely. For some examples, see Awkward, *Philadelphia Freedoms*; Baker, *Betrayal*; Dubey, "Speculative Fictions"; Gates, *Colored People*; Murray, "Time of Breach"; Reed and Warren, *Renewing Black Intellectual History*; Spillers, "All the Things"; and Warren, *What Was*.

25  The Reverend is explicitly associated with King in the chapter "Marching," where he takes part in organizing the 1963 March on Washington. Elsewhere, Sarah notes that others recognize her father as "the civil-rights minister," and that he subscribes to "a fixed optimism about the brotherhood of man" (Lee, *Sarah Phillips*, 55, 53).

26  Freud, "Mourning and Melancholia," 244–245.

27  Ibid., 245.

28  Judith Butler, *Psychic Life of Power*, 172.

29  Ibid., 170, 183.

30 Freud, "Mourning and Melancholia," 245.

31 Awkward, *Philadelphia Freedoms*, 145.

32 Freud, "Mourning and Melancholia," 256, 251.

33 This is the title of Murray's essay on contemporary novels about the Civil Rights era, including *Sarah Phillips* (Murray, "Time of Breach").

34 See, e.g., Marable, *Race, Reform, and Rebellion*; Steigerwald, *Sixties and the End of Modern America*.

35 Cvetkovich, *Depression*, 14.

36 Sedgwick, *Touching Feeling*, 16. In fact, Sedgwick's bias is that the logic of psychoanalysis is secondary to that of affect theory. She credits the psychologist Silvan Tomkins for clarifying this priority when she writes, "Common sense holds . . . that the drive system [of Freudian psychoanalysis] is the primary motivator of human behavior, to which the affects are inevitably secondary. Tomkins shows the opposite to be true: that motivation itself, even the motivation to satisfy biological drives, is the business of the affect system" (20).

37 In *Depression*, Cvetkovich includes a caveat about her use of the term "affect" that neatly captures my own approach to this conceptual domain. She writes, "I tend to use *affect* in a generic sense, rather than in the more specific Deleuzian sense, as a category that encompasses affect, emotion, and feeling, and that includes impulses, desires, and feelings that get historically constructed in a range of ways (whether as distinct specific emotions or as a generic category often contrasted with reason)" (4; Cvetkovich's italics).

38 Sedgwick, *Touching Feeling*, 21. Cvetkovich does something of this kind when she draws on Cornel West's formulation of "black sadness" to theorize a "political depression" grounded in ongoing traditions of anti-black racism. Rather than attending to processes and structures through which the injustices of the outside world become edifices of one's inner life, Cvetkovich emphasizes the ways in which feelings such as cynicism, "crankiness," and anti-sentimentality may be read as part of the texture of racism itself. She argues that a "rich vocabulary of affective life" is cultivated in the "strange but ordinary situations created by racism," providing an "important vantage point" from which to view a diverse and suggestive range of "modes of political response" other than "activism on the streets" (*Depression*, 125).

39 Warren, *So Black and Blue*, 13. This theme recurs as a dominant concern within Reed and Warren's *Renewing Black Intellectual History* and Warren's *What Was*, as well.

40 In "Elbow Room," McPherson indicates the editor's comments to the author by using italics; I have eliminated the editor's italics and have quoted conventionally by using quotation marks.

41 At the time of their meeting, the narrator describes Virginia as "a wounded bird fearful of landing with its wings still spread . . . in search of some soft, personal space to cushion the impact of her grounding" (McPherson, "Elbow Room," 260).

42 Cheng, *Melancholy of Race*, 16.

43 Muñoz, "Feeling Brown, Feeling Down," 679. Sara Ahmed offers a similar formulation when she describes racialized melancholia through the figure of "affect aliens"—discontent minority subjects who are "alienated through how [they] are affected by the world. . . . To be an affect alien is to experience alien affects—to be out of line with the public mood, not to feel the way others feel in response to an event" (Ahmed, *Promise of Happiness*, 157).

44 In her brilliant exegesis of "Elbow Room," Lubiano draws on Abdul JanMohammed's critique of colonial literary traditions to show how McPherson's fictional editor takes on the role of the civilizer, assuming as his duty the domestication of the narrator's unwieldy content. What the editor presents as an ideologically neutral commitment to aesthetics—particularly, the conventions/norms of realism, linearity, and closure—Lubiano reveals as the disingenuous imposition of "a form that pretends to be disinterested" in order to cultivate the myth of its own, universal truth. Form, here, "is an analogue for the idea of Western civilization and its ideology of beauty and morality." It is the instrument of a dominative will to paint the world through a singular story about "the privileged and the objects of their largess" ("Shuckin' Off," 168, 178).

45 The language of "hearing" and "feeling" the "frequencies" of racialized experience is borrowed from Muñoz's "Feeling Brown, Feeling Down," in which he conceptualizes racialized affect as "descriptive of the receptor we use to hear each other and the frequencies on which certain subalterns speak and are heard or, more importantly, felt" (Muñoz, "Feeling Brown," 677).

46 Randall, *Rebel Yell*. Further citations to this work are given in text. Though beyond the scope of the present chapter, it is worth noting that Andrea Lee has written her own, curious twenty-first-century rejoinder to *Sarah Phillips*. Her short story "The Prior's Room" re-stages much of the plot from the first chapter of *Sarah Phillips* ("In France"), but this time the part of the ingénue is played by a girl of Irish, Polish, and Filipino descent. In a familiar progression, Anna is an American teenager studying at Lausanne who begins a casual affair with an unlikeable French boy. The affair is built on mutual exoticization and youthful curiosity about sex, but where Sarah's relationship culminates in an ugly, racist insult and a compulsion to return home, Anna is gifted a pair of expensive jeans at the end of her brief liaison. Indeed, the story ends in analepsis, as a forty-something Anna recalls this long-ago lover as a "generous and benevolent [gatekeeper] to the world that has become hers" (Lee, "Prior's Room," 241).

47 See, e.g., Murray, "Time of Breach"; Warren, *What Was*; Awkward, *Philadelphia Freedoms*; Edwards, *Charisma*; and Patterson, *Exodus Politics*.

48 Browning, "Alice Randall Courts Controversy."

49 This quotation comes from a long section in *Rebel Yell* that Randall has italicized to distinguish it from the rest of the text. I have chosen to eliminate the italics and quote it conventionally using quotations marks.

50 Cheng, *Melancholy of Race*, 17.

51 Ibid.

52 Freud writes, "It is a matter of general observation that people never willingly abandon a libidinal position, not even, indeed, when a substitute is already beckoning to them. This opposition can be so intense that a turning away from reality takes place and a clinging to the object through the medium of a hallucinatory wishful psychosis" (Freud, "Mourning and Melancholia," 244).

53 Adam Phillips, *Beast in the Nursery*, 123.

54 Adam Phillips, *On Flirtation*, 24. I borrow this phrase from Phillips, who uses it to speak more specifically about dreams—a classic register of symptomatic "speech."

55 Ibid., 68.

56 Ibid., 78–79.

57 Ibid., 75.

58 Sedgwick describes a similar movement of shame, whose precision is informative. Imagining an audience to the embarrassing acts of "an unwashed, half-insane man," she writes: "I pictured the excruciation of everyone else in the room: each looking down, wishing to be anywhere else yet conscious of the inexorable fate of being exactly there, inside the individual skin of which each was burningly aware; at the same time, though, unable to stanch the hemorrhage of painful identification with the misbehaving man. That's the double movement shame makes: toward painful individuation, toward uncontrollable relationality" (*Touching Feeling*, 37).

59 Elsewhere in the scene, Randall writes, "You hate the fact that he has fucked and you haven't. You hate the way he swaggers through a world of grown folks and strands you in a world of children" (*Rebel Yell*, 362).

60 Jones, *Corregidora*, 103, 102.

61 Warren, *What Was*, 9.

## CHAPTER 4. READING AFRICAN AMERICAN LITERATURE NOW

1 Mat Johnson, *Pym*, 159, 8.

2 Ibid., 8.

3 Indeed, the entire novel may be read as an homage to Morrison, who devotes a chapter of her inquiry into "whiteness and the literary imagination" to an analysis of Poe's *Narrative*. Therein, she declares, "No early American writer is more important to the concept of African Americanism than Poe," and through her reading of Poe, she proposes to chart "a critical geography . . . to open as much space for discovery, intellectual adventure, and close exploration as did the original charting of the New World" (*Playing*, 32, 3). Chris Jaynes signals his indebtedness to Morrison on the very first page of the novel's main text, when he discloses his course title, "Dancing with the Darkies: Whiteness in the Literary Mind," and his subsequent voyage enacts something much like an intellectual adventure charted geographically (Mat Johnson, *Pym*, 7).

4 Mat Johnson, *Pym*, 23.

5 Ibid., 39.

6 Ibid., 108, 160.

7   Ibid., 35, 83, 29n, 39.

8   Charles Johnson, *Oxherding Tale*, xv. Johnson's novel was originally published by Indiana University Press, where his editor was John Gallman. It was subsequently re-printed by Grove Press in 1984, and by Plume in 1995.

9   Charles Johnson, "Interview" by Little, 232.

10  Keizer, *Black Subjects*, 48.

11  To be sure, *Oxherding Tale* is neither the first nor the only literary comedy about slavery, and although the comedic strain represents a minority trend among contemporary narratives of slavery, it is prevalent enough to constitute a recognized sub-genre. For a fascinating study of this topic, see Carpio, *Laughing*.

12  Charles Johnson, *Oxherding Tale*, 118. Further citations to this work will be given in text.

13  I borrow this phrase from Stanley Crouch's review of the novel, originally published in 1983 in the *Village Voice* (Crouch, "Charles Johnson: Free at Last!" 273).

14  Ottenberg, "Symbols and Ordeals."

15  Mitchell, *Freedom to Remember*, 21.

16  Morrison, *Beloved*, xviii.

17  Byerman, *Remembering the Past*, 107.

18  Keizer, *Black Subjects*, 72.

19  Byerman, *Remembering the Past*, 10.

20  My cursory definition of allegory borrows from Angus Fletcher's major study of the narrative mode. He writes, "In the simplest terms, allegory says one thing and means another. It destroys the normal expectation we have about language, that our words 'mean what they say.' When we predicate quality x of person Y, Y really is what our predication says he is (or we assume so); but allegory would turn Y into something other (*allos*) than what the open and direct statement tells the reader." In a note, he elaborates, "*Allegory* from *allos* + *agoreuein* (*other* + *speak openly, speak in the assembly or market*). *Agoreuein* connotes public, open, declarative speech. This sense is inverted by the prefix *allos*. Thus allegory is often called 'inversion'" (Fletcher, *Allegory*, 2, 2n.)

21  Kelley, *Reinventing Allegory*, 253. Kelley's discussion of contemporary allegory's tensile use of pathos further illuminates Johnson's narrative technique. She argues that contemporary allegory in particular is a double-voiced enterprise that works by yoking pathos to abstraction. In order to maintain credibility, she says, "allegory needs what ancient rhetoricians called pathos, the strong feeling that justifies exaggerated, even monstrous, figures" (9).

22  Ibid., 11.

23  Keizer, *Black Subjects*, 64.

24  See Hayward, "Something to Serve"; Keizer, *Black Subjects*; Rushdy, *Neo-slave Narratives*; and Retman, "Nothing Was Lost."

25  Hayward, "Something to Serve," 697.

26  Hartman, *Scenes of Subjection*, 3.

27 Hartman writes, at the outset of *Scenes of Subjection*, "Therefore, rather than try to convey the routinized violence of slavery and its aftermath through invocations of the shocking and the terrible, I have chosen to look elsewhere and consider those scenes in which terror can hardly be discerned—slaves dancing in the quarters, the outrageous darky antics of the minstrel stage, the constitution of humanity in slave law, and the fashioning of the self-possessed individual. By defamiliarizing the familiar, I hope to illuminate the terror of the mundane and quotidian rather than exploit the shocking spectacle" (ibid., 4).

28 Rushdy, e.g., opines that Evelyn's account of literary influence and her professional developments "reads like his [Johnson's] own *roman-a-clef*" (*Neo-slave Narratives*, 181).

29 Charles Johnson, "I Call Myself an Artist," 19.

30 Charles Johnson, *Oxherding Tale*, xiii.

31 Retman, "Nothing Was Lost," 429.

32 Freud, *Uncanny*, 124.

33 Ibid., 143.

34 Freud writes, "The process of repression is not to be regarded as an event which takes place *once*, the results of which are permanent, as when some living thing has been killed and from that time onward is dead; repression demands a persistent expenditure of force, and if this were to cease the success of the repression would be jeopardized, so that a fresh act of repression would be necessary. We may suppose that the repressed exercises a continuous pressure in the direction of the conscious, so that this pressure must be balanced by an unceasing counterpressure" ("Repression," 151).

35 Little, *Charles Johnson's Spiritual Imagination*, 103; Byrd, *Charles Johnson's Novels*, 94–95. For additional interpretations of the centrality of Buddhism and related Eastern philosophies in *Oxherding Tale*, see Gleason, "Liberation of Perception"; and William Nash, *Charles Johnson's Fiction*.

36 Jonathan Little notes that

> Reb's aesthetics are taken from a central parable from the "Inner Chapters" of Chuang Tsu's writing, a fourth-century B.C.E. Chinese Taoist. These influential chapters show Chuang Tsu "anticipating Zen Buddhism and laying the metaphysical foundation for a state of emptiness of ego transcendence." In this exchange, Prince Wen Hui's cook talks about his aesthetic techniques in carving an ox. Prince Wen Hui admires his cook's skill and mastery of his art. The cook tells the prince that "when I first began to cut up oxen, I saw nothing but oxen. After three years of practicing, I no longer saw the ox as a whole. I now work with my spirit, not with my eyes. My senses stop functioning and my spirit takes over." (*Charles Johnson's Spiritual Imagination*, 93)

37 Rushdy, *Neo-slave Narratives*, 190; and Keizer, *Black Subjects*, 68. For additional feminist and anti-racist critiques of Andrew's claims to *moksha*, see also Hayward, "Something to Serve"; and Hussen, "Manumission and Marriage?"

38  In a similar reading, William Gleason has aligned *Oxherding Tale*'s narrative proj-
    ect with Johnson's well-documented calls for "a broadened literary outlook that
    embraces (to quote Clayton Riley) the 'entire world—not just the fractured world
    of American racism and psychic disorder.'" With particular attention to Johnson's
    assimilation of Zen philosophy, Gleason argues that "*Oxherding Tale* attempts
    what Buddhists call opening the 'third eye,' or what Johnson sees as the final aim
    of serious fiction: namely, the liberation of perception" (Gleason, "Liberation of
    Perception," 705). For Johnson's essayistic elaboration on this literary ideal, see
    Charles Johnson, "Whole Sight."

39  Hayward, "Something to Serve," 701, 697.

40  Keizer uses this phrase to describe Minty in *Black Subjects*, 64.

41  Retman, "Nothing Was Lost," 432.

42  Storace, "Scripture of Utopia."

43  Charles Johnson, *Oxherding Tale*, 31.

44  Morrison, *Paradise*, 306. Further citations to the work are given in text.

45  Hilfrich, "Anti-Exodus," 330.

46  Lipsitz, *Time Passages*, 213.

47  Lipsitz's re-imagining of Foucaultian "counter-memory" offers a fitting theoretical
    frame for Patricia's notebooks. He writes:

    > Unlike historical narratives that begin with the totality of human existence
    > and then locate specific actions and events within that totality, counter-
    > memory starts with the particular and the specific and then builds outward
    > toward a total story. Counter-memory looks to the past for the hidden
    > histories excluded from dominant narratives. But unlike myths that seek
    > to detach events and actions from the fabric of any larger history, counter-
    > memory forces revision of existing histories by supplying new perspectives
    > about the past. . . . Counter-memory focuses on localized experiences with
    > oppression, using them to reframe and refocus dominant narratives purport-
    > ing to represent universal experience. (Ibid.)

48  Storace, "Scripture of Utopia."

49  Menand, "War between Men and Women," 79.

50  Dobbs, "Diasporic Designs," 113.

51  Edwards, *Charisma*, 178.

52  Jessee, "Contrapuntal Historiography," 105.

53  Hilfrich, "Anti-Exodus," 330.

54  Storace, "Scripture of Utopia."

55  Adam Phillips, *On Flirtation*, 23.

56  Freud, *Interpretation of Dreams*, 348–349.

57  Friedman, "Return of the Repressed in Women's Narrative," 142. I borrow this
    phrase from Friedman's description of the Freudian hermeneutic for dream analy-
    sis. She writes, "Beginning in determinacy, his method ends in indeterminacy.
    Dreams *have* 'authors,' 'intentions,' and 'meanings' to be decoded, he affirms. But
    their 'overdetermination' necessitates an unending 'overinterpretation,' in infinite

regress of interpretation that ultimately leads to the threshold of mystery" (Friedman's italics).

## POSTSCRIPT

1 Gates, *Figures in Black*, 14.
2 Alexander, *Black Interior*, 7.
3 Ibid., 5.
4 Morrison, "Site of Memory," 71.
5 My phrasing here borrows from Kevin Quashie's gorgeously realized monograph, in which he argues that "the inclination to understand black culture through a lens of resistance . . . practically thwarts other ways of reading." Beyond resistance, Quashie advocates for the idiom of "quiet," which he presents as "a metaphor for the full range of one's inner life—one's desires, ambitions, hungers, vulnerabilities, fears." Quiet, he elaborates, should not be confused with apolitical, since "the interior could be understood as the source of human action—that anything we do is shaped by the range of desires and capacities of our inner life" (Quashie, *Sovereignty of Quiet*, 4, 6, 8).
6 Best, "On Failing," 454.
7 Cheng, "Psychoanalysis without Symptoms," 92.
8 Quashie, *Sovereignty of Quiet*, 4.

# WORKS CITED

Abdur-Rahman, Aliyyah. *Against the Closet: Black Political Longing and the Erotics of Race*. Durham: Duke University Press, 2012.

Ahmed, Sara. *The Promise of Happiness*. Durham: Duke University Press, 2010.

Alexander, Elizabeth. *The Black Interior*. St. Paul: Graywolf Press, 2004.

Awkward, Michael. *Philadelphia Freedoms: Black American Trauma, Memory, and Culture After King*. Philadelphia: Temple University Press, 2013.

Baker, Houston A., Jr., *Betrayal: How Black Intellectuals Have Abandoned the Ideals of the Civil Rights Era*. New York: Columbia University Press, 2008.

———. *Blues, Ideology, and Afro-American Literature: A Vernacular Theory*. Chicago: University of Chicago Press, 1984.

Bambara, Toni Cade. *The Salt Eaters*. New York: Random House, 1980.

Baraka, Amiri. "Afrikan Revolution." In William J. Harris ed., *The Leroi Jones/Amiri Baraka Reader*, 243–248. New York: Basic, 1991.

Best, Stephen. "On Failing to Make the Past Present." *Modern Language Quarterly* 73.3 (2012): 453–474.

Bradley, David. "The Business of Writing: An Interview with David Bradley." By Susan L. Blake and James A. Miller. *Callaloo* 7.2 (1984): 19–39.

———. *The Chaneysville Incident*. New York: Harper Collins, 1981.

Brand, Dionne. *A Map to the Door of No Return: Notes on Belonging*. Toronto: Vintage Canada, 2001.

Brown, Wendy. *Edgework: Critical Essays on Knowledge and Politics*. Princeton: Princeton University Press, 2005.

———. *Politics out of History*. Princeton: Princeton University Press, 2001.

———. "Wounded Attachments." In *States of Injury: Power and Freedom in Late Modernity*, 52–76. Princeton: Princeton University Press, 1995.

Browning, Maria. "Alice Randall Courts Controversy with *Rebel Yell*." Review of *Rebel Yell* by Alice Randall. *BookPage*, October 2009. http://bookpage.com.

Butler, Judith. *The Psychic Life of Power: Theories in Subjection*. Stanford: Stanford University Press, 1997.

———. *Undoing Gender*. New York: Routledge, 2004.

Butler, Octavia. "Interview with Octavia E. Butler." By Charles Rowell. *Callaloo* 20.1 (1997): 47–66.

———. "Interview with Octavia E. Butler." By John C. Snider. In Conseula Francis ed., *Conversations with Octavia Butler*, 213–218. Jackson: University Press of Mississippi, 2010. First published online at www.scifidimensions.com, June 2004.

——. *Kindred*. Boston: Beacon Press, 2003. First published New York: Doubleday, 1979.

——. "Octavia Butler: Persistence." *Locus Online*, June 2000. www.locusmag.com.

Byerman, Keith. *Remembering the Past in Contemporary African American Literature*. Chapel Hill: University of North Carolina Press, 2005.

Byrd, Rudolph P. *Charles Johnson's Novels: Writing the American Palimpsest*. Bloomington: Indiana University Press, 2005.

Carpio, Glenda R. *Laughing Fit to Kill: Black Humor in the Fictions of Slavery*. New York: Oxford University Press, 2008.

Caruth, Cathy. "Introduction." In Cathy Caruth ed., *Trauma: Explorations in Memory*, 3–12. Baltimore: Johns Hopkins University Press, 1995.

——, ed. *Trauma: Explorations in Memory*. Baltimore: Johns Hopkins University Press, 1995.

Cheng, Anne Anlin. *The Melancholy of Race: Psychoanalysis, Assimilation, and Hidden Grief*. New York: Oxford University Press, 2000.

——. "Psychoanalysis without Symptoms." *Differences: A Journal of Feminist Cultural Studies* 20.1 (2009): 87–101.

Christian, Barbara. "Fixing Methodologies: *Beloved*." *Cultural Critique* 24 (1993): 5–15.

Cole, Alyson M. *The Cult of True Victimhood: From the War on Welfare to the War on Terror*. Stanford: Stanford University Press, 2007.

Crouch, Stanley. "Charles Johnson: Free at Last!" Review of *Oxherding Tale* by Charles Johnson. In Rudolph Byrd ed., *I Call Myself an Artist: Writings by and about Charles Johnson*, 271–279. Bloomington: Indiana University Press, 1999. First published in *Village Voice*, July 19, 1983.

Cvetkovich, Ann. *An Archive of Feelings: Trauma, Sexuality, and Lesbian Public Cultures*. Durham: Duke University Press, 2003.

——. *Depression: A Public Feeling*. Durham: Duke University Press, 2012.

Dash, Julie, dir. *Daughters of the Dust*. New York: Kino International, 1991.

Davis, Thadious. *Southscapes: Geographies of Race, Region, and Literature*. Chapel Hill: University of North Carolina Press, 2011.

Dayan, Joan. "Paul Gilroy's Slaves, Slave Ships, and Routes: The Middle Passage as Metaphor." *Research in African Literatures* 27.4 (1996): 7–14.

Delany, Samuel. *The Game of Time and Pain*. In *Return to Nevèrÿon*, 9–23. Hanover: Wesleyan University Press, 1987.

Dobbs, Cynthia. "Diasporic Designs of House, Home, and Haven in Toni Morrison's *Paradise*." *MELUS* 36.2 (2011): 109–126.

Dubey, Madhu. *Black Women Novelists and the Nationalist Aesthetic*. Bloomington: Indiana University Press, 1994.

——. *Signs and Cities: Black Literary Postmodernism*. Chicago: University of Chicago Press, 2003.

——. "Speculative Fictions of Slavery." *American Literature* 82.4 (2010): 779–805.

Edwards, Erica R. *Charisma and the Fictions of Black Leadership*. Minneapolis: University of Minnesota Press, 2012.

English, Darby. "A New Context for Reconstruction: Some Crises of Landscape in Kara Walker's Silhouette Installations." In *How to See a Work of Art in Total Darkness*, 71–137. Cambridge: MIT Press, 2007.

Eyerman, Ron. *Cultural Trauma: Slavery and the Formation of African American Identity*. Cambridge: Cambridge University Press, 2002.

Felman, Shoshana. "The Betrayal of the Witness: Camus' *The Fall*." In Shoshana Felman and Dori Laub, *Testimony: Crises of Witnessing in Literature, Psychoanalysis, and History*, 165–203. New York: Routledge, 1992.

———. *The Juridical Unconscious: Trials and Traumas in the Twentieth Century*. Cambridge: Harvard University Press, 2002.

———. "Turning the Screw of Interpretation." *Yale French Studies* 55/56 (1977): 94–207.

Fletcher, Angus. *Allegory: The Theory of a Symbolic Mode*. Princeton: Princeton University Press, 2012. First published Ithaca: Cornell University Press, 1964.

Freeman, Elizabeth. *Time Binds: Queer Temporalities, Queer Histories*. Durham: Duke University Press, 2010.

Freud, Sigmund. "A Child Is Being Beaten: A Contribution to the Study of the Origin of Sexual Perversions." In James Strachey ed., *The Standard Edition of the Complete Psychological Works of Sigmund Freud*, 17:179–204. London: Hogarth Press, 1974.

———. *The Interpretation of Dreams: The Complete and Definitive Text*. Edited and translated by James Strachey. New York: Basic, 2010.

———. "Mourning and Melancholia." In James Strachey ed., *The Standard Edition of the Complete Psychological Works of Sigmund Freud*, 14:243–258. London: Hogarth Press, 1974.

———. "Repression." In James Strachey ed., *The Standard Edition of the Complete Psychological Works of Sigmund Freud*, 14:146–158. London: Hogarth Press, 1974.

———. *The Uncanny*. Translated by David McLintock, with an introduction by Hugh Haughton. New York: Penguin Classics, 2003.

Friedman, Susan Stanford. "(Self)Censorship and the Making of a Modernist." In Susan Stanford Friedman ed., *Joyce: Return of the Repressed*, 21–57. Ithaca: Cornell University Press, 1993.

———. "The Return of the Repressed in Women's Narrative." *Journal of Narrative Technique* 19.1 (1989): 141–156.

Gates, Henry Louis, Jr. *Colored People: A Memoir*. New York: Vintage, 1995.

———. *Figures in Black: Words, Signs, and the "Racial" Self*. New York: Oxford University Press, 1987.

Gerima, Haile, dir. *Sankofa*. Washington, D.C.: Mypheduh Films, 1993.

Gilman, Sander. *Difference and Pathology: Stereotypes of Sexuality, Race, and Madness*. Ithaca: Cornell University Press, 1985.

Gilroy, Paul. *The Black Atlantic: Modernity and Double-Consciousness*. Cambridge: Harvard University Press, 1993.

Giovanni, Nikki. "Reflections on April 4, 1968." In *Black Feeling Black Talk Black Judgment*, 54–55. New York: Morrow Quill, 1979. First published New York: Harper, 1971.

Gleason, William. "The Liberation of Perception: Charles Johnson's *Oxherding Tale*." *Black American Literature Forum* 25.4 (1991): 705–728.

Grier, William, and Price M. Cobbs. *Black Rage*. New York: Basic, 1968.

Halberstam, Judith. *The Queer Art of Failure*. Durham: Duke University Press, 2011.

Hall, Jacquelyn Dowd. "The Long Civil Rights Movement and the Political Uses of the Past." *Journal of American History* 91.4 (2005): 1233–1263.

Hartman, Saidiya. *Lose Your Mother: A Journey along the Atlantic Slave Route*. New York: Farrar, Straus & Giroux, 2007.

——. *Scenes of Subjection: Terror, Slavery and Self-Making in Nineteenth-Century America*. New York: Oxford University Press, 1997.

Hayward, Jennifer. "Something to Serve: Constructs of the Feminine in Charles Johnson's *Oxherding Tale*." *Black American Literature Forum* 25.4 (1991): 689–703.

Higginbotham, Evelyn Brooks. *Righteous Discontent: The Women's Movement in the Black Baptist Church, 1880–1920*. Cambridge: Harvard University Press, 1994.

——. "Wrestling with Respectability in the Age of #BlackLivesMatter: A Dialogue." By Kimberly Foster. *For Harriet*, October 2015. http://forharriet.com.

Hilfrich, Carola. "Anti-Exodus: Countermemory, Gender, Race, and Everyday Life in Toni Morrison's *Paradise*." *Modern Fiction Studies* 52.2 (2006): 321–349.

Hirsch, Marianne. "The Generation of Postmemory." *Poetics Today* 29.1 (2008): 103–128.

——. "Maternity and Rememory: Toni Morrison's *Beloved*." In Donna Bassin et al. eds., *Representations of Motherhood*, 92–110. New Haven: Yale University Press, 1994.

——. "Surviving Images: Holocaust Photographs and the Work of Postmemory." *Yale Journal of Criticism* 14.1 (2001): 5–37.

Hogue, Lawrence. "The Limits of Modernity: Andrea Lee's *Sarah Phillips*." *MELUS* 19 (1994): 75–90.

Holland, Sharon Patricia. *The Erotic Life of Racism*. Durham: Duke University Press, 2012.

Hussen, Aida Ahmed. "'Manumission and Marriage?': Freedom, Family, and Identity in Charles Johnson's *Oxherding Tale*." *African American Review* 42.2 (2008): 239–253.

Jessee, Sharon. "The Contrapuntal Historiography of Toni Morrison's *Paradise*: Unpacking the Legacies of the Kansas and Oklahoma All-Black Towns." *American Studies* 47.1 (2006): 81–112.

Johnson, Charles. "I Call Myself an Artist." In Rudolph Byrd ed., *I Call Myself an Artist: Writings by and about Charles Johnson*, 3–30. Bloomington: Indiana University Press, 1999.

——. "Interview with Charles Johnson." By Jonathan Little. In Rudolph Byrd ed., *I Call Myself an Artist: Writings by and about Charles Johnson*, 225–243. Bloomington: Indiana University Press, 1999.

——. *Oxherding Tale*. With a new introduction by Charles Johnson. New York: Plume, 1995. First published Bloomington: Indiana University Press, 1982; subsequently published New York: Grove Press, 1984.

———. "Whole Sight: Notes on the New Black Fiction (1984)." In Rudolph Byrd ed., *I Call Myself an Artist: Writings by and about Charles Johnson*, 85–90. Bloomington: Indiana University Press, 1999.

Johnson, Mat. *Pym*. New York: Spiegel & Grau, 2012. First published New York: Spiegel & Grau, 2011.

Jones, Douglas A. "The Fruit of Abolition: Discontinuity and Difference in Terrance Hayes' 'The Avocado.'" In Soyica Colbert et al. eds., *The Psychic Hold of Slavery: Legacies in American Expressive Culture*, 39–52. New Brunswick: Rutgers University Press, 2016.

Jones, Gayl. *Corregidora*. Boston: Beacon Press, 1975.

Kawash, Samira. *Dislocating the Color Line: Identity, Hybridity, and Singularity in African-American Narrative*. Stanford: Stanford University Press, 1997.

Keizer, Arlene R. *Black Subjects: Identity Formation in the Contemporary Narrative of Slavery*. Ithaca: Cornell University Press, 2004.

———. "Obsidian Mine: The Psychic Aftermath of Slavery." *American Literary History* 24.4 (2012): 686–701.

Kelley, Theresa M. *Reinventing Allegory*. New York: Cambridge University Press, 1997.

Kenan, Randall. "Let the Dead Bury Their Dead." In *Let the Dead Bury Their Dead: Stories*. 1st Harvest ed., 271–334. San Diego: Harcourt Brace Jovanovich, 1993.

———. *A Visitation of Spirits*. New York: Grove Press, 1989.

La Capra, Dominick. *History in Transit: Experience, Identity, Critical Theory*. Ithaca: Cornell University Press, 2004.

———. *Writing History, Writing Trauma*. Baltimore: Johns Hopkins University Press, 2001.

Laplanche, J., and J.-B. Pontalis, *The Language of Psycho-analysis*. New York: Norton, 1974.

Lee, Andrea. "The Prior's Room." In *Interesting Women: Stories*, 223–241. New York: Random House, 2002.

———. *Sarah Phillips*. With a new foreword by Valerie Smith. Boston: Northeastern University Press, 1993. First published New York: Random House, 1984.

Lenzer, Gertrud. "On Masochism: A Contribution to the History of a Phantasy and Its Theory." *Signs* 1.2 (1975): 277–324.

Levine, Caroline. *Forms: Whole, Rhythm, Hierarchy, Network*. Princeton: Princeton University Press, 2015.

Leys, Ruth. *From Guilt to Shame: Auschwitz and After*. Princeton: Princeton University Press, 2007.

Lipsitz, George. *Time Passages: Collective Memory and American Popular Culture*. Minneapolis: University of Minnesota Press, 1991.

Little, Jonathan. *Charles Johnson's Spiritual Imagination*. Columbia: University of Missouri Press, 1997.

Litwack, Leon. "Trouble in Mind: The Bicentennial and the Afro-American Experience." *Journal of American History* 74.2 (1987): 315–337.

Lotman, Jurij. *The Structure of the Artistic Text*. Translated by Ronald Vroon. Ann Arbor: University of Michigan Press, 1977. Originally published as *Struktura khudozhestvennogo teksta*, Providence: Brown University Press, 1971.

Lubiano, Wahneema. "Shuckin' Off the African American Native Other: What's 'Po-Mo' Got to Do with It?" *Cultural Critique* 18 (1991): 149–186.

Luckhurst, Roger. *The Trauma Question*. New York: Routledge, 2008.

MacIntyre, Alasdair. "The Virtues, the Unity of a Human Life, and the Concept of a Tradition." In *After Virtue: A Study in Moral Theory*, 3rd ed., 204–225. Notre Dame: University of Notre Dame Press, 2007. First published Notre Dame: University of Notre Dame Press, 1981.

Marable, Manning. *Beyond Black and White: Transforming African-American Politics*. New York: Verso, 1995.

———. *Race, Reform, and Rebellion: The Second Reconstruction in and beyond Black America, 1945–2006*. Jackson: University of Mississippi Press, 2007.

Marriott, David. *Haunted Life: Visual Culture and Black Modernity*. New Brunswick: Rutgers University Press, 2007.

Marshall, Paule. *Praisesong for the Widow*. New York: Plume, 1983.

McBride, James. *Song Yet Sung*. New York: Riverhead, 2008.

McCormick, Adrienne. "Is This Resistance? African American Postmodernism in *Sarah Phillips*." *Callaloo* 27.3 (2004): 808–828.

McDowell, Deborah E. "Negotiating between Tenses: Witnessing Slavery after Freedom—*Dessa Rose*." In Deborah E. McDowell and Arnold Rampersad eds., *Slavery and the Literary Imagination*, 144–163. Baltimore: Johns Hopkins University Press, 1987.

McPherson, James Alan. "Elbow Room." In *Elbow Room*, 256–286. New York: Fawcett, 1986. First published Boston: Little, Brown, 1977.

Menand, Louis. "The War between Men and Women." Review of *Paradise* by Toni Morrison. *New Yorker*, January 12, 1998, 78–82.

Michaels, Walter Benn. *The Shape of the Signifier: 1967 to the End of History*. Princeton: Princeton University Press, 2004.

———. *The Trouble with Diversity: How We Learned to Love Identity and Ignore Inequality*. New York: Holt, 2007.

Mitchell, Angelyn. *The Freedom to Remember: Narrative, Slavery, and Gender in Contemporary Black Women's Fiction*. New Brunswick: Rutgers University Press, 2002.

———. "Not Enough of the Past: Feminist Revisions of Slavery in Octavia E. Butler's *Kindred*." *MELUS* 26.3 (2001): 51–75.

Morris, Susana M. *Close Kin and Distant Relatives: The Paradox of Respectability in Black Women's Literature*. Charlottesville: University of Virginia Press, 2014.

Morrison, Toni. *Beloved*. With a new foreword by Toni Morrison. New York: Vintage, 2004. First published New York: Knopf, 1987.

———. *The Bluest Eye*. New York: Holt, Rhinehart & Winston, 1970.

———. *Jazz*. With a new foreword by Toni Morrison. New York: Vintage, 2004. First published New York: Knopf, 1992.

———. *Paradise*. New York: Plume, 1997.

———. *Playing in the Dark: Whiteness and the Literary Imagination*. New York: Vintage, 1993.

———. "The Site of Memory." In *What Moves at the Margin*, 65–80. Jackson: University Press of Mississippi, 2008.

Moten, Fred. *In the Break: The Aesthetics of the Black Radical Tradition*. Minneapolis: University of Minnesota Press, 2003.

Muñoz, José Esteban. *Cruising Utopia: The Then and There of Queer Futurity*. New York: NYU Press, 2009.

———. "Feeling Brown, Feeling Down: Latina Affect, the Performativity of Race, and the Depressive Position." *Signs* 31 (2006): 675–688.

Murray, Rolland. "The Time of Breach: Class Division and the Contemporary African American Novel." *Novel: A Forum on Fiction* 43.1 (2010): 11–17.

Musser, Amber Jamilla. *Sensational Flesh: Race, Power, and Masochism*. New York: NYU Press, 2014.

Nash, Jennifer C. *The Black Body in Ecstasy: Reading Race, Reading Pornography*. Durham: Duke University Press, 2014.

Nash, William R. *Charles Johnson's Fiction*. Urbana: University of Illinois Press, 2003.

Naylor, Gloria. *Mama Day*. New York: Ticknor & Fields, 1988.

Nielsen, Aldon Lynn. "Wasness." Review of *What Was African American Literature?* by Kenneth W. Warren. *Los Angeles Review of Books*, June 13, 2011. https://lareviewofbooks.org.

Ottenberg, Eve. "Symbols and Ordeals." Review of *Oxherding Tale* by Charles Johnson. *New York Times Book Review*, January 9, 1983. www.nytimes.com.

Patterson, Robert J. *Exodus Politics: Civil Rights Leadership in African American Literature and Culture*. Charlottesville: University of Virginia Press, 2013.

Perry, Phyllis Alesia. "Confronting the Specters of the Past, Writing the Legacy of Pain: An Interview with Phyllis Alesia Perry." By Corinne Duboin. *Mississippi Quarterly* 62.3/4 (2009): 633–653.

———. *Stigmata*. New York: Hyperion, 1998.

Phillips, Adam. *The Beast in the Nursery: On Curiosity and Other Appetites*. New York: Vintage, 1998.

———. *Becoming Freud: The Making of a Psychoanalyst*. New Haven: Yale University Press, 2014.

———. *On Flirtation: Psychoanalytic Essays on the Uncommitted Life*. Cambridge: Harvard University Press, 1994.

———. *Promises, Promises: Essays on Psychoanalysis and Literature*. New York: Basic, 2001.

Phillips, Caryl. *Crossing the River*. New York: Vintage, 1995.

Poe, Edgar Allan. *The Narrative of Arthur Gordon Pym of Nantucket*. New York: Harper & Bros., 1838.

Quashie, Kevin. *The Sovereignty of Quiet: Beyond Resistance in Black Culture*. New Brunswick: Rutgers University Press, 2012.

Randall, Alice. *Rebel Yell*. New York: Bloomsbury, 2009.

Rankine, Claudia. *Citizen: An American Lyric*. Minneapolis: Graywolf Press, 2014.

Reed, Adolph, Jr., and Kenneth W. Warren, eds. *Renewing Black Intellectual History: The Ideological and Material Foundations of African American Thought*. Boulder: Paradigm Publishers, 2010.

Reid-Pharr, Robert. *Once You Go Black: Choice, Desire, and the Black American Intellectual*. New York: NYU Press, 2007.

Retman, Sonnet. "'Nothing Was Lost in the Masquerade': The Protean Performance of Genre and Identity in Charles Johnson's *Oxherding Tale*." *African American Review* 33.3 (1999): 417–437.

Rody, Caroline. *The Daughter's Return: African American and Caribbean Women's Fictions of History*. New York: Oxford University Press, 2001.

Rushdy, Ashraf H. A. *Neo-slave Narratives: Studies in the Social Logic of a Literary Form*. New York: Oxford University Press, 1999.

———. "'Relate Sexual to Historical': Race, Resistance, and Desire in Gayl Jones' *Corregidora*." *African American Review* 34.2 (2000): 273–297.

———. *Remembering Generations: Race and Family in Contemporary African American Fiction*. Chapel Hill: University of North Carolina Press, 2001.

Scott, Darieck. *Extravagant Abjection: Blackness, Power, and Sexuality in the African American Literary Imagination*. New York: NYU Press, 2010.

Scott, Daryl Michael. *Contempt and Pity: Social Policy and the Image of the Damaged Black Psyche*. Chapel Hill: University of North Carolina Press, 1997.

Sedgwick, Eve. *Touching Feeling: Affect, Pedagogy, Performativity*. Durham: Duke University Press, 2003.

Sharpe, Christina. *Monstrous Intimacies: Making Post-slavery Subjects*. Durham: Duke University Press, 2010.

Smith, Valerie. "Foreword." In *Sarah Phillips* by Andrea Lee, i–xxiv. Boston: Northeastern University Press, 1993.

Snitow, Ann. Review of *Beloved* by Toni Morrison. In Henry Louis Gates, Jr., and Kwame Anthony Appiah eds., *Toni Morrison: Critical Perspectives Past and Present*, 26–31. New York: Amistad, 1993. First published in *Village Voice Literary Supplement*, September 1987.

Spillers, Hortense. "All the Things You Could Be by Now, If Sigmund Freud's Wife Were Your Mother." In *Black, White, and in Color: Essays on American Literature and Culture*, 376–427. Chicago: University of Chicago Press, 2001.

Steigerwald, David. *The Sixties and the End of Modern America*. New York: St. Martin's, 1995.

Storace, Patricia. "Scripture of Utopia." *New York Review of Books*, June 11, 1998. nybooks.com.

Stockton, Kathryn Bond. *Beautiful Bottom, Beautiful Shame: Where "Black" Meets "Queer."* Durham: Duke University Press, 2006.

Stowe, Harriet Beecher. *Uncle Tom's Cabin*. Boston: John P. Jewett & Co., 1852.

Tate, Claudia. *Psychoanalysis and Black Novels: Desire and the Protocols of Race*. New York: Oxford University Press, 1998.

Tillet, Salamishah. *Sites of Slavery: Citizenship and Racial Democracy in the Post-Civil Rights Imagination*. Durham: Duke University Press, 2012.

Walker, Margaret. *Jubilee*. New York: Mariner, 1999. First published Boston: Houghton Mifflin, 1966.

Warner, Michael. "Uncritical Reading." In Jane Gallop ed., *Polemic: Critical or Uncritical*, 13–39. New York: Routledge, 2004.

Warren, Kenneth W. *So Black and Blue: Ralph Ellison and the Occasion of Criticism*. Chicago: University of Chicago Press, 2003.

——. *What Was African American Literature?* Cambridge: Harvard University Press, 2011.

Washington, Mary Helen. "Young, Gifted and Black." Review of *Sarah Phillips* by Andrea Lee. *Women's Review of Books* 2.6 (1985): 3–4.

Weiss, Margo. *Techniques of Pleasure: BDSM and the Circuits of Sexuality*. Durham: Duke University Press, 2011.

Woolfork, Lisa. *Embodying American Slavery in Contemporary Culture*. Urbana: University of Illinois Press, 2008.

# INDEX

Perry, Phyllis Alesia, *Stigmata* (see *Stigmata*)
Phillips, Adam, 8, 125
Phillips, Caryl, 43
Poe, Edgar Allan, 131–132, 189n3
postmemory, 25–29, 30, 36, 38, 40, 42, 45, 46, 50. *See also* rememory; trauma
prohibitive reading, 5–7, 14, 16, 19, 25–29, 32–36, 41–42, 45, 50, 53, 97, 129, 138, 140–141, 150, 154, 178n33
protest novel, 146–147, 150, 169, 174–175n13
psychoanalysis, 8, 14, 37; critiques of, 7–8, 22–24, 108–109, 184n2, 187n36; and literary criticism, 10–12, 16, 167, 170–172, 175n19, 175n20; theory of humiliation, 125; usefulness for African American Studies, 9; working through, 57. *See also* depression; Freud, Sigmund; masochism; melancholia; trauma
*Pym* (Johnson), 131–133, 134, 189n3

Quashie, Kevin, 193n5
queer: desire, 48, 68, 70; identity, 48; temporality, 43–45, 48–51, 68–69; theory, 43–45, 55, 58, 66, 68–69, 88–89, 183n47

race: in cultural imagination, 7, 8, 47, 95–96, 101, 106, 110, 157, 158, 176n33, 178n30; epistemology of, 9, 16, 23, 28, 115–116; and identity, 5, 48, 100, 104–107, 154–155, 177–178n24; and literary history, 39–40, 120, 132, 169–170, 176n30. *See also* racism
racism, 7, 41, 55, 70, 93–94, 132–133, 139, 181n6; emotional effects of, 108–109, 112–116, 187n37, 188n43, 188n45; erotics of, 75, 76; and identity formation, 98, 100, 108, 113, 116, 123–126; and psychoanalysis, 7–8, 23; and violence, 75, 90–91, 120, 159. *See also* race
Randall, Alice, *Rebel Yell* (see *Rebel Yell*)
reader: affective experience of, 20–21, 25, 36, 38, 41, 113, 118, 137–140, 142–145,

151; as fictional character, 7, 132–133, 155; implied, 14, 174n8; inculcation of, 2–5, 18, 25, 28, 37, 53, 68, 138, 173n5; interpretive labor of, 34, 42–43, 116, 131, 133, 140, 150, 156, 157, 166–168, 171–172; relationship to history, 35, 137–140
*Rebel Yell* (Randall), 15, 96, 119–129
recognition: denial of, 60, 63, 72, 77, 86, 123, 181n18; fantasy of historical, 13, 37, 41, 62–64, 71–73, 85, 142; misrecognition, 109, 113–114, 117–118; political, 28, 60, 62–64
Reed, Adolph, Jr., 178n30
Reid-Pharr, Robert, 18, 41, 43, 178n33
rememory, 22, 25–26, 30, 32, 44. *See also* postmemory; trauma
repression: historical, 4, 53, 66–68, 164, 183n40; psychoanalytic, 10, 113, 126, 151–152, 168, 191n34, 192–193n57 (*see also* melancholia); reader's, 4, 53, 118, 173n5; of sexuality, 46, 74–75; textual, 10, 138, 147–148, 152, 166
respectability, 13, 55, 180n2
Rody, Caroline, 177n12
Rushdy, Ashraf H. A., 24, 78, 82, 155, 173n5

Sacher-Masoch, Leopold, 59
*Sarah Phillips* (Lee), 93–109; companion text to, 188n46; contemporary racism in, 93–95, 99–100, 109, 118; critical perspectives on, 94–95, 176n30, 185n5; presentism in, 11, 15, 94–96, 112, 118; and racial depression, 109 (*see also* depression); and racial melancholia, 99–100, 102–107, 119–120 (*see also* melancholia)
Scott, Darieck, 55, 57, 88–91, 183n56
Scott, Daryl Michael, 23
Sedgwick, Eve, 108–109, 126, 187n36, 189n58
Sharpe, Christina, 24, 55–56, 58, 183n40
serial dreams, 10, 167, 176n27

## ABOUT THE AUTHOR

Aida Levy-Hussen is Associate Professor of English at the University of Wisconsin–Madison.

CPSIA information can be obtained
at www.ICGtesting.com
Printed in the USA
FFOW02n1454270217
32908FF